⋙ TOO ⋘
SWEET

KEITH ELLIOT GREENBERG

TOO SWEET

INSIDE THE INDIE WRESTLING REVOLUTION

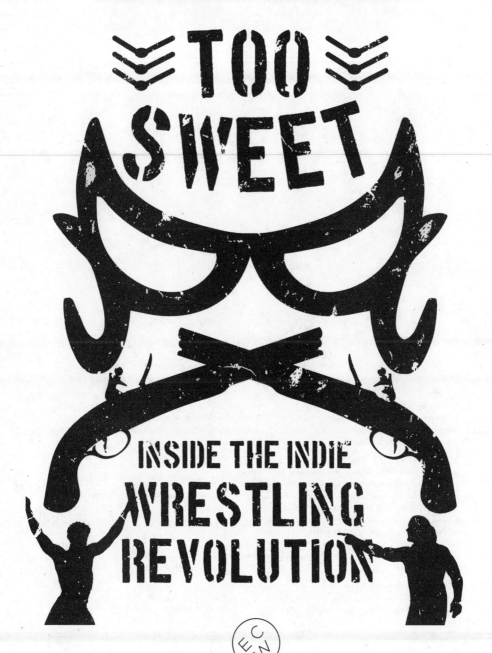

Published by ECW Press
665 Gerrard Street East
Toronto, Ontario, Canada M4M 1Y2
416-694-3348 / info@ecwpress.com

Editor for the Press: Michael Holmes
Cover design and artwork: Jessica Albert
Unless otherwise noted, all photos courtesy of Kevin Quiroz

LIBRARY AND ARCHIVES CANADA
CATALOGUING IN PUBLICATION

Title: Too sweet : inside the indie wrestling revolution / Keith Elliot Greenberg.

Names: Greenberg, Keith Elliot, 1959- author.

Identifiers: Canadiana (print) 20200235044 | Canadiana (ebook) 20200235052

ISBN 978-1-77041-518-8 (softcover)
ISBN 978-1-77305-577-0 (PDF)
ISBN 978-1-77305-576-3 (ePUB)

Subjects: LCSH: Wrestling. | LCSH: Wrestling—History.

Classification: LCC GV1195 .G74 2020 | DDC 796.812—dc23

PRINTED AND BOUND IN CANADA

PRINTING: MARQUIS   5 4 3 2 1

"We didn't do it for the money. We did it for the applause."
— Maurice "Mad Dog" Vachon (1929–2013)

CHAPTER 1

"The Bad Boy" Joey Janela was nervous. He paced. He sat. He stood up. He reached into his pocket and pulled out a pack of cigarettes, tapping it against the inside of his palm. With the butt shoved under his lip, he stepped outside the Sears Centre Arena and lit up.

He could see the cars converging on the utilitarian glass and concrete building, angling for spots in the parking lot. From a distance, he heard the doors creaking open, slamming shut, voices talking, laughing, chanting.

Wooooo!

After 12 years in the wrestling business, the sounds were familiar to him. So was the general look of the crowd: long hair and shaved heads, motorcycle boots and sneakers, hard bodies bursting through muscle shirts and balloon-shaped physiques wedged into wrestling tees. Occasionally, an attractive woman tottered by on high heels, holding the hand of a boyfriend rushing to keep up with his wrestling buddies. The parade of fans didn't stop.

Janela pulled out his ponytail and shook his long brown hair from side to side. When the "Most Badass Professional Wrestler in the

World" finally went back into the building, he passed the other wrestlers in the halls: Cody, the Young Bucks and Kenny Omega — the biggest stars on the North American indie scene — Kota Ibushi and Kazuchika Okada from Japan, Rey Fenix, Penta El Zero and Bandido from Mexico. Outside of World Wrestling Entertainment (WWE), these were some of the most important names in the business. And Janela, the five-foot-eight scrapper from South Jersey, who still lived at home with his mother, was among them. In fact, some of the fans had specifically come to suburban Chicago *because* Joey Janela — who earned social media infamy by being tossed from a roof into the flaming bed of a pickup truck — was included in this historic September 2018 show, known as *All In*.

Fifteen minutes later, Janela headed back outside for another smoke. The crowd had not abated. In fact, it had gotten larger. "Wow," he said, the jitters again tingling through his body. "This is *big*."

In fact, it was the largest show not staged by WWE or WCW — WWE's chief rival until 2001 — in 25 years.

"There's something happening here that hasn't happened in a long time," said Awesome Kong, the charismatic Amazon who later signed with All Elite Wrestling (AEW), the company that grew out of *All In*. "It's kinetic. There's an energy. There's a sheer will of wanting something different to succeed. And this all started on a dare."

I first subscribed to Dave Meltzer's *Wrestling Observer* newsletter in the 1980s, after I began writing for *WWF Magazine*, before the lawsuit with the World Wildlife Fund that forced the World Wrestling Federation to become WWE. Although the *Wrestling Observer* has a significant online presence, I still look forward to the paper edition each week, an exhaustive collection of wrestling history, match results, business analysis and gossip in single-spaced seven-point type. Meltzer, who has lectured at Stanford University's Graduate School of Business, also popularized a star rating system for major matches, one that even the performers who claim to hate him take extremely seriously. While I was working on this book, Meltzer and I were guests on a public access show in which he was asked about his taste in movies and bands. He paused and fumbled for words. *A movie?* But when it comes to professional wrestling, not to mention MMA and old-school roller derby, nobody knows more — or ever will.

In May 2017, Meltzer was asked on Twitter about whether Ring of Honor, the primary American indie league at that time, could draw more than 10,000 fans. "Not any time soon," he responded. Cody Rhodes — the youngest son of the "American Dream" Dusty Rhodes and an indie prince since he parted ways with WWE the year before — then tweeted, "I'll take that bet, Dave."

For the next 16 months, Cody and the Young Bucks, brothers Nick and Matt Jackson, worked to prove that Dave Meltzer was wrong, as well as to create *All In.*

The effort became "a worldwide movement for professional wrestling [and] everyone that wants an alternative," Kenny Omega, who went into *All In* wearing the vaunted International Wrestling Grand Prix (IWGP) Heavyweight Championship for the New Japan Pro-Wrestling promotion, told the group's website. "Especially in America because in America, you're kind of forced to believe that WWE is the best." *All In*, he continued, was "a rally to show support for people who have a different vision."

Initially, the three men rejected outside efforts to fund the experiment and relied on their families and friends. Cody's sister, Teil, created the name *All-In*, the Bucks' father, Matt Massie Sr., the musical score. Alabama mortgage broker Conrad Thompson, a wrestling podcaster who married the legendary Ric Flair's oldest daughter, Megan, coordinated Starcast, the fan convention surrounding the event. Cody's wife, Brandi — a WWE-trained wrestler herself — and Matt Jackson's wife, Dana, were deeply involved in organizational decisions.

Like Cody, WWE Hall of Famer Jeff Jarrett had grown up in the wrestling business, learning promotion from his father, Jerry Jarrett, and step-grandfather, Eddie Marlin, in the old Memphis wrestling territory. "I love to see guys take risks," he observed. "Sometimes, that gets you into big trouble. Sometimes, it pays off. Reward is always measured by your level of risk. But when I saw *All In* lining up, I felt they had a pretty good chance. The concept was good. The independent wrestling revolution started quite a few years ago. Now we were on the cusp of a wrestling boom."

Since the advent of television, promoters had used the medium to generate interest in upcoming matches. But Cody, Omega, the Bucks and assorted friends had begun reaching their audience another way: through a YouTube series they'd branded *Being the Elite*, or *BTE*, all shot on the wrestlers' cell phones as they traveled around the world. Each installment combined documentary elements — the guys sitting on airplanes, lounging in hotel rooms and preparing for matches backstage — comedy sketches and wrestling highlights. "We didn't treat *Being the Elite* like pro wrestling," Matt explained. "'Ah, it's just wrestling.' You put together these angles, and there's plotholes, and you just don't care. *Being the Elite* was more like Netflix, HBO, Showtime. We tried to tie up every loose end, pay attention to every detail. When we started building the *All In* card, we said, '[How] can we blow off the stories that fans have been following on *Being the Elite*?' We wanted people to be satisfied after watching six months of episodes. We wanted them to feel rewarded in the end."

Former Ring of Honor owner Cary Silkin, a friend of the Jackson brothers, tried offering advice. "They did everything wrong," Silkin said. "I suggested they shouldn't put tickets on sale on Sunday afternoon. But it didn't matter. They could have put tickets on sale at three in the morning. They had the spirit of the people with them."

Within the first 30 minutes that tickets were available, 10,541 were sold. In total, 11,263 fans filled the Sears Centre Arena, the maximum that the fire department would allow. Even the suites were overflowing.

Over the course of the Starcast weekend, nearly $500,000 worth of merchandise was sold. Ninety minutes before bell time, not one *All In* t-shirt was available.

When the show finally took place, Jarrett noted, *All In* was "independent wrestling's version of *WrestleMania*. From top to bottom, the card was stacked. And the vibe in the arena, the energy in the building, carried you through the matches."

Silkin compared the "rock 'n' roll frenzy" in the building to watching Jethro Tull performing "Locomotive Breath" live. "I've never seen a crowd — Bruno Sammartino in Madison Square Garden, Hulk Hogan and Roddy Piper, ECW, Led Zeppelin, Metallica in 1987, the Yankees in the World Series — hot like this from beginning to end. Never, never, never."

Yet, backstage, Cody appeared nonchalant, as if this most public testament to the vitality of indie wrestling was preordained. To those who knew his father, as both a headliner and a booker — the person responsible for outlining matches and storylines — the similarity was striking. "I was watching Cody back there," former WCW World Heavyweight Champion Diamond Dallas Page said on announcer Jim Ross' podcast, "and everyone's coming up to him and asking him everything, and he was getting ready for the biggest match of his life, but having fun . . . just like Dusty used to do."

Dusty Rhodes was an essential player in the National Wrestling Alliance (NWA), a conglomeration of international promotions all sharing a touring world champion. The "American Dream" had captured the belt on three separate occasions before its meaning was eclipsed by honors affiliated with the World Wrestling Federation. In 2017, Smashing Pumpkins lead singer Billy Corgan purchased the NWA name. What he needed was a vehicle to resuscitate its meaning.

All In's main event, featuring Cody challenging Nick Aldis for the NWA World Heavyweight Championship, seemed to satisfy Corgan's goal. "The people who have an emotional attachment to the belt remember the glory years of the NWA when Dusty was on top," Jarrett said. "A member of that family involved in the match meant a resurgence of the belt. *All In* would not have been anywhere near as special without Cody, and I think Nick would agree with me on that."

Aldis, a chiseled Brit previously known as Magnus, had been defending the NWA strap on indie shows sometimes consisting of several hundred fans. "There are so few things of historical value that WWE doesn't own," he told *TVInsider*'s Scott Fishman. "With the right presentation and with a fresh coat of paint [. . .] we are reminding people of what this name means, what this championship means."

Despite the variety of styles highlighted at *All In*, the NWA championship clash drew the most intrigue. "When Cody and I stood in the ring and they rang the bell, and the whole place is standing before we even touched, that was the ultimate validation for me," Aldis told *Inside the Ropes* podcast host Kenny McIntosh. "'There is still a place for storytelling and building anticipation.' It's not just about a match. It's not all about athleticism. It's about a moment."

When Aldis locked a bloody Cody in the figure four, the way Ric Flair frequently did to Dusty, the two performers were perennially bonded. "We'll always have that point forever," Aldis said. "And he told me that. He said, 'We shared a moment that so few people in our business get to experience . . . you gave it to me. I'll always remember that.' That's the art of doing business. That's what this business is about."

Watching the match turned veteran women's star Angelina Love into a fan again. "For every indie wrestler," Love said, "*All In* symbolized hope, possibility, giving back to the fans and giving back to the other wrestlers."

Omega told the New Japan website that even when he wasn't in the ring, he felt a sense of love from the crowd, an affirmation that his decision to go his own way on the indies was right: "We changed the face of professional wrestling with that show. We did something no one else could do."

Leaving the Sears Centre Arena that night, Joey Janela could feel that both his life and indie wrestling were headed in directions he had never before imagined. "I now knew," he reflected, "that the impossible was possible."

CHAPTER 2

On the day before the first card not promoted by the McMahon family in Madison Square Garden in nearly 60 years, Bully Ray — known as Bubba Ray Dudley during his time in WWE — stood in a hallway in the fabled arena, contemplating the changes he'd witnessed since he first entered the business in 1991, at the tail end of wrestling's territory days.

"We're going as an industry where we should go," he stated. "In all different directions."

The WWE Hall of Famer was preparing for his six-man "New York street fight" the next night at the *G1 Supercard*. A dual promotion between Ring of Honor and New Japan Pro-Wrestling, it deliberately took place on the same weekend tens of thousands of fans were in town for *WrestleMania 35* in nearby New Jersey. If anyone questioned the viability of indie wrestling, the fact that the Garden was sold out was evidence that the terrain had shifted.

"Years ago, the term 'indie' was derogatory," said Matt Striker, a performer who has commentated for WWE and New Japan, along with other groups. "'Oh, that's indie. He's indie.' It almost meant that you weren't there yet, not ready. Now, being independent is a positive thing. You look at the indie scene and you see talent that's totally athletic, totally charismatic, totally engaging."

Only those still locked into the past continue to cling to the old connotations of "indie." During a live Q&A for *Inside the Ropes* in late 2018, Cody recalled how his mother, the wife of the late "American Dream" Dusty Rhodes, struggled to grasp the altered landscape. "My mom always tells me," he said, imitating a southern accent, "'Are you still doing independent wrestling?'"

But rugged journeyman Dan Maff, a staple on the northeast indies for two decades, took great pride in what he'd accomplished in church basements and high school gyms. "I trained at a place called the Doghouse in New York, and we always said, 'The indies matter.' Look at what's going on in wrestling right now. Who are the top guys and where did they start? It's all generated from the indies."

The seeds of this book were germinated during *WrestleMania 34* weekend in New Orleans. Afterwards, Michael Holmes, my editor at ECW Press — the acronym comes from the Toronto-based company's background as a literary magazine, by the way, and originally stood for Essays on Canadian Writing, not Extreme Championship Wrestling — and I were discussing what we'd witnessed while walking through the French Quarter. We noted that we'd seen almost as many t-shirts for the Bullet Club — then the primary faction in New Japan and Ring of Honor — as those for John Cena, Roman Reigns and Braun Strowman. Professional wrestling was experiencing a transformation, we agreed, and maybe it was time for an indie book.

But what exactly is *indie*?

"I hate the term 'indie wrestling,'" Championship Wrestling from Hollywood owner and *NWA Power* announcer David Marquez told me a few months later, as rain beat down on the awning above us at our outdoor table at the Rainbow on Sunset Boulevard. "It's kind of like painting yourself in a box. It's like saying 'backyard wrestling,' which sounds very limited. Why can't we just say there's a renaissance in pro wrestling?"

With all due respect to David, and all the wrestlers and fans who feel the same way, this book will define "indie wrestling" in its widest sense, the way one might use the term "Christian" to represent Roman

8

Catholics, Seven Day Adventists, Baptists, Mormons and Unitarians. In the course of my research, I saw New Japan's exalted IWGP Heavyweight belt change hands for the first time on American soil in midtown Manhattan. In Jersey City, in a post-midnight, anarchic free-for-all dubbed the Greatest Clusterfuck Battle Royal, I watched legless Dustin Thomas execute a 619, senton bomb and corkscrew dive. I interviewed the husband and wife owners of Pro Wrestling EVE, a British promotion with a feminist bent that donates its proceeds to a number of charities, including one called Bloody Good Period. At an event put on by Germany's wXw group, I sat next to a guy who described himself as the first Canadian ever to wrestle in China. I know some will read this and feel angry for not being included. So let me apologize in advance. The indies are so diverse and vast that I knew from the beginning that I wasn't going to get to everybody. The goal is to provide an overview of the general scene and a snapshot of a very unique time, arguably the most epochal one since WWE ended the Monday Night Wars by absorbing WCW in 2001.

"I see a time of change, tumultuous change," said Excalibur, cofounder of Pro Wrestling Guerrilla (PWG) and a commentator for All Elite Wrestling (AEW). "Never in my career did I expect to see this many opportunities for this many people. For the longest time, everybody was fighting for a finite amount of spots. Getting to WWE seemed to be the only pathway to success. Now, the possibilities are changing by the day."

As a wrestling fan himself, AEW CEO and president Tony Khan said he understood why other enthusiasts "wanted and needed something different, authentic and better for far too long." Followers were "underserved and perhaps even disappointed," he continued, by the "scripted, soapy drama" they saw on their televisions each week.

"If WWE was really on point, there wouldn't be a reason for an indie boom," opined Jac Sabboth, an indie promoter in Queens and owner of Wrestling Universe, a store completely devoted to wrestling merchandise, on Francis Lewis Boulevard. "Not all fans want PG-13. They want hardcore. They want luchadores. They want Japanese strong style. WWE is too predictable. I can call every match at *WrestleMania*. There was just a hunger for more."

Shawn Spears, who was known as Tye Dillinger before joining AEW, claimed an ingenuity deficit had led many fans to tune out. "If you're watching the product and two guys come out and you're already able to tell the finish of the match based on entrances alone, that's a problem," he told entertainment reporter and AEW backstage interviewer Chris Van Vliet. "We're giving the audience an opportunity to change the channel."

Nick Jackson of the Young Bucks elaborated on this concept. "People were tired of the same old bookings, the same old characters."

"It's fatigue, too," his brother, Matt, added, "because WWE has so much content. When you have to fill so many hours, things can feel redundant. You want it to be fresh."

As a result, Nick Jackson said, fans began searching elsewhere. "The alternative became things outside WWE, and that's what pushed everything to where it is now."

Yet, according to former WWE Cruiserweight champion Rich Swann, the appetite for other options doesn't necessarily bode doom for the company most indie standouts grew up watching. "WWE is a machine," he said in 2018. "At this point, there's nobody who will ever be able to compete with them."

It was a truth not lost on Ring of Honor COO Joe Koff. But he believed that companies with lesser bureaucracy enjoyed an elasticity that the pillar of the grunt'n'groan circuit didn't. "WWE's an ocean liner. When they have to make a move, it really takes a lot of time. We're a cigarette boat. We can swerve in. We can swerve out."

For Chris Jericho, who was among the rare personalities to shuttle between WWE and New Japan in the new millennium, the choices enriched the pro wrestling ecosystem. "If you're in the jungle and there's a wild lion and a wild boar and a rhino," he told *Busted Open Radio*, "you don't have to be friends with each other, but you can also exist in the same jungle."

With its family-friendly advertisers, WWE deliberately appealed to a younger audience, said Striker. "The money is coming from the 12-and-under crowd. '*Mommy, Daddy, buy me that.*' And then, if you go to an indie show, you're going to see an adult male in a black t-shirt who wants to be part of something special. WWE is always going to be the New York Yankees. But the Washington Nationals still draw money."

The beneficiaries of these circumstances, Jericho stressed, were younger talent. "The best thing that can happen is there are more places where guys can make a legitimate living," he told *Rolling Stone*. "I always say to guys, 'The WWE isn't going anywhere. It will be here for the rest of our lives and our children's lives. Go experience the world. Go see what's out there. Go make a name for yourself, which makes you even more valuable when you come into the WWE.' That's what I did."

So did Swann, who was signed by WWE after a tryout in September 2014. "I started my career in places like Combat Zone Wrestling, where blood and guts was glorified to the utmost," he said during a Major League Wrestling (MLW) show, toweling off in the changing area of a Queens nightclub, while father and son team Samu and Lance Anoa'i — of the celebrated Wild Samoan wrestling clan — discussed whether to stop off in Chinatown on the way home, and first cousins Teddy Hart and Davey Boy Smith Jr. chatted with Brian Pillman Jr., whose late father lived among their wrestling forebears in Calgary. "I've had a taste of Ring of Honor. I've dipped my feet and honed my craft in Dragon Gate, Japan. That's what got me to WWE."

Following his release in 2018, he returned to a rejuvenated scene. "It's almost like the independent circuit has turned upside down. There's so much talent, it's like the world doesn't know what to do with it. We now know the independents can draw people to professional wrestling. Everything doesn't have to be planned out. Sometimes, people want to see the nitty gritty."

In 1998, at age 18, Teddy Hart, nephew of five-time World Wrestling Federation Heavyweight champion Bret "Hit Man" Hart and the oldest grandchild of family patriarch Stu Hart, was the youngest person ever signed to a developmental contract by the mega-promotion. But attitude and behavioral issues drove him to the margins of the industry. As I researched this book, though, one indie wrestler after another spoke up for Teddy's generosity in sharing knowledge that not only came from being one of the indies' best workers, but also the lessons he learned in both storytelling and backstage politicking. He hated to lose and wasn't always enthusiastic about "selling" — bouncing around for his opponent and grabbing body parts in agony — but 15 minutes in the ring with Teddy Hart was the industry equivalent of a seminar at Oxford.

"Within the last 10 years," he said, "I think the indie scene has become the best wrestling in the world. The hungriest, most risk-taking guys are all trying to make a name for themselves. You've got savvy fans who chant 'you fucked up,' 'you can't wrestle' and 'don't come back' if you do something wrong. But they'll give you a standing ovation and chant your name when they know you've put your heart into your match.

"Once you taste an independent crowd, it's a hell of a drug.

"I'm watching the progression of professional wrestling, and it's evolving into something really cool. Today, the fans aren't asking whether it's real or not. They recognize that this is an art, this is theater, this is gymnastics, this is a public speaking space with a lot of improv, and you combine so many facets of athleticism to make it work."

Downstairs, at the MLW show, Joey Ryan — who owns the unique distinction in professional wrestling for his bionic penis gimmick — stood at the merch table, comparing the rise of the indies to the general trend in independent arts. "Look at movies, music, theater. It's easier to gain visibility today without necessarily having a mainstream outlet."

New Jersey's Pro Wrestling Magic promotion threads an occult theme through its storylines. Its primary title is the Pro Wrestling Magic Dark Arts Championship. Matches take place at a building called the Pro Wrestling Magic Kingdom. When a wrestler executes a daring move, fans — some of whom attend every card — intone, "This is magic," as opposed to, "This is awesome."

"When wrestling is done right, there's nothing like it," said the group's announcer James Baxter. "It doesn't matter if it's a death match or a technical match. If you're giving people something they've been missing, it works."

Baxter, who also works for the Unsanctioned Pro outfit in Columbus, Ohio, credits the appeal of the indies to its unpredictability. "Anyone can show up. When you get what you didn't know you wanted, it's unbelievable."

Simon Gotch worked for WWE from 2013 to 2017, primarily as a member of the Vaudevillians tag team, a duo whose antiquated outfits and hairstyles seemed to honor the pastime's carny roots. "The biggest difference is creative freedom," he said. "On the indies, you're your own boss, and you're in charge of your own marketing. It's your job to sell yourself, no different than if you're trying to sell a character in a movie or a comic book or a video game.

"When you see me wrestling on the indies, I do whatever I want. It's not necessarily WWE-friendly. My matches can go long, with a lot of mat work, a lot of rough strikes, throws, submissions. No one's telling me what to do as a performer, so I have the opportunity to at least show what I'm capable of."

Before a typical WWE promo, "you got to have a lighting guy over there, you have to have a sound guy over there," Jon Moxley, who worked as Dean Ambrose for the company between 2011 and 2019, said on the *Wade Keller Pro Wrestling Podcast.* "It takes a team of six guys for some reason. These guys are all pros and good at their jobs, and they make you look great. But if one little thing is off, Vince [McMahon] will say, 'Hey, you have to redo it.'" As a result, he continued, there was less time to concentrate on the upcoming performance in the ring, "which is stupid."

During his time in WWE's highly touted NXT division — a league with a disproportionate amount of onetime indie stars — Sami Callihan, who was then known as Solomon Crowe, claimed to have encountered the same creative obstructions as Gotch. "It's one of the reasons I quit," he said. "[Now], I don't have the shackles. I don't have the restraints. My opponent and I can just listen to the fans, let them tell us what they want, let them call our match for us. If I truly believe in something, I can go out there and paint my picture, tell my story. I can perform my art the way I want to perform my art. I don't want the narrative someone else wants. I want the narrative the way I want it to be. Because my narrative in my mind is correct."

When wrestlers are given that kind of leeway, Baxter said, the fans reap the rewards. "The unadulterated passion these guys show is amazing. It doesn't matter if there are four people in the audience. The effort the wrestlers put in . . . it's like you're at a stadium rock show."

Gene Snitsky's most memorable angle in WWE occurred in 2004 when he blasted the "Big Red Monster" Kane from behind with a chair, causing him to smash into future WWE Hall of Famer Lita. According to the plot, the collision forced Lita to miscarry. Snitsky's catchphrase then became a highly defensive, "It wasn't my fault."

After his release in 2008, the hulking, long-bearded Pennsylvanian returned home, working for smaller wrestling groups as well as appearing in music videos, commercials, movies and TV shows. When we saw each other in the spring of 2019, he was running a military surplus store in Hamburg, Pennsylvania, where the World Wrestling Federation had taped its *All-Star Wrestling* program until 1986, and working an indie once or twice a month. "I try to take shows within driving distance of my home," he said, pointing out his wife, Caroline. "As you can see, my wife's really hot, and I prefer snuggling with her to Afa Jr." He was referring to his sometime travel partner, Afa Anoa'i, Jr., another member of the Wild Samoan dynasty.

His morning began with him deadlifting 600 pounds, squatting 500 and benching 425. Then, he and Caroline began what should have been a two-and-a-half hour ride to Brooklyn. They were making good time when they discovered that the Bayonne Bridge, connecting New Jersey to Staten Island, was closed, and they had to find a long, roundabout way to get to the show. "It was an adventure," Snitsky joked.

Legendary Action Wrestling (LAW), a small, family-oriented promotion, was holding this particular card at a soccer facility located on a rooftop in Sunset Park, an industrial neighborhood with views of the Statue of Liberty. While a tiny ring with loose ropes was set up on artificial grass on one field, Mexican and Caribbean immigrants played on adjoining pitches. By my estimation, there were approximately 100 fans at the wrestling show, largely people from the neighborhood and their kids.

Most of the wrestlers appeared to be trainees. Moves were limited. But with the reasonable cost of admission, the crowd was completely engaged and having a great time.

At 49 years old, Snitsky had a philosophical view about appearing on this type of indie. "The biggest difference between this and WWE are the accommodations. I wouldn't call them top-notch. You're changing in a men's-room stall. You go from working in front of 10,000 to 15,000 fans to working here. It's where you start and where you end up. But you're performing and you're meeting fans. I wouldn't be here if I wasn't enjoying myself."

At the request of my friend Dante Jase, the usual ringside commentator, I agreed to call his match against Mr. Ruda, a heel manager who tried antagonizing the largely minority audience with pro-Trump slogans. The fans appeared apolitical, but I did utter a few jokes about trying to "make Sunset Park great again," harking back to the days when the neighborhood was called Finn Town and Little Norway. I'd planned to make another crack about the community's original inhabitants, the indigenous Canarsee band, for whom a small chunk of Brooklyn is named, but got so caught up in the action, I forgot.

During another match, I watched the bottom rope fall off. With no ring crew available to fix it, the wrestlers worked around the inconvenience. Just behind me, a woman in a burka rocked a newborn in a stroller, while her other three kids laughed and ran around the ring. But when her son, who I guessed was around four, kicked one of the fallen heels when he tumbled to ringside, she grabbed her baby and scurried toward the ring, separating her offspring from the competitors.

This was how the indies used to be, a sprinkling of recognizable names with green and sometimes unknown talent. While these types of shows will always exist, the genre is now known for so much more. "The indies went from the Kamalas and Brutus Beefcakes," Joey Janela noted, invoking the names of two WWE stars from the '80s and '90s, "to becoming a breeding ground for the future."

As a result, promoters no longer have to book former WWE personalities to draw a house. "There are indie legends now," said David Fuller, owner of Iconic Heroes of Wrestling Excellence (IHWE) in Fort Worth, Texas. "And when one of these guys has a great match with one of the really talented regional wrestlers, the people will pay to see the local guy the next time."

Because of online streaming services, fans in other parts of the world can also grow to appreciate that performer's abilities. In 2019, FITE TV COO Mike Weber said his company, which also telecasts boxing and MMA, had 125 wrestling organizations under contract, offering cards from such assorted leagues as Booker T's Houston-based Reality of Wrestling; the Shine women's promotion, Backbreaker Wrestling in Griffith, Indiana; and Southern Legacy Wrestling in Munford, Alabama.

"So many of these wrestlers have good full-time jobs or own companies," Weber said. "But they do it out of their love for wrestling. Not many expect to make a living from this. But they want to be a part of it."

In the years before he signed with AEW, Jimmy Havoc worked as a project manager, projectionist and teacher in his native England. "I still remember how excited I was," he said, "when the bookings got so frequent that I didn't have to do my other jobs."

Fellow Brit "The Villain" Marty Scurll recalled viewing the indies as a place to learn his trade. While that purpose still exists, he said, "the independents are also a platform where guys can actually make money. Each one of us is running his own business."

Between September 28 and November 1, 2018, "The Innovator of Violence" Tommy Dreamer had just four days off. "I'm 47 years old," he said in the midst of that run, "and, last year, I did 187 independent wrestling events all over the world, including working for my own promotion," House of Hardcore.

At the time, Dreamer viewed himself as part of a continuum, playing the part of the wizened veteran for the younger talent, a role once occupied by Terry Funk in Extreme Championship Wrestling (ECW). "I'm working my ass off and trying to help the next generation of stars."

Besides the in-ring lessons, there were teachings about backstage etiquette, along with the catechism of fan interaction. "The thing about independent wrestling is that it's such an intimate setting," observed John Thorne, owner of Cleveland's Absolute Intense Wrestling (AIW). "You're so close to the people. Heels get on the mic and yell things, and an individual fan will yell back, and the wrestler will answer him. It's an interactive experience."

In between the matches, the spectator can often find that same wrestler at the merchandise table and engage in a civil dialogue. "My one gripe about the intimacy is that it leads to seeing people out of character, which takes the mystery away," Baxter said. "At the same time, I've seen guys have an interesting conversation with a fan before a show, then come out at intermission to continue. That's when you really feel that this is a community."

With the code of kayfabe — keeping fans in the dark about pro wrestling's predetermined nature — diminished, equal friendships between spectators and performers are now possible. Said Janela, "I talk to the fans more than I talk to the wrestlers."

San Diego–based veteran B-Boy views some of those fans as a resource. "They can tell you about other shows they've seen, other promoters. They give you input. It doesn't mean they're always right. You don't have to listen to them. But it's good to have them there."

Another line that's eroded is the one separating indie fans from those of larger organizations. "There used to be the same mentality among indie fans that you'd find in people who loved these fringe bands before they struck it big," noted Derek Sabato, *Wrestling Observer* producer and a referee for Combat Zone Wrestling (CZW) and CHIKARA. "'How can you be a fan? I was here first?' Now, the world is smaller, and everyone on the scene wants people watching them. If you're really a fan, you want new people discovering the wrestlers you love. The barrier between these two types of fans is less than it's ever been before. It's no longer *us versus them*."

3
CHAPTER

The indie wrestling revolution would have occurred with or without Cody. The ocean had already swelled, due to the shifting contours of the sandbank below. As the wave peeled, though, it was the self-professed "Prince of Pro Wrestling" riding back and forth across the crest.

Although trained by his father, as well as Al Snow, Rock 'n' Roll Express member Robert Gibson, "Nightmare" Danny Davis and Randy Orton, Cody drew much of his creative inspiration from film producer, actor and YouTube personality Adi Shankar, whose work includes *The Grey, Dredd, Castlevania* and unauthorized Bootleg Universe satire films like *Venom: Truth in Journalism* and *The Punisher: Dirty Laundry*. "He's somebody I've learned a lot from," Cody told *Bleacher Report*, "because these old [wrestling] models . . . it's not the way the business is going to be five to ten years from now. If you hire wrestlers and don't give them the freedom of expression, you're doing yourself a disservice. This era of trying to control every aspect of creation kills creativity."

Yet, as much as he embraced disarray, Cody also treasured the old-school wrestling principles espoused by The American Dream. Cody's theme music referenced Dusty's classic 1985 promo in which he compared the "hard times" experienced by unemployed auto workers to his own travails with then–NWA World Heavyweight champion, Ric Flair: "My father said, 'Hard times breed better men.'"

"Dusty never smartened me up to anything," he said during his *Inside the Ropes* Q&A in Dublin in 2018, romanticizing the days when wrestlers kayfabed their own families. "I think he thought, *he'll figure it out*. We never talked about sex. He never told me about Santa Claus. He kind of just waited. And wrestling, he waited way too long. I wanted to believe . . . I was one of those kids."

After a segment that Dusty booked involving Vader breaking Sting's ribs, Cody inquired about the six-time WCW World Heavyweight champion's future. "Well, Sting's going to drink a lot of milk," Dusty said, "and I'm pretty sure he'll be at work next week."

A few weeks later, Cody broke his leg. "In the hospital bed, I was screaming at my mother, 'We have to go get milk.'"

Born Cody Garrett Runnels the same year as the "hard times" promo, there were few places he could go to escape the pull of the wrestling business. Dusty's tag-team partner Terry "Magnum TA" Allen was the boy's godfather, and his uncles were Fred "Tugboat" Ottman and Jerry Sags of the Nasty Boys. Although Cody spoke of college and spent some time in L.A., trying to break into acting, his fate was determined early. As a junior and senior at Lassiter High School, he won the Georgia state wrestling tournament at 189 pounds. During the same period, he refereed for Turnbuckle Championship Wrestling (TCW), the Marietta-based indie his father owned from 2000 to 2003. At age 17, Cody legally changed his surname to Rhodes, the moniker his father — born Virgil Riley Runnels Jr. — had been using since 1968. He debuted in WWE in 2008, soon forming a team with the sons of "Million Dollar Man" Ted DiBiase and Afa the Wild Samoan.

He'd also hold the WWE World Tag Team and Intercontinental titles. WWE was "a great place to learn, travel and grow up across TV sets," he tweeted in 2018. "[It] helped shape the business side of me forever."

In 2011, CM Punk predicted that he and Cody, along with Beth Phoenix, Zack Ryder, Daniel Bryan and the high-flying team of Air

Boom — Kofi Kingston and Even Bourne (Matt Sydal) — represented WWE's future. "It was definitely time for change," Cody told *Inside the Ropes*. "I think Punk was ready, but I don't think everybody else . . . definitely not me, definitely not Sydal . . . were ready for that amount of responsibility, to take the reins."

For a while, Cody teamed with his half-brother, Dustin, who'd been playing the platinum-suited, androgynous Goldust on and off since 1995. Born 16 years apart and raised by different mothers, the pair didn't completely mesh. In 2014, Cody was turned into Stardust — a nickname Dusty had used at one point of his career. Like Goldust, Stardust wore a bodysuit and face paint. Inspired by Jim Carrey's portrayal of the Riddler in *Batman Forever*, he'd distort his face into a demented grimace and prattle on about the "Fifth Dimension" and the "Cosmic Key."

"It was supposed to be a temporary thing so the brothers could turn on each other," Cody's wife, Brandi, told *Inside the Ropes*. "It was supposed to be a short-lived story. And I thought, 'That would be cool. That could be really cool.' And then it seemed like everybody lost interest in it except for the people who were in it. He developed this insane character that, literally, as soon as he put the outfit on, he became that. Now, he's lost. How does that happen?"

Cody remembered being "angry after each show."

According to the plot, Cody had transformed into Stardust and lost sense of who he'd been and where he'd come from. He began ditching Goldust in the ring during tag team matches. During one promo building up to the sibling showdown, Stardust announced, "Cody Rhodes is dead and, as far as I'm concerned, so is my father," while Dusty looked at him, despairingly.

Dustin wanted the tension to lead to a clash at *WrestleMania*. "We kept getting told, 'No, it's not big enough,'" Dustin recounted on Chris Jericho's *Talk Is Jericho* podcast. "And I had that said to me more times than I wanted to hear. *If you just got behind the story and you pushed it just a little bit, the interest would be there.*"

Instead, the duo met at the *Fast Lane* pay-per-view in February 2015. "It was horrible," Dustin said. "Neither one of us liked it. It just did not click. It wasn't special. I think we were both upset because it was not *WrestleMania* and here we are stuck on *Fast Lane*, which sucked. And we weren't anywhere close to the main event. It was just like, no story behind it, put them out there, let brother do brother, see where it lays and it was horrible."

Four months later, Dusty passed away. In the aftermath, his youngest son lobbied to become Cody Rhodes again. He told *The Ringer* that WWE's writing team didn't even make an effort to humor him. During one meeting, he said, he was seated across from a writer who pretended to type on a laptop that wasn't turned on.

That's when Cody began planning his exit from the company, gleaning advice from Kevin Owens, who, as Kevin Steen, had been a superstar on the indie circuit. Owens, who'd been trained by Dusty, gave Cody the names of promoters, along with suggestions about what to charge and the best way to market merchandise.

On May 16, 2016, Cody found himself at the Greensboro Coliseum in North Carolina, a building steeped in family lore. It played host to *Starcade '83*, a closed-circuit event that predated *WrestleMania I*, where "Nature Boy" Ric Flair captured the NWA World Heavyweight belt — at this point, the most prestigious championship in wrestling — from Harley Race in a steel cage, with former titlist Gene Kiniski serving as referee. Dusty had developed the *Starcade* concept and booked the entire show two months before Hulk Hogan's World Wrestling Federation Championship victory over the Iron Sheik in Madison Square Garden signaled that the industry's power was swiveling to the McMahon family. On November 28, 1985, Dusty was back in Greensboro for another *Starcade*, this time unseating Flair for the NWA title.

Thirty-one years later, Cody sat in the Greensboro Coliseum dressing room, digesting the news that WWE's writers hadn't pencilled him in to that night's edition of *Monday Night Raw*. Staring into his locker, he pondered the outfit he'd created for the return of Cody Rhodes, along with Stardust's makeup and bodysuit. His mind swirled with images of the men who'd headlined cards at the arena: Ricky "The Dragon" Steamboat, Wahoo McDaniel, Rowdy Roddy Piper, Jack Brisco. "What would any of those guys have done if they thought they had a brand, if they thought they had value?" he told *The Ringer*.

Five days later, he informed the world that he was moving in another direction. "The past 10 years have been quite the trek," he tweeted, "but as of early today, I have asked for my release from WWE."

Expectations were low. Sure, Cody was a gifted hand, and there was the potential for him to entertain a certain fragment of fans by wrestling his way. But he was a WWE midcarder, the kind of performer whose sibling-rivalry match was relegated to an unfamiliar pay-per-view, and there were questions over whether he could draw on the indies.

But Cody would be different than Chris Masters, MVP and Mr. Kennedy. He'd find allies who shared his fervor, ethic and ambition. He'd enter the indie scene in the midst of its ascension. And he'd come in with an understanding that the unfortunate booking decisions of the past could be remedied by a calculated social media strategy.

"Of course, he was Dusty's son, and it was right after Dusty died, and there was a romance there," noted Championship Wrestling from Hollywood owner David Marquez. "But watching Cody on social media became very appealing. Young people were saying, 'Look, he's saying "fuck you" to the establishment. Let's support him.' We saw him grow into a man there."

4
CHAPTER

The indie wrestling revolution could not have occurred during the era of the "Monday Night Wars," when fans were dependent on watching the sport of kings on a major cable network. Nor would it have blossomed during the prior era, when a secure television slot — even on the murkiest UHF station — encouraged viewers to attend live events.

"Newspapers and Saturday morning television used to promote wrestling," remembers Jeff Jarrett, referring to the days when his father was tag-teaming with Tojo Yamamoto in Tennessee, Kentucky and Indiana. "And now, none of those are used."

Instead, promoters, particularly those on the indie circuit, have become reliant on social media. "Twitter is the new dirt sheet," Joey Janela said, wielding the term resentful promoters gave Dave Meltzer's *Wrestling Observer* newsletter after it began exposing kayfabe. "We hang out with fans now. You give them information about something we heard and they tweet. They're the new Meltzer."

Observed Kevin Gill, a commentator for New Jersey–based Game Changer Wrestling (GCW), "Nowadays, if the fans don't tweet, it didn't happen."

Outlets like Facebook and Instagram have enabled individual wrestlers to directly share their messages with individual fans. "There's a lot more opportunity to get ourselves and our brands over," said Jimmy Havoc.

Unlike network television, social media posts are uncensored. "You can do whatever you want, like Donald Trump," David Marquez said in 2019. "When he wants to create a commotion or distraction, he deliberately says something silly.

"But fans are now following people they may have never seen in public, people they only know from the internet. And they're also exposed to different styles of wrestling than what they've seen on TV or what's available at shows close to where they live."

This has allowed inexperienced wrestlers to sharpen their proficiency between the ropes. "Everyone studies each other's work on YouTube," said GCW referee Ryan Torok, "so when two guys finally get in the ring together and call their spots, each knows what the other can do."

As fan tastes broaden the pressure on wrestlers to exhibit a more extensive inventory of maneuvers increases. "We're not only studying new moves, but wrestling from years ago, particularly wrestling from Japan and Mexico," said Davey Boy Smith Jr. "You go to an indie show, and you see wrestlers who do a lot of cross-training, a lot of mixed martial arts, different forms of gymnastics. So you combine that with the matches you can learn from on the internet, and you have a group of wrestlers who are more advanced and are really stepping it up."

When Simon Gotch began wrestling in 2001, he'd purchase VHS tapes to acquaint himself with pro wrestling in different parts of the world. "If you wanted a promoter to notice you, you had to make a VHS tape of three matches, a promo and a highlight reel. Then you'd mail it with an eight-by-ten photo. Nowadays, it's instantaneous. There are so many platforms that allow you to promote and distribute your product. And that's what's allowed independent wrestling to go from something regional to an international phenomenon."

The other advantage that the internet provides is that wrestlers now have a forum to discuss the virtues and vices of particular promoters. "When everyone talks," said referee Derek Sabato, "the scammers get exposed, and the ethic is higher."

Even the most scrupulous promoters are subject to intensive enquiry. "The fans are so invested in the show, you'd think they owned the company," observed Mike Petkovich, promoter and producer of AAW — formerly All American Wrestling — based in the Chicago suburb of Merrionette Park. "You see them smiling at the show and then they go online and it's like you murdered wrestling."

Tom Green, who began promoting in Indiana in 2007, maintained that social media changed long-held convictions about how professional wrestling was supposed to be presented. "If you were a performer and got a booking somewhere, you were at that promoter's whim," he said. "There was the 'right way' of doing things. Now, we have proof that nobody really knows what the right way is, and we're seeing experimentation on every level.

"As the world gets smaller through social media, people tend to follow individuals rather than companies, which benefits the performers and takes away some of the power from promoters. If you're a wrestler, you can pick up your phone, cut a 30-second promo and put it online instantly for fans who are specifically following you. Then, instead of the promoters pushing the wrestlers to fans, the fans are pushing their favorites to the promoters."

But how does a wrestler rise to that level of internet adoration? "The platform exists," said Joey Janela. "A relatively unknown name can find a new audience very fast. It's up to the wrestler to steal the show."

In late 2019, for example, amid the buzz about the emergence of AEW and its head-to-head television rivalry with NXT, hardcore followers were sharing clips of Michigan indie sensation Danhausen bizarrely doing the tequila dance while kicking the hell out of his opponents.

Noted Janela, "These opportunities couldn't have happened 20 or 30 years ago. Me, Cody, the Bucks, we all happened to be in the right place at the right time, just like Mick Foley, The Rock and 'Stone Cold' Steve Austin during the [WWE] Attitude Era."

5
CHAPTER

"Life . . . begins as a cell," Jeff Jarrett said, explaining the beginnings of the indie wrestling revolution. "Something microscopic, something that cannot be seen by the eye. But it is there. It has started."

Despite its carny beginnings and the eccentricities of its impresarios, the business — at least in North America — has had a delineated structure since 1948, when seven promoters parleyed at the President Hotel in Waterloo, Iowa. Facing threats from other companies in their respective regions, the conclave agreed to carve out territories around the United States. Tony Stecher, for example, was based in Minneapolis, while Pinky George operated out of Des Moines. No one would invade the other's sectors, they pledged. And if a rival promoter tried running opposition, the rest of the pack would assist, dispatching their headliners to stack an ally's cards and, if necessary, blacklisting wrestlers who chose to work for the wrong league.

This was the beginning of the National Wrestling Alliance (NWA), a cabal that would eventually include nearly 40 separate territories in such far-flung locations as Japan, Mexico, the Dominican Republic, Australia and New Zealand. Every affiliate had its own stars, feuds and titles. But the NWA Heavyweight Championship was the most distinguished honor of all. Each territory received visits from the NWA kingpin, who'd generally wrestle the area's top star. Although the champion almost always left with the belt, the goal was to give the contender enough offense to *almost* win, enhancing his status in the eyes of the local fans. For the rare instances in which a challenger tried "going into business for himself" and overpowering the titlist, NWA promoters only elected champions who could "shoot" — that is to say, break bones and apply torture holds in defense of the title and organization.

From time to time, though, promoters splintered off from the consortium, crowning their own champions and forming their own acronyms. Verne Gagne, along with partner Wally Karbo, did this in 1960 when he awarded himself the American Wrestling Association (AWA) belt. Eventually, the title was defended in cities such as Minneapolis, Chicago, Omaha, Milwaukee, Winnipeg, Salt Lake City and Denver. In 1963, Vincent James McMahon, father of WWE boss Vincent Kennedy McMahon, and Toots Mondt claimed the entire American northeast, promoting shows from Bangor, Maine, to Washington, DC, under the auspices of what was then called the World Wide Wrestling Federation (WWWF).

Still, both the AWA and WWWF showed deference to the rules engraved during that fateful meeting in Waterloo. Gagne and McMahon generally constrained their expansionist tendencies, attended the NWA's yearly convention and eagerly assisted when an outlaw outfit — a renegade company that flouted the codifications of the wrestling establishment — breached an NWA territory.

Less than a year after the WWWF's formation, the new organization was threatened by an outlaw group that included a well-known promoter from below the Mason-Dixon Line. Headlining the outsider's cards was Antonino Rocca, the Italian-Argentinian high-flier who had set attendance records at Madison Square Garden for McMahon and Mondt in 1959 and 1960. But by 1961, "Nature Boy" Buddy Rogers was the tandem's new favorite. On several occasions, the promoters requested that Rocca "do the job" — aka lose — to the flaxen-haired star, a task the man once known as "The Television Kid" performed with reluctance. When Bruno Sammartino, who beat Rogers for the WWWF Heavyweight

Championship in May 1963, was portrayed as the territory's new ethnic hero, Rocca grew embittered.

Meanwhile, Charlotte-based promoter Jim Crockett Sr. — whose son and namesake would battle the younger Vince McMahon for promotional dominance in the 1980s — invaded the New York area, securing a sponsor, Schaefer Beer; a home venue, Sunnyside Gardens in Queens, and a TV station, WOR, Channel 9, which began broadcasting *All-Star Wrestling with Antonino Rocca*, hosted by local DJ Lonnie Starr, in the fall of '63.

The top heel was Karl Von Hess, who'd earned McMahon's ire after refusing to job to Bruno. In order to enhance his Nazi gimmick, Von Hess turned a West Virginia weightlifter named Sam Slay into his "brother," Adolf. There were other recognizable names as well: "Cowboy" Bob Ellis, who'd main-evented against Buddy Rogers at Madison Square Garden in 1962; "Handsome" Johnny Barend; Mike and Doc Gallagher; and George Becker, who primarily worked for Crockett in the Carolinas. Most of the cards, however, were rounded out by wrestlers with little drawing power.

The group gained some initial attention, but there wasn't enough depth to sustain interest. By January 1964, the promotion had lost its television spot, its sponsor and Sunnyside Gardens. With Crockett abandoning the experiment, Rocca tried promoting by himself, even staging a card at the Singer Bowl during the 1964 New York World's Fair. But with Bruno Sammartino taking on challengers like Gorilla Monsoon, Freddie Blassie and Waldo Von Erich in Madison Square Garden — on shows that also featured Killer Kowalski, Haystacks Calhoun and Bobo Brazil — Rocca's outlaw group was soon forgotten by all but a few fans of obscure wrestling trivia.

The Atlanta wrestling war of 1972 to 1974 is far better remembered and had an impact not only on the Georgia Championship Wrestling (GCW) territory, but also the cable exposure its successor, World Championship Wrestling (WCW), would receive during its rivalry with the World Wrestling Federation.

Ray Gunkel, a former Amateur Athletic Union (AAU) champion in freestyle wrestling, had been a GCW regular since 1957, when he dethroned the territory's co-owner Don McIntyre for the league's top title, the Southern Heavyweight Championship. Eventually, he purchased a piece of the territory, taping its television shows in the studios of Atlanta station WTCG, which communications mogul Ted Turner would transform into "superstation" TBS as cable TV became a staple of American homes.

On television, Gunkel's tag team partner was Buddy Fuller, a member of a storied family of wrestlers whose surnames included Welch, Hatfield, Fields and Golden. Behind the scenes, the two were also business partners. According to multiple sources, their feelings for one another ranged from benign distrust to outright hatred.

Each was anxious to amass allies. As Buddy Fuller's sons, Ron and Rob — later Colonel Rob Parker in WCW — came of age, their father conceived a plan to push them hard in GCW. Gunkel objected, having a separate vision of the promotion's direction, which included bringing in the territory's booker, Tom Renesto of The Assassins tag team, as a partner who could neutralize Fuller's influence.

On August 1, 1972, following a heavy meal at Mrs. Wilkes Dining Room in Savannah, Georgia, 48-year-old Gunkel wrestled Ox Baker at the city's Civic Center. Returning to the dressing room, he showered and talked business. While conversing about the night's gate receipts, he suddenly fell out of his chair and hit the floor. According to the autopsy, Gunkel, who already had hardened and plaque-filled arteries, developed a gumball-sized hematoma after Baker bounced off the ropes and smashed into his opponent's chest. The hematoma swelled, dislodged and caused a fatal heart attack.

Interestingly, Ox Baker was associated with another in-ring death the year before, when a ruptured appendix claimed the life of Alberto Torres three days after he battled the bald Fu-Manchued lout in a Nebraska tag team match. Promoters created a mythology around the incidents, proclaiming that Baker used his heart punch to slaughter both men. In 1974, Baker sparked a riot in Cleveland after interrupting a match and repeatedly heart punching Ernie "The Cat" Ladd.

Gunkel's wife, Ann, an Atlanta businesswoman and former model, inherited her husband's share in GCW. But at Ray's funeral, one of her friends claimed to overhear Florida promoter Eddie Graham and Lester

29

Welch, Buddy Fuller's uncle, plotting a takeover. Aligning themselves with Fuller and Atlanta frontman Paul Jones, they soon attempted to purchase Ann's share of the business. She refused to sell. Rather, she planned to start her own group with Renesto.

Although GCW enjoyed the affiliation of the NWA, Ann was well liked by the wrestlers and convinced the majority of the roster to boycott a GCW show in Columbus, Georgia, on November 22, 1972. The dissidents then joined Ann Gunkel's All-South Wrestling Alliance.

For the next two years, All-South and GCW ran competing shows around the state. As a member of Atlanta's business community, Ann was friends with Ted Turner and persuaded him to bestow her with the Saturday evening time slot previously allotted to GCW. But Buddy Fuller also knew Turner, who agreed to bring GCW back and air its broadcasts immediately afterwards. This was exactly the type of scenario the NWA founders had envisioned. Seeing a member besieged, the organization saturated Georgia with talent such as Jack Brisco, Bill Watts and Mr. Wrestling #2. Unable to replenish its cards with comparable attractions, All-South grew static. By the fall of 1974, Ann surrendered.

GCW quickly seized All-South's timeslot. Now, instead of watching the competing promotions back to back, fans received 120 straight minutes of GCW. In 1982, at Ted Turner's request, the group's name was changed to World Championship Wrestling to reflect the entrepreneur's global objectives. With the exception of a small window in 1984 and 1985, when the World Wrestling Federation maneuvered itself into the two hour space, the Saturday evening broadcast would become WCW's most high-profile showcase on cable television until the Monday Night Wars ignited in 1995.

In 1955, Ed Don George, who held several versions of the world championship before the formation of the NWA, sold his wrestling territory based in Buffalo, New York, to Pedro Martinez. Unhappy with the fees charged by the NWA — on cards featuring the NWA World Heavyweight champion, the organization took 2 percent of the gate, while the titlist received 8 percent — Martinez broke off from the group. For the first several years, cards centered on Martinez's son-in-law Ilio

DiPaolo. Like Rocca, DiPaolo appealed to both Italians and Hispanics; he was born in Italy, lived in Venezuela and wrestled in the Dominican Republic. In Buffalo, DiPaolo became an institution, opening a popular restaurant outside the city when he went into semi-retirement in 1965.

By 1972, Martinez's National Wrestling Federation (NWF) was holding events in Upstate New York, Ohio and western Pennsylvania. "We were stretched pretty thin back then," his son, Ron, a host of the league's television shows, told *SLAM! Wrestling*'s Steve Johnson. "We were trying to run Cleveland and Pittsburgh TV, both on Saturday afternoon, as well as Akron, Ohio, on Saturday night, plus the odd spot show around Pittsburgh, also on Saturday night."

Unlike weaker outlaw groups, the NWF had a collection of top talent, including Ernie Ladd, Waldo Von Erich, Black Jack Lanza, Bulldog Brower, Dick the Bruiser, Mighty Igor, Abdullah the Butcher and the Fabulous Fargos, consisting of Don Kait and a young Greg "The Hammer" Valentine. The main draw of the promotion was Martinez's financial partner, Johnny Powers. In a quest to build his reputation in the United States, Antonio Inoki captured the NWF Heavyweight Championship from Powers in 1973, and he brought it to Japan, where it was defended long after the NWF folded a year later; the final titlist, Shinsuke Nakamura, unified it with the IWGP Heavyweight crown in 2004.

In 1975, Martinez joined with Eddie Einhorn to start a new group, the International Wrestling Association (IWA), using talent already affiliated with the NWF. Like Ted Turner and AEW's Tony Khan, Einhorn was a sports executive — he'd started the TVS television network devoted to college sports, was involved with the upstart World Football League and later was minority owner of the Chicago White Sox — who sought to transmogrify the wrestling business. Defying the territorial system embraced by the NWA, AWA and WWWF, the IWA's goal was to become a national company. Although promoters generally paid talent a percentage of the gate — and transportation and lodging were generally the wrestlers' problems — the IWA promised guaranteed money and also paid for hotel rooms and rental cars.

In New York, the IWA's television show, hosted by Jack Reynolds and Tex McKenzie, aired on WOR, the same station that broadcast *All-Star Wrestling with Antonino Rocca* a dozen years before. Locked out of

31

Madison Square Garden because of the WWWF's longtime association with the arena, the IWA went across the river to Roosevelt Stadium in Jersey City, drawing 14,000 for a bout featuring IWA World Heavyweight champion Mil Mascaras defending the gold against former WWWF titlist Ivan Koloff. But national expansion did not occur as quickly or nimbly as anticipated. Facing money losses, Einhorn abandoned the venture after a few months.

With Powers as booker, the group concentrated on the Mid-Atlantic states but encountered resistance from arenas loyal to the promoter there, Jim Crockett Jr., son of Rocca's onetime business partner. In 1976, IWA Tag Team champions Geeto and Bolo Mongol, turned up on the Charlotte territory's television show with the belts, billing themselves as the International Tag Team title holders. After losing an anti-trust case against Crockett, the IWA closed in 1978.

The television show, however, took on a new life when old episodes began airing in Nigeria and Singapore, enabling Powers to defend the strap in Africa as late as 1982. What fans didn't realize was that Mascaras claimed to have never lost the belt either. He continued to appear as champion in Mexico and Japan, including a 2016 Korakuen Hall bout when "The Man of 1,000 Masks" was 74 years old.

Even when he was playing minor league baseball, the future Randy "Macho Man" Savage would slip a mask on and appear on the undercards of shows featuring his father, *Ripley's Believe It or Not*–endorsed sit-up champion Angelo Poffo. The hooded Spider was far skinnier than the Macho Man, but just as intense. Even before the bell rang, he frantically ran the ropes. Although spectators knew nothing about him, he made them curious to see more.

But after Randy finally gave up baseball in 1975 — symbolically destroying his bats and other equipment — to devote himself to his father's vocation, promoters did not seem in any rush to propel him to main events. Frustrated by their myopia, Angelo began International Championship Wrestling (ICW) in 1978 to highlight Randy and his younger brother, "Leaping" Lanny Poffo, later known as "The Genius."

Perhaps more than any promotion, ICW defined the term "outlaw." Based in Lexington, Kentucky, the ICW held shows in towns reserved for the Knoxville, Nashville, Memphis and Indianapolis territories, along with Verne Gagne's AWA, with cards generally featuring all three Poffos, along with names like the original Sheik, Crusher Broomfield (a younger version of the One Man Gang), "Hustler" Rip Rogers, future NWA Heavyweight champion "Rugged" Ronnie Garvin, Bob Roop, Ox Baker, "Professor" Boris Malenko and "Pistol" Pez Whatley. The announce team included Randy's real-life girlfriend, Liz Hulette, who'd become "Miss Elizabeth" in the World Wrestling Federation.

One of the group's strategies for drawing crowds was having its talent deprecate the headliners from the rival territories, throwing out challenges and even breaking kayfabe by revealing some wrestlers' actual names. When the Memphis promotion held shows in Lexington, the ICW crew bought tickets, daring the performers to fight as they entered the Rupp Arena or heckling them from ringside. Some of the Memphis team were so unnerved, particularly by Savage, that they began carrying guns.

Upon learning that "Superstar" Bill Dundee had emblazoned the words "Macho Man" on his trunks, Savage committed himself to escalating the tension. While leaving the gym in Henderson, Tennessee, one day, Dundee said that he encountered a mob of ICW wrestlers. He had his arms folded against his car, he recounted, and was talking to Pez Whatley and Lanny Poffo's tag team partner, George Weingeroff, when Savage sucker punched him. Scrambling to his car, Dundee said that he managed to grab his .38 and hold it on Angelo Poffo until Randy agreed to back off.

In a more popular rendition of the encounter, Savage confronted Dundee in the parking lot. Intimidated, Dundee is said to have pulled his gun. In the fracas that followed, Savage allegedly wrested the .38 away and pistol-whipped Dundee, putting him out of commission for several weeks.

Once, when Randy Savage and I were in the same car, and he was relaxed and talking about other things, I tried getting the true tale out of him. "There are a lot of different versions of that story," he answered. End of topic.

As with the other outlaw groups, ICW was eventually worn down by its more proven competition. In the course of this wrestling war, though, Savage had emerged in the eyes of local fans as a fearsome character. When Angelo decided to shut the operation down, he and Randy "invaded" the Memphis TV show, causing a commotion at the announce table, where Randy grabbed a framed photo of the territory's number one babyface, Jerry "The King" Lawler, and busted it with his forehead. Behind the scenes, the recent animosities were written off as "just business." Because of his feud with Lawler — and a memorable bout featuring Randy and Lanny against the Rock 'n' Roll Express — Savage received the attention that Angelo was seeking by forming ICW. Shortly after the first *WrestleMania*, the Macho Man began his Hall of Fame career in the World Wrestling Federation.

By this point, the sons of Vincent James McMahon and Jim Crockett Sr. had renewed the conflict that started with the defection of Antonino Rocca. The Hatfields and McCoys analogy is appropriate here, since one of the actual Hatfields, Virgil "Speedy" Hatfield, was married into the Welch and Fuller clan. As Vincent Kennedy McMahon stockpiled talent from the various territories — including the AWA, from which he lured Hulk Hogan, Jesse "The Body" Ventura and announcer "Mean" Gene Okerlund, among others — and ran shows wherever he wished, Jim Crockett Jr. became the most powerful promoter in the NWA, co-opting the Georgia, Florida, Oklahoma and Kansas City circuits. But all that expansion was expensive. By 1988, Crockett was out of cash and sold his wrestling business to Ted Turner, who'd use his checkbook and broadcasting network to turn WCW into the World Wrestling Federation's most serious rival.

Somewhere in this time period, the word "indie" replaced the term "outlaw." Not that anyone really cared about that scene at the time.

Shane "Hurricane" Helms grew up in Crockett Country and started wrestling in 1988. "The indie scene was abysmal," he said. "It was hard to find good trainers. And [because of the Hulk Hogan era] it was still a big-man's business. It was just a bunch of big guys who wanted to beat me up."

Getting paid was a challenge. "I remember a promoter handing me an envelope with five dollars in it. I said, 'You needed an envelope for that?' Another time, I was working a loop, wrestling Friday night and two times on Saturday. I was supposed to get paid after the last show. Then they said that they'd pay me at the end of the month. And I finally did get an envelope from them. But when I opened it up, there was a really strange Bible tract inside."

It took a man as deranged as Herb Abrams to attempt to start a wrestling company in this atmosphere. Herb had owned a women's clothing store in Flushing, Queens, close to where I grew up, and I remember him bringing in Chief Jay Strongbow and Billy White Wolf, the WWWF World Tag Team champions from December 1976 to August 1977. I'm not sure if Abrams sold any dresses that day, but, if memory serves me correctly, my art teacher from Bayside High School, Mr. Stock, was in attendance.

In famed wrestling photographer and writer Bill Apter's book, *Is Wrestling Fixed? I Didn't Know It Was Broken!*, he recalled Abrams' pledge to become a promoter one day. In that instance, at least, Herb was telling the truth.

Convinced that he was a legitimate challenger to Vince McMahon, Abrams had procured the Universal Wrestling Federation (UWF) name. Both Bill Watts, whose Oklahoma-based UWF was one of the most compelling leagues of the 1980s, and Jim Crockett Jr., who eventually purchased the company and folded it into his own, had neglected to trademark the acronym, and Abrams hoped to capitalize on the group's reputation. Reaching into his personal coffers, he compiled an impressive talent list of ex-WWFers: former champions Bob Backlund and Ivan Koloff, as well as Bam Bam Bigelow, Paul "Mr. Wonderful" Orndorff, Don "The Magnificent" Muraco, Bob Orton Jr., B. Brian Blair, Billy Jack Haynes, Ken Patera, "Captain" Lou Albano and others. Colonel DeBeers, a top AWA contender several years earlier, and Steve "Dr. Death" Williams, a centerpiece of Watts' UWF and a formidable presence in the NWA, were on the roster, along with a young, daring Mick "Cactus Jack" Foley. Even Andre the Giant showed up in a non-wrestling role.

Debuting in 1990, Abrams' television show initially featured the promoter sharing announcing duties with "Living Legend" Bruno

Sammartino, whose post-WWF career had left him disaffected toward the McMahon family. Some shows were shot in a Manhattan hotel ballroom populated with models clearly paid to play audience members. When Dave Meltzer's newsletter criticized Herb's program, the promoter named a jobber "Davey Meltzer" and had Steve "Dr. Death" Williams destroy him and shove a version of the *Wrestling Observer* into his mouth. Abrams also offered Williams an extra $100 to break the nose of opponent Steve Ray — not to be confused with WWE Hall of Famer Stevie Ray of Harlem Heat — because Herb was convinced that his wife was having an affair with the buffed blond showman. Williams allegedly took the money but only pretended to harm his adversary.

Attempting to penetrate the pay-per-view market, the UWF held a show called "Beach Brawl" in 1991, drawing just 500 fans to the 4,000-seat Manatee Civic Center in Palmetto, Florida.

Still, the UWF sputtered on until 1994, closing after a live cable TV special drew 600 to the MGM Grand — where AEW would pull approximately 12,000 fans to its *Double or Nothing* pay-per-view in 2019.

Two years later, 41-year-old Abrams was hanging out with two prostitutes in his New York office. Naked, with cocaine stuck to a lubricant smeared all over his body, he began demolishing furniture with a baseball bat. Police were summoned, and he died of a heart attack in their custody.

The story, however, does not end there. In 2019, a man claiming to be Herb Abrams Jr. boasted that he was reviving the UWF in Southern California. Although Abrams was said to have no children, his surviving relatives quickly took to Facebook to decry the promoter as a fraud. When the SoCal Uncensored website contacted a venue where a UWF show was supposed to be held, they discovered that no wrestling card had been scheduled — even though non-refundable tickets were being sold online. As SoCalUncensored continued its probe, it traced Herb Abrams Jr.'s account to a San Diego figure on the fringes of the business who'd previously been sued for making equally preposterous assertions.

CHAPTER 6

Wrestler and promoter Vance Nevada remembered the cloud of gloom hanging over the western Canadian indies in the 1990s. "People were lamenting the death of the business," he said, "blaming Vince McMahon for killing it, saying they'd never have a chance again."

Back then, talent still spoke carny in the dressing room — a form of pig Latin punctuated by Zs that excluded outsiders from understanding the wrestlers' conversations. "You had the old-school promoters who were all about kayfabe, who'd fine you if you were seen in a restaurant with your opponent," Nevada said. Babyfaces and heels changed on opposite sides of the building, and someone ran back and forth, exchanging messages.

Fans who suddenly came into money and decided to enter the wrestling business were branded "money marks" since the performers understood that these devotees were oblivious to the reality that, once they were finished exhausting their savings, their access to the industry would end. "They'd book a bunch of fly-in talent," Nevada said, "and burn out."

After viewing hours of VHS tapes of hardcore encounters from Japan, one striver booked a card consisting of nothing but cage matches in Winnipeg. "Winnipeg can be a pretty conservative place," Nevada said, "and after the first blood-and-guts match, about half of the crowd walked out. I was on another card that drew about 25 people. After that show, everyone went out, and the promoter said, 'You know what? The bar tab is on me.' It took about an hour for him to realize that's not something you say to a group of wrestlers."

Other promoters demanded that wrestlers sign exclusive contracts despite the fact that their shows were weeks or even months apart. "They didn't want you working anywhere else without their permission," Nevada said. "One guy actually took me to small claims court for breach of contract after I took a booking somewhere else. He didn't show up on the court date, and the judge threw out the case. But these were the kinds of things that would happen."

On numerous occasions, Nevada partook in Winnipeg promoter Tony Condello's infamous "death tours" of Inuit communities in northern Manitoba. It was forbidding territory, with few hotels or restaurants. Wrestlers either slept in arenas or in their cars on the side of the road. Each was required to pack at least one bag of food to sustain themselves. But Nevada learned a lot. "The good thing was that there were still guys on the scene who'd worked for [promoter] Al Tomko in Vancouver and Stu Hart in Calgary. So you had guys who'd been through the territory system and watched it die. But they were holding on, hoping it came back." Over the years, these performers had had the opportunity to wrestle stars like former NWA World Heavyweight champion Gene Kiniski and ex-WWWF kingpin Stan "The Man" Stasiak, along with Bret Hart and the British Bulldogs before they moved on to the World Wrestling Federation. "They had all that experience. So they were there to watch your match and give you feedback."

Raised in the rural town of Souris, Manitoba, the real-life Vern May lived in a region where he could receive WWF, AWA and the Hart Family's Stampede promotion on television. "We had three hours of wrestling we could watch," he said, "and all very different products."

One day in high school, a kid saw Vern sketching pictures of wrestlers in class and mentioned that his cousin was local grappler Chi Chi Cruz. Although billed as a native of East L.A., Cruz was actually from Hartney, Manitoba. On Cruz's recommendation, Vern began training with Ernest Rheault in the town of Somerset in 1993. "The training back then was designed to weed you out if you couldn't survive it. I'd estimate that 75 percent of all the aspiring superstars quit the camp before completion. Of the remaining 25 percent, only about 10 percent would make it past their first year and, typically, a few more would drop off before the end of year two."

Although 17-year-old Vern survived training school, his repertoire was limited. "They taught me a headlock, takedown, hip toss and that was it. Then, they released me to the wolves."

Weighing just 150 pounds, he described his role as "a milk and cookies babyface, cannon fodder for the veteran heels." Working for the River City Wrestling group, Vern generally worked every second Thursday in front of 300 to 400 fans. Most of the other wrestlers had day jobs. But Vern was determined to make wrestling his life. He developed his "Mr. Beefy Goodness" Vance Nevada character into a self-absorbed heel who was infinitely more interesting than the teenager portraying him. "The name was given to me as a rib. There'd been a really terrible wrestler out of Vancouver who'd also used the name 'Nevada,' so maybe they were trying to tell me something."

From Winnipeg, he began working in other parts of Canada, including Emile Dupree's Grand Prix summertime promotion, which ran in hockey arenas throughout Canada's Maritime region. Wherever he traveled, he encountered one constant. There were Vance Nevadas everywhere — people willing to make virtually any concession to enjoy even a small taste of the wrestling business.

David Fuller's mother passed away when he was 15. A native of Fort Worth, Texas, Fuller remembered Steve Austin feuding with his trainer "Gentleman" Chris Adams at the Dallas Sportatorium during the final incarnation of World Class Championship Wrestling. Once Austin's "Stone Cold" character developed in the WWF, Fuller "began living vicariously through him."

At home, Fuller's father regaled the grieving boy with stories about watching Johnny Valentine and Wahoo McDaniel's bloody clashes over the Texas Heavyweight title, circa 1970. When David found out that Valentine — who'd been paralyzed in a 1975 private airplane crash that nearly ended "Nature Boy" Ric Flair's career — was running a small training school in Fort Worth, the teen sought out the legend. "I was about five-foot-five and maybe 100 pounds," Fuller recalled. "I begged him and begged him to join until he said yes. Valentine was in his wheelchair, and couldn't do much. But I'd run the ropes and take Johnny's forearm. His wife, Sharon wasn't a worker, but she could put you in a headlock 'til you screamed. I think she was the one who told me, 'You don't really have the body for this, but I think you could become a promoter.'"

Fuller took the advice seriously.

In November 1998, 16-year-old Fuller and his friends Danny Casey and Ronnie McMurray heard about an available ring and rented it for $100. They set it up in Ronnie's backyard, then attended a weekly Friday night indie show located in North Richland Hills. "You want some money?" Fuller asked the talent when they went out to the gimmick table during intermission. "Come on down."

The trio agreed to hold their debut card on a Saturday afternoon, allowing the wrestlers to work their regular Friday show and a Saturday night indie about 90 minutes away. If the few dollars they were offering wasn't enough, they told the wrestlers that they could crash at Ronnie's house. "We drew about 30 people and at the end of the show, the owner just left the ring there," Fuller recounted.

"I don't have anywhere else to put it," he told the kids. "I guess it's safe here."

After two more shows, the boys started charging five dollars a ticket. They rented 50 chairs and filled every seat.

"At the other indie shows, the ring announcer would say, 'Don't throw anything in the ring,'" Fuller said. "We told the fans, 'Do anything you want.'"

Fuller was in the wrestling business. He and his friends created a primitive website and a name: Iconic Heroes of Wrestling Excellence (IHWE). One day, they received a message from hardcore warrior Dylan

Keith Summers, aka Necro Butcher, who'd later be shown taking a staple gun to Mickey Rourke in the 2008 movie *The Wrestler*. Summers lived in Killeen and was in the mood to work. They gave him $10. A reporter from the *Fort Worth Star-Telegram* was there when Necro Butcher turned up with a garbage can full of weapons, smashing a light tube over his foe Damon Richards' back and lacerating him with one of the edges. There seemed to be no such thing as bad publicity. "This story comes out about these teenagers who have their own wrestling promotion in their backyard," Fuller said. "More people started coming to our shows. Now we could pay the wrestlers between $50 and $60.

"But the one indie that we'd been getting most of our wrestlers from wasn't happy. 'Who's this 16-year-old kid using our talent in his friend's backyard?' They sent me an email banning me from coming to their shows. There was no social media back then. We printed their email in our program, which I think we were selling for a dollar. People started passing it around, and WFAA [Dallas' ABC affiliate] did a story on us."

Of course, the good times could only last so long. "We began bringing in outside talent. If you spend $600 a show and you only charge five dollars a ticket, you do the math. There were neighbors complaining about cars parking up and down the street, noise, people getting hit with barbed wire bats. The cops were coming around and it was too much."

From his very first card, Fuller had felt an affinity with Rodney Mack, an indie star who'd eventually perform in WWE with his wife, Jazz. When the couple went on the road, they occasionally asked Fuller to accompany them. Sometimes, Necro Butcher came along too. "I did refereeing, ring announcing, play by play. I sold gimmicks. I did security. I got thrown in a mud pit one night by a bunch of women. I didn't want to cut myself for the longest time because I was scared of it. But I did whatever was asked of me. You didn't cover up for chair shots. *'You're a man. Take it.'*"

By the time he graduated high school, Fuller was vastly different from the sad boy consoling himself by watching "Stone Cold" Steve Austin on *Monday Night Raw*. But he still loved wrestling. And wrestling loved him back.

There's also a similar story from some 1,200 miles away, in Ohio.

At the height of WWF's Attitude Era, in the late 1990s, 15-year-old John Thorne got on the internet to see if he could rent a wrestling ring. Within hours, he received a reply from a guy who ran a wrestling school. For $300, Thorne could have a ring *and* a crew of wrestlers. They wouldn't get paid, their promoter told them, but it was still a good deal. With all that exposure, they'd probably get other wrestling gigs.

Now, all Thorne needed was a venue. Opening the yellow pages, he began looking up church phone numbers. A sanctuary in the Cleveland suburb of Brecksville agreed to let him use the gym for $200.

"I promoted a totally untrained event, mainly using my friends from high school," said Thorne, the promoter for Absolute Intense Wrestling (AIW). Among the competitors that night was Thorne's classmate Matt Capiccioni, who'd later work as Matt Cross in Ring of Honor and Son of Havoc in Lucha Underground. "It was his first time in a ring ever. Totally untrained."

Thorne has witnessed considerable change in the industry since his church wrestling days. "In 1999, you'd put the word 'wrestling' out there and a couple of hundred people showed up," Thorne said. "So you had a bunch of 15-year-olds trying to promote a wrestling event, and the crowd is into everything. We had one guy come out with a live chainsaw, and he left it running during the match. Today, even on the smallest indie, people would be worried about the liability. But nobody thought about that back then. At least, nobody I knew."

During the same period, Vance Nevada pursued bookings in the United States. He was en route to a show in Fond du Lac, Wisconsin, with another Winnipeg wrestler, when the two were stopped at the border. "Of course, I was working without a visa," he said. "Obviously, no indie promoter is going to shell out more than he's paying you to get you a visa. So someone had called ahead to alert the authorities.

"Our car was ripped through, and we were put in separate holding rooms for hours. Then someone came back and gave my colleague the opportunity to withdraw his application to enter the U.S. I was given a five-year ban from coming into the country — all over petty wrestling politics."

This was as much a part of the industry as the excitement of cutting a promo in front of a screaming crowd. Tony Condello, who was born in Calabria, Italy, and had a very distinct accent, told Nevada about rival promoters calling venues, mimicking his voice and cancelling events. "A promoter saw his marriage destroyed due to a rib," or practical joke, Nevada said, "after another promoter sent a girl to his house to tell his wife she was pregnant."

It was the kind of hoax competing carnival operators had pulled — a reminder that no amount of money, television contracts or stockholders could fully eradicate wrestling's origins. But the carny aspect of pro wrestling also leads to great pride in the little tricks that hypnotize the public — and keep them coming back — as well as membership in a fraternity that includes anyone bold enough to take a bump in a pair of spandex. "One of the things I always found fascinating is that when you crossed paths with someone who was legitimately successful — either a well-traveled guy who regularly worked Japan or a WWE name now on the indies — they were often the most humble people you'd ever meet," Nevada said. In the ring, these performers were frequently eager to have compelling matches against opponents who had nothing but regional reputations. "They knew that Vince McMahon didn't have scouts watching to see how we were performing in Moose Jaw, Saskatchewan. They were doing this for *you*."

7
CHAPTER

Tension always crackled in Philadelphia, a city steeped in gang-sterism, gunplay, political corruption and racial strife. Only in Philadelphia would the city's first African-American mayor, Wilson Goode, have his police drop a bomb from a helicopter to punish the black militant group, MOVE, destroying more than 60 homes in the process. Whether they were watching wrestling, hockey or Roller Games — a frenzied off-shoot of roller derby — Philadelphia fans were generally unsatisfied unless there was the potential for the riot squad to rush in with nightsticks flailing. The late Gootch Gautieri, a Roller Games villain who used to pepper the female players with profanities that sometimes made the air, said that he'd travel to Philadelphia with bodyguards, and once utilized his skates to bloody the face of a fan who rushed onto the track. Recalled Philadelphia Warriors sweetheart Judy Arnold, "The Philly crowds always wanted us to smash someone."

Given the city's mentality, it was a good place to start an indie, even when independents in other locations were floundering. A fan named Joel Goodhart was convinced that both the WWF and WCW were ignoring the unique sensibilities of fans in the City of Brotherly Love.

So in 1989, he founded the Tri-State Wrestling Alliance (TWA) to service a region that included Delaware and South Jersey. Forging ties with the few territories that still existed, the TWA promoted shows that featured matches like Jerry "The King" Lawler — then the champion of the United States Wrestling Association (USWA), an allegiance of the dying Memphis and Dallas groups — against Kerry Von Erich; AWA World Heavyweight titlist Larry Zbyszko versus David Sammartino, Bruno's son; NWA Pacific Northwest Heavyweight champion Billy Jack Haynes versus Brian "Crush" Adams; Abdullah the Butcher versus Bam Bam Bigelow; and Lawler against his first cousin, the Honky Tonk Man.

Goodhart also had a radio show that, in those days before the internet, provided a lot of elusive wrestling information. But like so many before and since, investing in the wrestling business was a losing proposition for the amiable promoter. In 1992, he sold the company to his partner, pawnbroker and real estate agent Tod Gordon, who initially used the TWA Championship belt in the newly named Eastern Championship Wrestling.

"People have to remember that ECW was just a small indie, running once a month," noted Tommy Dreamer.

Operating out of an old freight warehouse that also functioned as a bingo hall, Eastern Championship Wrestling (ECW) initially featured such former WWF stars as Jim "The Anvil" Neidhart, "The Magnificent" Muraco and the first ECW champion, Jimmy "Superfly" Snuka. "Hot Stuff" Eddie Gilbert, a creative performer and wrestling strategist, had been the booker in a number of territories, including Memphis, where Paul Heyman worked as his assistant. Now, Heyman reprised the partnership in Philly.

When Gilbert and Gordon had a disagreement, Heyman assumed full booking duties, executing every wrestling fantasy he'd been conceptualizing since he first saw George "The Animal" Steele devour a turnbuckle on TV.

Philadelphia was a city built for a guy like Paul Heyman, who'd been hanging around the wrestling business since childhood, sometimes going berserk in Madison Square Garden while his lawyer father indifferently read the *New York Times* beside him. Starting out as an errand boy for a number of wrestling managers — including "Classy" Freddie Blassie, who used to let the underage Heyman drive his car — Heyman became a ringside photographer with a legitimate WWF press pass, as well as a manager in numerous territories, including WCW.

I'd observed him long before we ever had a conversation, and I once attended a party he threw during the final days of the renowned New York nightclub Studio 54. Other guests included Dusty Rhodes, Ric Flair and Magnum TA. Heyman became acquainted with them after inviting himself to a Jim Crockett Promotions production meeting. While at the party, I overheard a conversation:

"You know, he actually has a great wrestling mind."

"Yeah, but look how he fuckin' behaves himself."

With ECW, Heyman developed a promotion that behaved exactly the way he did, and altered the business in ways that are still felt today.

Unlike other indies who built their shows around former WWF stars, Heyman's policy was to have the onetime headliners chokeslammed by a six-foot-eight leviathan called 911. And he began luring talent not associated with one of the "big two" companies: the Sandman, Public Enemy (Rocco Rock and Johnny Grunge) and the "homicidal, suicidal, genocidal" Sabu, whose hardcore worldview was imparted to him by his uncle, the original Sheik, who'd extended his career by having short matches that involved throwing fireballs and carving up opponents with a pencil hidden in his trunks.

Terry Funk, a former NWA World Heavyweight champion, admired the promotion's attitude, as well as the overall mentality of the competitors, and he enthusiastically bled and took bumps for them. On August 13, 1994, he and tag team partner Mick Foley, then known as Cactus Jack, had just wrestled Public Enemy, when Funk asked a fan to toss him a steel chair. Impressed with the spectator's zeal, Funk then demanded that *everybody* throw chairs. Terry was knocked out by the onslaught, but finished the night as happy as the spectators.

Two weeks later, Heyman and Gordon conceived the plot that would rebrand ECW forever, rebelling against both tradition and nostalgia to desecrate what was arguably the industry's most cherished symbol.

Up until 1991, WCW had remained the largest member of the NWA. On television, the NWA and WCW titles were regarded as one and the same. But after champion Ric Flair had a screaming argument with

WCW president Jim Herd, the Nature Boy left with the "Ten Pounds of Gold." Officially, the WCW World Heavyweight Championship was removed from Flair, while the few promotions that stayed in the NWA continued to recognize him as the titlist. Ultimately, the NWA stripped him of the prize when he brought it with him to the World Wrestling Federation a few months later. A new NWA World Heavyweight champion was eventually crowned in Japan. In September 1993, WCW officially resigned from the NWA.

As part of Jim Crockett Jr.'s sale of his wrestling business to Ted Turner in 1988, Crockett signed a three-year non-compete agreement. In 1994, after the non-compete had expired, Crockett decided to rebuild the NWA. He approached the NWA's president, New Jersey promoter Dennis Coralluzzo, and asked him to organize a tournament comprised of wrestlers from the various indies maintaining links to the once mighty organization. ECW wrestler Shane Douglas was scheduled to defeat 2 Cold Scorpio in the finals and become the new NWA kingpin. But Douglas and Coralluzzo had had issues. After Douglas allegedly no-showed a number of Coralluzzo's events, the promoter had contacted several NWA-allied groups and urged them not to hire the man who'd later be called "The Franchise." As a result, it wasn't difficult for Gordon and Heyman to convince Douglas to participate in their plot to sabotage the tournament.

As planned, on August 27, 1994, Douglas won the finals in front of a highly partisan crowd at ECW's home arena, but he shocked fans by tossing the NWA belt on the ground and proclaiming that he had no desire to represent a dead organization. The great NWA champions of the past, he continued, could kiss his ass. Picking up the ECW Championship, he boasted that this was the only title that mattered.

Oh, and one more thing: henceforth, Eastern Championship Wrestling would be referred to as *Extreme* Championship Wrestling.

Paul Carboni had grown up in the Philadelphia area and became a wrestling fan only two years earlier when he developed a fascination with the Ultimate Warrior amidst the hype leading to *SummerSlam '92*. Now a high school teacher in Aston, Pennsylvania, he still romanticizes Douglas' battered ECW belt. "The side plates were falling off," he said. "Everything was low budget. It just represented everything an indie is supposed to be."

47

In reality, ECW was different than most indies, and fans began to travel to the ECW Arena to witness angles and matches unlike anything they'd ever seen. After an American teenager was caned for vandalizing property in Singapore, for example, the Sandman began wielding a "Singapore cane" in his confrontations. In one incident, he repeatedly lashed Tommy Dreamer, who'd yet to expose the depths of his personality. That changed when, as blood poured down Dreamer's back, he exercised his grit by begging Sandman for more torture.

ECW encouraged fan participation. Spectators handed the gladiators stop signs, cheese graters and frying pans to use as weapons in brawls. When someone executed a move that was particularly bold, disciples chanted the promotion's letters, along with mantras like "He's hardcore" and "We want blood."

Observed Mark Pollesel, owner of Ottawa indie, Capital City Championship Combat, or C4, "For all the good of ECW, they brought out a certain type of *smark*," an obnoxious mark (the derogatory carny term for fan) who naively thinks he's "smart" to the inner workings of the business. "Those 'You fucked up' chants were funny at first, but these guys were working their asses off. Why kill the mood by pointing out every mistake?"

Jac Sabboth had opened his first sports card and comic book store in New York City in 1993, offering wrestling action figures and magazines along with other memorabilia. He credited ECW with changing his inventory choices: "Once ECW hit, the wrestling stuff started to consume the store. We became a wrestling store that sold comics and cards." Then, the comics and cards went away. The shop went through a number of name changes before it was finally christened The Wrestling Universe, pulling fans who attended ECW's shows at the promotion's satellite facility, Lost Battalion Hall, on Queens Boulevard, along with wrestlers who, Sabboth discovered, were also collectors.

By 1995, Tod Gordon was out, and Heyman took over ECW. He invested in storylines surrounding the cult figures he promoted: Bubba and D-Von Dudley, Rob Van Dam, "The Human Suplex Machine" Taz (an extra "z" would be added to his name in WWF), the Gangstas, The Eliminators, the Blue Meanie, Stevie Richards, Nova, and spectacular technical wrestlers like Dean Malenko, Chris Benoit, Chris Jericho,

Lance Storm and Eddie Guerrero. When the inevitable occurred, and ECW standouts were absorbed by the WWF and WCW, Heyman built more stars: Rhyno, Ballz Mahoney, Spike Dudley and Angelica — future WWE Hall of Famer Lita.

After WCW fired a hunky blond wrestler called "Stunning" Steve Austin, he showed up in ECW and vented about the Atlanta company's backstage politics. It was this previously unseen demonstration of Austin's personality that prompted the WWF to give him a shot.

One of the few times that ECW was forced to apologize occurred after an angle that saw Raven "crucify" the Sandman. But generally, shock value ruled. ECW showcased wrestling's first lesbian kiss — between Kimona Wanalea and Beulah McGillicutty. This was not intended to foster sensitivity toward the LGBTQ community but, rather, the goal was to appeal to prurient impulses.

Tommy Dreamer made out with both of them afterwards.

If Heyman had one notable flaw, though, it was that he was an awful businessman. ECW was always losing money, and Heyman had to constantly come up with little tricks to keep paying the bills. Vince McMahon secretly kicked in some funds; ECW had had a working relationship with the WWF, which acknowledged the Philadelphia company's role in stimulating the Attitude Era. When TNN — the television network that was later rebranded Spike — began televising the promotion, it appeared that an infusion of cash would come with it. But Heyman's personality hadn't changed since he was standing on chairs, shouting for the heels in Madison Square Garden. The TNN executives' objections to some of ECW's content was met with incendiary insolence from Heyman. Plus, ECW could not attract WWF-level ratings. In October 2000, TNN cancelled the show.

The company limped along for the next few months until its pay-per-view, scheduled for March 2001, was cancelled. The WWF ended up with ECW's tape library and other intellectual properties and created an underwhelming storyline in which the group's wrestlers merged with performers from the recently vanquished WCW to mount an invasion.

Heyman would play a variety of on- and off-camera roles in WWE, even participating in an effort to revive ECW on the Syfy network in 2006. But after some initial curiosity, neither the fans nor the wrestlers really seemed that into it. More compelling were the old ECW broadcasts that ran on the WWE Network, programs that enabled viewers to travel back into the relatively recent past to experience a promotion that changed tastes, broke barriers and created the paradigm for indie wrestling.

8

CHAPTER

parks from the ECW inferno spread in multiple directions. Less than an hour from Philadelphia, in Wilmington, Delaware, the East Coast Wrestling Association (ECWA) lured some of the best technical wrestlers in the world to its annual Super 8 Tournament, first held in 1997. Over the years, the event became a showcase for the top indie performers, with names like Christopher Daniels, Low Ki, Petey Williams, Davey Richards, Jerry Lynn and Tommaso Ciampa taking the honors.

"Those Super 8 shows were the real deal," recalled Philadelphia-area fan Paul Carboni. "We were going to wrestling shows every Saturday night, either ECWA, ECW or CZW [Combat Zone Wrestling]."

In North Carolina, Shane "Hurricane" Helms had become acquainted with Matt and Jeff Hardy and Shannon Moore on the indies. All were fans of styles common in Japan and Mexico, where smaller, audacious wrestlers could sell out the house. "Nowadays, I would have met them on the internet," Helms said. "Back then, you'd have to search until you found them."

Every two weeks, Helms and Moore made the nine-and-a-half hour trek to Nashville to work for Music City Wrestling. "The payoff was $40. There weren't developmental territories back then, but we heard that Music City was one the places that WCW and the WWF paid attention to."

By Helms' estimation, the caliber of wrestlers he encountered was below the standards of the Carolinas. "There were guys who didn't know how to catch the high fliers, who we couldn't trust to be our base. I had guys dropping me on the floor."

But he included his Music City highlights on the VHS tape he sent to WCW as the company expanded its roster of cruiserweights. "We heard stories that people would look at these tapes and throw them in the garbage. Matt Hardy was known as High Voltage in OMEGA (the indie that the Hardyz started in 1997 in their hometown of Cameron, North Carolina), and WCW stole his name. As 'Stone Cold' Steve Austin would say: 'D.T.A. — don't trust anybody.'"

Nonetheless, WCW hired Helms and Moore in 1999, matching them up with Evan Karaigas in a boy band knockoff unit called 3-Count.

In Montreal, which had long offered a style of wrestling that appealed to the Quebecois palate, a generation of fans raised on the WWF were done with performers like Gilles "The Fish" Poisson and Michel "Justice" Dubois. "We wanted to be like ECW," said Manny Elefthriou — aka PCP Crazy Fuckin' Manny — cofounder of the International Wrestling Syndicate (IWS).

The IWS started as a lark for a collection of students at Dawson College, a school appealing to the city's Anglophone community, on the grounds of a former nunnery. In 1998, Edward Derozowsky, aka SeXXXy Eddy, got into a worked on-air feud with a fellow deejay on the campus radio station. The pair ended up brawling at the college's annual picnic, incorporating an ironing board, ladder and filing cabinet. The next year, he founded the Dawson Wrestling Federation, using the school newspaper to build interest in the upcoming matches. In its first and last contest on campus, Eddy executed a move he labeled the "garbage-sault," holding a garbage can over his head as he moonsaulted onto his foe. A video of the incident quickly circulated around the city's wrestling community.

A short time later, Manny was in a place called Wally's Pub when a mutual acquaintance introduced him to Eddy. "You guys should hang out together," Manny was told. "He knows as much about wrestling as you do."

As they chatted, Manny noticed that there were four pillars holding up the ceiling. "We wondered if we drilled holes into those pillars and put some ropes up, maybe we could make a wrestling ring. And that's what we did."

Teaming up with another friend named Nixon Stratus, the two presented a card called *Blood, Sweat & Beers '99*. Although many attendees enjoyed the action, the bar's other patrons were revolted. "They told us it was because of the thumbtacks and the blood," Manny said. "But the thing that made them the most angry — no one ever confirmed this, but it's the truth — was that we were English."

Manny continued, "At that time, there was probably about 20 indie companies fighting for the same fans. The biggest thing was the shit-talking that we were a bunch of kids who didn't know what we were doing. Which was 100 percent true. We weren't even trained yet. But the people were into us."

The promotion went through a succession of names. It was the Internet Wrestling Syndicate before the International Wrestling Syndicate. Fans called the group Le Fed Canadian Tire because of the auto parts inserted into the matches. In 2000, Wally's Pub closed, and the company moved to other venues, renting an authentic ring from former Montreal star Paul LeDuc.

Around this time, Wild Rose Productions, a local porn company, partnered with IWS. "They were looking to branch out from porn," Manny said. "And they had a lot of skills we didn't. They helped us build this really good website. Eventually, we did a live web show — back when no one else was doing it. And they'd send these hot girls to our shows to get involved in our matches."

The affiliation with the porn industry enhanced the reputation that the IWS was trying to cultivate. During one show, Eddy pinned Manny after a frog splash from the balcony. At another, a fan suffered a heart attack. In November 2001, Carl LeDuc, Paul's son, refused to do a job for Eddy, causing an altercation backstage. The younger LeDuc then went out to the ring and began tearing down the company and its fans, mixing real-life details with wrestling hype. Eventually, Manny handed LeDuc a handful of money and had security escort him from the building.

With the relationship with the LeDuc family shattered, IWS was left without a ring. The company briefly rented from another indie, then commissioned local wrestler Iceberg to build one exclusive to IWS.

As with ECW, the controversies only drew a more militant fan base. By age 16, future WWE star Sami Zayn was sneaking into the group's 18-and-over shows. "He was training with a small local federation in a guy's backyard," Manny said. "Before our shows, he'd come to the arena and help put up the ring. He'd lead chants. During breaks, he'd run up and do a 450 splash in the middle of the ring. And I'd chase him away. *'Get the fuck out of the ring. What the fuck is wrong with you?'*"

Sometime in 2002, one of the scheduled wrestlers didn't show up. "His opponent said, 'Just put the kid in the ring.' So we put a mask on him, and he started doing all these crazy moves he'd learned from watching [Mexican high-flier] Super Crazy. He told me he didn't know what to do next, so he yelled, '*Ole, ole, ole, ole.*'" The term became his catchphrase. "And then, he was a professional wrestler."

For the next 11 years, the Syrian-Canadian's hooded character, El Generico, would become one of the most sought-after commodities on the indies. In 2003, he and Kevin Steen — the future Kevin Owens — would have the first of hundreds of matches that would continue after both were in WWE.

At the time, a mysterious fan who used the online name "Llakor" regularly posted detailed reviews of IWS shows on his blog, *When We Were Marks.* "He invested hours and hours of his time and energy into writing . . . anything to let the world know about these crazy kids in Montreal who were trying to make some noise," Zayn tweeted in 2013. "He did this not because he had to or because anyone had asked him to, but because he genuinely believed in us. He helped my career a lot, particularly in the early stages."

Manny wondered about the man's identity until they finally met. His name was Michael Ryan and Manny described him as "this geeky

Comic Con kind of guy who seemed to be in his forties when we were in our twenties. He volunteered to be our publicist."

According to associates, Michael Ryan found interactions with normal people challenging, and seemed to live for those moments when he could immerse himself in wrestling. He was also involved in the Young Cuts Film Festival, a yearly Montreal gathering highlighting directors below the age of 30. In 2013, his absence was noticed at an area indie show. He also missed a scheduled card game, as well as several appointments. After failing to reach him, an area promoter called the police in St. Sauveur, Quebec. When they entered his apartment, they discovered that he'd died of a heart attack related to his diabetes.

Wrote Kevin Steen on Twitter, "Michael 'Llakor' Ryan did so much for me and my career, more than he ever knew. Never got the chance to tell him."

By the time of Ryan's death IWS had gone through numerous incarnations and worked with dozens of promotions, among them Ring of Honor, Pro Wrestling Guerrilla, CHIKARA, wXw in Germany and AAA in Mexico. At CZW's third annual *Tournament of Death* in Smyrna, Delaware, in 2004, Eddy was wrestling the Arsenal and sliced open an artery on the left forearm. "Blood started shooting out," Manny remembered. "Instead of panicking, he held his forearm up and squirted it into his mouth.

"People were saying, 'Who are these crazy Canadians?' There was a CZW show coming up at the old ECW Arena, and they asked me to bring my four best wrestlers. I brought Eddy, Excess 69, Kevin Steen and El Generico. They had a wild four-way match that had the fans chanting, 'IWS.' No one in the U.S. could name a Canadian indie and now we had a cult following. Seventy-five percent of our DVD sales were in the United States. We were selling DVDs in Japan and Italy. Our guys started getting booked everyplace. We could see there was an explosion going on."

When WWE would come to the Bell Centre — site of the 1997 Montreal Screwjob, in which the departing Bret "The Hit Man" Hart lost his WWF belt to Shawn Michaels after Vince McMahon ordered a timekeeper to ring the bell in the middle of the match — the IWS performers saturated the building with fliers. "It's easier now because you can do a Facebook ad," Manny said. "But we still have a flier team and 6,000 fliers whenever *Raw* comes to town. If no one knows what you're doing, no one's going to come."

To a certain extent, IWS' triumphs have come at the expense of "The Mountie" Jacques Rougeau, a former WWF Intercontinental and Tag Team champion, whose family ran Quebec's Les As De La Lutte (All-Star Wrestling) promotion in the 1970s. In 2001, Rougeau was overseeing his own indie when two of his students defected at an IWS event and joined the rival league.

Most humiliating for Rougeau was that IWS represented everything that he detested about the new direction of the industry. His Spectacle Familial Jacques Rougeau league banned punching, kicking, profanity and alcohol in the arena. "If you're a wrestling promoter, you should give back to the community," said Rougeau, whose father and uncle, Jacques Sr. and Johnny, were Montreal headliners and maternal great-uncle, Eddie Auger, wrestled until days before his death from pancreatic cancer. "Get involved with youth hockey, Big Brothers/Big Sisters. If you're just going in and asking for money, you better be doing something exceptional."

The high point of Rougeau's promotional career occurred in 1997, the same year as the Montreal Screwjob. Playing the Quebecois hero, Rougeau booked himself in the main event against Hulk Hogan, then the WCW World Heavyweight champion, on loan from the Atlanta-based conglomerate. The undercard featured local wrestlers like Nelson Veilleux, Sunny War Cloud, Jacques Compois, Richard Charland and Pierre Carl Ouellet — later known as PCO — along with such WCW stars as "The Giant" Paul Wight — the Big Show in WWE — Harlem Heat, Lex Luger and Ric Flair. Hogan later told *Slam! Wrestling* that he received "a ton of heat" from WCW management for allowing Rougeau to pin him in the non-title match. "It was business and it was the right thing to do," the Hulkster said. "Jacques was working very, very hard for wrestling in Montreal."

Jacques' ultimate goal was following the tradition of promoters like Stu Hart and Fritz Von Erich, who were able to build territories around their sons. Unfortunately, Jacques' boys, Jean-Jacques, Emile and Cedric, did not share the same love for the business as the Rougeaus of generations past. Cedric was listed as six-foot-seven and 325 pounds, and Jacques was certain that there was a role for him in NXT — a position that would increase interest in Spectacle Familial Jacques Rougeau. But after breaking his leg while trying to execute a 450 splash off the ropes, he fell behind in his cardio at the WWE Performance Center. Privately, each of the Rougeau sons confided to their father that they had no heart for the barnstorming that Jacques and his brother, Raymond, did during their early days. "In Stampede [the Hart family's Calgary-based territory], you'd do Lethbridge on Monday, Red Deer on Tuesday, Saskatoon on Wednesday, Regina on Thursday, Calgary on Friday and Edmonton on Saturday," Rougeau said, "all for $35 a night. My sons didn't want to pay their dues that way.

"They just lost interest. It never was their dream. It was Daddy's dream."

In 2018, the promotion ran a farewell show, after which 58-year-old Jacques, 28-year-old Jean-Jacques, 25-year-old Cedric and 18-year-old Emile retired. "This is a very sad time in my life," Jacques confided. "Sometimes, when I'm home, I start to cry. Seventy-five years of the Rougeau family went down the drain. But I can't make my sons do something if they don't want to do it."

Meanwhile, after declaring itself defunct in 2010, IWS returned four years later, even procuring the services of WWE United Kingdom champion Pete Dunne for a match with IWS Canadian titlist Matt Angel in 2018.

In 2017, the IWS began taping a monthly television show for the French language network RDS. Despite the Anglophone sensibilities of the group's owners, the ring announcer introduced the combatants in French. Shows were taped without commentary, before a French-speaking team inserted their own play-by-play in the patois of *La Belle Province*.

"If you can't see AEW or Ring of Honor or WWE in Montreal, come to see us," Manny urged. "House shows, we draw 250 people. Large shows, maybe 1,000. But in the summer, if there's a music festival, we can get 7,000 people to stand there and watch what we're doing."

Before a Metallica show, the promotion set up a ring where they knew thousands of fans would be waiting for hours to enter the concert. "It's not about putting on a show," Manny stressed. "It's about creating an atmosphere. If you believe in what you're doing, it doesn't matter if the match in the ring sucks. The fans will scream their heads off anyway."

When the Rougeaus folded up operations, Jacques' former student, Martin Villeneuve purchased the ring and started Gatineau Professional Wrestling (GPW) — named for the group's home base, the Knights of Columbus hall in Gatineau, Quebec, near Ottawa — with Derick Clement, Guillaume Charbonneau and Eric Carpentier. To save money, all four partners vowed to wrestle multiple times, under a variety of identities, on the same card. On GPW's debut show, on October 21, 2018, Villeneuve was both the masked Mummy, as well as a heavily made-up character called The Crow. Clement used the names Predator and Thunder, while Charbonneau played a sheriff and the hooded Knightman. Carpentier wrestled as the crazed Justin Sane and appeared under another guise as a manager for wrestler Paul Jones.

GPW's G-rated dogma was identical to the philosophy espoused by Rougeau. With an audience consisting almost exclusively of French-speakers, GPW tried to replicate the days when Les As De La Lutte and the Vachon clan's Grand Prix promotion were competing for dollars in the province. "It's old-fashioned," Villeneuve said. "You don't see 10 near-falls with kickouts. When a guy hits his big finisher, the match is over."

Before each show, competitors were warned to avoid busting each other open or fighting in the crowd. "If you do anything to make me lose my sponsors," Villeneuve emphasized, "you're off the card."

With some five other indies in the Ottawa area, Villeneuve theorized that promoters were all capitalizing on the "Steen effect" — after Steen successfully transformed into Kevin Owens in WWE. "Everyone here saw him on indies, but with spectacular moves you don't see him use that much anymore. So the fans know that, when they come to one of these shows, they're going to see every wrestler giving it their all, hoping that somebody from WWE finds out about them."

GPW's first show drew 450 fans, and Villeneuve was heartened that 100 chose to purchase tickets to the next card before they left the building. As he went through the task of purchasing championship belts, ringside barricades and screens to wall off the wrestlers' changing area, he worried about how many fans would continue to support his product. "We have 600 people who already like our Facebook page," he said, "so you hope they keep sharing the information we put up. And then, you have to ask yourself how much money do you really want to spend. You can draw 2,000 fans, but spend so much, you would have been better off getting 400 fans into a smaller building that was cheaper to rent."

But profit was low on the list of incentives driving GPW. "I'm not going to become a millionaire from this," Villeneuve, a full-time paint store owner, said. "We all have our outside jobs, but this is our passion."

"You start out thinking you're going to make money in wrestling," said Jian Magen, cofounder of Toronto's Twin Wrestling Entertainment (TWE) with his identical sibling, Page. "But there's not really money to be made at this level. So you have great experiences, make lifelong friends, bring joy to people, raise money for charity. After our last show, we ended up buying a school bus for special needs kids. Is there anything really better than that? Not for me."

I first met the Magen twins when I was working on the autobiography of the man they regard as their uncle, the Iron Sheik (the Magens' father, Bijan, had been a table tennis champion in Iran and practiced at the same facility where a young Khosrow Vaziri wrestled). I loved the Sheik's stories — brutally driving a member of the NFL's Pittsburgh Steelers to tears for daring to disrespect Bruno Sammartino, forcing a fan to exercise until he vomited in the gym, slamming the great shooter, Karl Gotch, so hard that he farted, calling the Fabulous Moolah a whore, sneaking an 8-ball of coke across the border for Jake "The Snake" Roberts, invoking the names of Adolf Hitler and Osama bin Laden during a wedding speech — but, unfortunately, the book was never published. While no one ever verified this, I have the impression that somebody very high up at WWE read the manuscript and determined that, when the positives were weighed against the negatives, the Sheik's unvarnished story didn't really help the brand.

To this day, it remains the greatest unpublished treasure in the annals of wrestling journalism. And that's not a work. It's a shoot.

Either way, the Magens and I became friends. They put me up at their homes while I was visiting Toronto. I appeared in the documentaries they produced about the Sheik and the seminal Sweet Daddy Siki. Perennial hustlers, they've called me regularly to talk about everything from their plans to import talent from the Islamic Republic of Iran to invigorating the post-wrestling career of former WWF valet Virgil — a goal that was realized, to a certain extent, in AEW when Chris Jericho included the performer, now known as Soultrain Jones, in the Inner Circle posse.

At an event the twins promoted specifically for Orthodox Jews — the Magens are descended from a Jewish community that has been in Persia since approximately the eighth century BCE — Jian Magen donned a singlet and put an aging, bearded rabbi through a table. Joey Janela later told me that of all the warped angles he'd seen in his corner of the indie world, that ranked among the funniest.

Because of their father's connection to the Sheik, the Magen twins loved wrestling since early childhood. When the WWF was in Toronto, the Sheik and his tag team partner, Nikolai Volkoff, would go to their house for Persian meals. The boys attended most of the shows at Maple Leaf Gardens, even standing at reverent attention when the Sheik attempted to draw heat by playing the "Imperial Anthem of Iran," recited during the days of the Shah:

Long live our King of Kings
And may his glory immortalize our land
For Pahlavi improved Iran
A hundredfold from where it once used to stand

At Thornlea Secondary School, the pair was always putting on impromptu matches in hallways. "We'd be walking around with garbage cans and hitting each other with chairs in the middle of the day,"

Jian said. "It was out of control. But we were drawing. The kids wanted to see it."

One day, while waiting for the bus home, the brothers spotted a poster for an indie show featuring a number of former WWF stars. When they arrived at the event, though, they were stunned to be part of a crowd that numbered no more than 50. On the weekends, the pair was pulling more than 10 times as many teens to their all-ages deejay events, all with some kind of underlying wrestling theme.

"We called our company 'Suck It Productions,'" Jian said, evoking DeGeneration X's catchphrase during the WWF's Attitude Era. "We'd do wrestling-style fliers. If a deejay was named Eric B, we'd call him Eric "Koko" B," after future WWE Hall of Famer Koko B. Ware.

Occasionally, the Magens turned up at a rival school, taunting some kid as he left for the day. A crowd would gather, anticipating a fight. If a teacher intervened, the twins cursed him out. Then the twins — and the kid they seemed to be mocking — would reach into their bags and pull out fliers, inviting everybody to an upcoming event. "He was part of the act," Jian boasted. "People went crazy. It was like the Carolinas in the '70s, with Ric Flair and Ricky Steamboat on top."

Convinced that they could create the same excitement as wrestling promoters, the Magens had gathered phone numbers at the poorly attended indie show. "We were looking for ring crew guys, someone to rent us a ring, people who knew Rick Martel and Jimmy Snuka and other wrestlers we might want to work with."

When the WWF ran its *Breakdown: In Your House* pay-per-view in 1998, the two drove to Copps Coliseum in Hamilton, Ontario, hoping to widen their circle. Before they left the parking lot, they spotted two kids they recognized from a bar mitzvah party the brothers had organized the night before. "None of us had tickets," Jian said. "We went over and promised to get everyone in. I knew the mother, and she was just happy to unload the kids for a few hours. She gave us money to scalp tickets and buy snacks."

Jian and Page began testing the arena's doors, seeing if anything would open. Eventually, one portal did, and the brothers led the adolescents into the building. After purchasing the kids some t-shirts, the pair struck up a conversation with a WWF employee. "He said they needed seat fillers for the first section. Anytime someone stood up during the show, they put us in their seats, so the arena always looked full on TV."

When the fans returned, the Magens and the bar mitzvah kids hung off to the side, as the WWF employee imparted the lessons he'd obviously heard from someone else. "You hear those boos?" he asked during one match. "There's *money* behind those boos. Vince is going to take that kid and turn him into the biggest babyface there ever was because he can hear the money."

"Hey," Jian ventured. "If we were doing our own show, how much would it cost to get, I don't know — like a Tito Santana or King Kong Bundy?"

"What do you need them for? You've got Edge, Christian, Val Venis and Trish Stratus all in Toronto. They do outside appearances all the time. I'll give you the number for talent relations. Here's my card. Tell them you spoke to me."

Then, to the brothers' astonishment, the employee apologized for monopolizing the twins' night out and took them into the dressing room area, where they saw people like Triple H, Mankind and The Rock stretching, chatting and commenting on the matches. Recalled Jian, "The bar mitzvah kids were going out of their minds."

Ultimately, 1,500 fans turned up to the Magens' show to see a main event pitting Edge against Andrew "Test" Martin at the Garnet A. Williams Community Centre in the Toronto suburb of Thornhill. In the semifinal, the Magen twins wrestled each other. "We brawled all over the building," Jian said, "until my mother — unscripted — ran out to the ring and told us to stop."

The referee ruled the finish a double-DQ.

Most of the rest of the card consisted of local talent hired by a woman the pair had met at the sparse indie show. "She gave us this list of how much everything would cost: $250 for the ref, $400 for this wrestler, $350 for that wrestler. Years later, we found out she was paying the guys something like $20 each. But we didn't know. We even tipped her $2,500 because we thought she was a saint."

In college — Jian attended York University and Page went to Dawson College, just like SeXXXy Eddy and PCP Crazy Fuckin' Manny — the pair learned that every school had an entertainment budget and, for an agreed-upon fee, the brothers could stage wrestling events, largely featuring the WWF talent they idolized in the '80s. "By then, we knew what things really cost," Jian said.

In addition to the university circuit, the Magens began putting on cards at birthday parties, shopping malls and trade shows. They also built their business arranging deejays, musicians and dancers to perform at weddings and bar mitzvah parties. Sometimes, they'd give away tickets to their wrestling shows as prizes to the bar mitzvah attendees. When the youngsters showed up with their parents, the crowd would be reminded that, if anyone in Toronto were having a bar mitzvah, Magen Boys Entertainment was the way to go.

Initially, the pair's wrestling company was called the Twin Tower Wrestling Federation, featuring a logo of the Twin Towers in the center of a target. Shortly after the real Twin Towers collapsed in 2001, the Iron Sheik was passing through Canadian customs, wearing his signature kaffiyeh. When a border service agent asked the purpose of his visit, he replied, belligerently, in his Iranian accent, that he was working for the Twin Tower Wrestling Federation.

The Magens knew it was time to change the company's name.

The group expanded, running cards outside the Toronto area, renting rings locally and using area wrestlers. At a show in Thunder Bay, the pair used a contingent of Winnipeg performers, including Kenny Omega, and worked with a promoter familiar with the lakeside city. "I was asked to go to his hotel room for a meeting," Jian said, "and he began trying to shake me down for money we didn't agree to. Every time I'd mention the fee his contact had given us, the guy would say, 'He was wrong.' Finally, he opened up his briefcase and showed me his gun. So I paid him. When I did, he looked at me and said, 'Don't you ever come back to Thunder Bay again.'"

It's a refrain that the brothers continue to use. If one makes a mistake, the other says, "Don't you ever come back to Thunder Bay again."

Still, the incident changed something for the Magens. Everything had been so much fun until this point that the brothers were able to ignore the fact that wrestling could be a dodgy business. "There were lots of lessons learned," Jian noted. "They were harsh lessons."

During the summers, the brothers would split up and run dual shows on the same day at different summer camps, then drive through the night to the next venue. During one of these trips, Page Magen had his back broken in a car accident that killed the driver. Another time, "a very careless hardcore wrestler smashed a dirty ladder into my friend's temple, and he was bleeding so much, I thought he was going to die," Jian said.

After another card, the profits disappeared. "We were pretty sure one of the boys took it," Jian said. "So we started to slow down and concentrate more on our other business. But the truth is that once you're in it, wrestling never leaves you. It's such a great life, even after things go wrong. I can remember just laughing while walking out of a club party with Billy Gunn and Brutus Beefcake in their gimmicks. We did comedy roasts with the Iron Sheik. We had famous wrestlers crash weddings. I helped John Morrison produce a wrestling horror film. When Impact Wrestling came to Toronto, I was used as a backstage interviewer and got involved in an angle where someone got thrown in a pool."

In 2019, he reflected on how much wrestling had occupied his thoughts during his 40 years on earth. "Wrestling's just so tied into everything. Who knows what else we're going to do? We're certainly not done yet. We might just be getting started."

9
CHAPTER

The absorption of WCW and ECW into the World Wrestling Federation in 2001 put an end to not just the Monday Night Wars, but also the battle Vince McMahon began two decades earlier by boldly trespassing territorial boundaries. While talent like Booker T, Stacy Keibler, Diamond Dallas Page and Rhyno found work in the WWF, other wrestlers from the now-conquered companies were driven underground to scratch out a living. "When Vince bought his competition, the independent scene that we see today truly started," said Jeff Jarrett, who was fired by McMahon on live television the night WWF merged with WCW. "With Vince taking over everything, there were a lot of guys looking for work."

WCW Cruiserweight champion Shane Helms was among those given a job in the WWF. But because of the boy band gimmick he had in WCW — and his status as a smaller wrestler — he was uncertain of the position he'd attain in his new company. "It was the hardest time to get over," he said. "WCW was gone. ECW was gone. There was just that one company with a stacked roster."

For his first few house shows in the WWF, Helms maintained the "Sugar Shane" character he'd portrayed in WCW. But since Vince McMahon's son also happened to be named Shane, Helms — whose birth name was actually Gregory Shane — was told to use the first name on his birth certificate. "They stripped me of my name," he said, "my championship, my music and my finisher. They wanted to call me 'Hollywood Helms.' But Hulk Hogan was 'Hollywood Hogan' in WCW, and those were some gigantic shoes to fill. And there was nothing about my [southern] vernacular that said Hollywood. So I asked [director of creative writing] Stephanie McMahon about 'Hurricane.' And she said she'd bring it up to Vince."

About an hour later, Vince passed Helms backstage and growled approvingly, "*Hurricane* Helms."

Given his Green Lantern tattoo and the comic book t-shirts he tended to wear off-screen, Helms was informed that he'd be playing a character who was convinced that he was a superhero. "Promos were not as scripted as they are now," he said. "On one interview, I started talking about the Green Lantern as a real person, and they liked it. Today, you'd try something like that at the [WWE] Performance Center before they'd ever let you do it on *Raw* or *SmackDown*. So I was lucky."

Hurricane Helms blended into the role nicely, as the World Wrestling Federation became World Wrestling Entertainment. But the entire time, he was aware of how close he'd come to turning invisible on the indies. "When I started wrestling, there was no such thing as an independent wrestling superstar," Colt Cabana, who debuted in 1999, pointed out to *Vice Sports*.

"If you were on the indie circuit, you were kind of lost," said journalist Kenny Herzog, whose pro wrestling stories have appeared in *The Ringer* and *Rolling Stone*. "I remember going to a small show in Queens in 2002 and seeing Ballz Mahoney and Sabu from ECW. WWE had already picked up the WCW and ECW guys they wanted. If you hadn't been selected, where did you fit in? You were like the [2016 Green Party presidential candidate] Jill Stein of wrestling."

Matt Striker was still working primarily as a school teacher in Queens in the early 2000s and had never experienced the excitement of performing for a major promotion. As a result, he was grateful for every wrestling gig he procured. "Ignorance is bliss," he said. "I was so naive,

I had no idea. I would get in my car and drive from New York City to Atlanta. I'd sleep on the side of the road, holding a butter knife. I had a VHS tape in my car in case a promoter wanted to see more of me, and I thought it was the greatest thing in the world. I remember I had an opportunity to referee a match with Jimmy 'Superfly' Snuka, and I was driving home, saying, 'Wow, I made it.'

"Before this, I had no idea that anyone could become a wrestler. I just thought you were born Hulk Hogan or you weren't. For me, being in the indies, that was the reward. Just being let through the door was enough for me."

But there were unsatisfied spectators who sought a different style of wrestling than the product shown on *Monday Night Raw* and *SmackDown*. Recalled "The Villain" Marty Scurll, "When WCW and ECW ended, fans who wanted an alternative were still there."

Although Chris Jericho had a secure position in WWE, he remained a fan as well. Because of this, the lack of high-profile choices disturbed him. "The worst thing that happened in a lot of ways was when WWE bought WCW in 2001," he told *Rolling Stone*. "There's nothing better than having variety."

From his Wrestling Universe store in Queens, Jac Sabboth understood how desperately his customers missed ECW. In 2001, he began promoting Impact Championship Wrestling (ICW), using intrepid performers like Low Ki, Xavier and Amazing Red. "No one knew who these guys were," Sabboth said. "But the fans definitely came back to see them a second time. All of these guys were doing things people hadn't seen before, and it was the ECW influence that inspired them. ECW was gone, but the fans still wanted it. They still want it today."

In 2001, Combat Zone Wrestling (CZW) held its *Cage of Death 3* show at the old ECW Arena, hoping to appeal to those hardcore fans. "They wanted to fill the void left by ECW," said Derek Sabato, a CZW producer from 2001 to 2009. "CZW took ECW's timeslot on Philly TV. And now, they were doing this show not in Jersey, not in Delaware, but the place where it all happened, in Philadelphia itself.

"Clearly, there was a demand for this type of wrestling. There hadn't been any hardcore shows — with light tubes and fire — in Philly since ECW. There was a tremendous buzz and a gigantic walkup. The show started two hours late and didn't end until 2 a.m. But they burned everybody out. The next show went from 1,500 to 500. They fucked up badly."

Herzog compared the indie mood during this period to the atmosphere surrounding a punk band yet to sign with a commercial label. "If you were part of that scene, you could be very proud of what you helped cultivate and nurture. But if you zoom out, it really was obscure to most people."

As with punk, there was no shortage of capable performers who never rose above a certain grade. Trent Acid had begun wrestling at 14 and became one of the early stars of CZW. In 2002, he and his partner in the Backseat Boyz, Johnny Kashmere, joined Ring of Honor, where they won the Tag Team Championship the next year. But as the indies gained momentum, Trent's substance abuse issues began to cripple him. In 2010, he was arrested for heroin possession and sentenced to 23 months of incarceration, as well as court-ordered rehab. Before he could start his sentence, he died of an overdose.

CZW and Ring of Honor each celebrated Acid with a ten-bell salute, and a tribute show was held at the ECW Arena to raise money for his funeral expenses. As others stepped in to replace him, though, his name was invoked with increasingly less frequency.

In 2002, Jeff Jarrett and his father, Jerry, started the company that became Impact Wrestling, Total Nonstop Action (TNA). "I knew without a number two, there's no such thing as a number one," Jarrett said. "I wasn't classifying TNA as a number two. But I was very happy just to get in the game."

Given its suggestive acronym, TNA offered a bolder product than WWE. Initially billed as NWA-TNA, the company promoted NWA World Heavyweight and NWA World Tag Team Championship bouts until the arrangement with the storied organization ended in 2007. Still, fans never seemed to equate titlists like Jarrett, Christian Cage — of Edge and Christian fame — and Abyss to such kingpins as Lou Thesz, Dory Funk Jr. and Dusty Rhodes. Another miscalculation was bypassing television for inexpensive, weekly pay-per-views. While the concept made sense, TNA needed TV to get fans interested.

Eventually, TNA was televised in the United States on Spike TV, holding matches in the same type of six-sided ring periodically used by

Mexico's AAA group. The hexagonal shape was particularly advantageous during cruiserweight matches, allowing high-fliers to soar from a number of directions.

Almost from the beginning, there were financial challenges. Several months after the company's founding, Panda Energy International — a Dallas-based company known for eco-friendly power plants — acquired controlling interest in TNA. Even after Panda divested in 2012, Dixie Carter, daughter of the corporation's founder, Robert Carter, remained a majority shareholder and on-air personality.

As with WCW, TNA erred by stockpiling former WWE headliners, including Hulk Hogan, Ric Flair, Kurt Angle, Mr. Anderson (known as Mr. Kennedy in WWE), Jeff Hardy, Rikishi and Kevin Nash, creating the impression that the outfit was acquiring castoffs. Even Matt Morgan, Orlando Jordan and other wrestlers who'd never enjoyed leading positions in WWE were given jobs. Despite a hard-working roster that boasted future WWE standouts like AJ Styles, Samoa Joe, Bobby Roode, Xavier Woods and Drew McIntyre, TNA came to be regarded as second-rate.

Said Philadelphia-area fan Paul Carboni, "I was rooting for TNA to go out of business because it would have freed up two hours of my week."

The company had a dismal record promoting Japanese talent. When future IWGP Heavyweight champions Shinsuke Nakamura, Kazuchika Okada and Hiroshi Tanahashi were brought to TNA in 2008, they were either ignored or demeaned. Nakamura was consigned to the company's ancillary television show, *TNA Xplosion*, while Okada was forced to portray a character based on the Green Hornet's Asian sidekick, Kato. After being buried in tag team matches and a 10-man X-Division bout, Tanahashi cut his tour short and returned home.

Ironically, TNA's international endeavors are remembered fondly. Its reality show, *TNA British Bootcamp* — featuring Marty Scurll and Rockstar Spud (Drake Maverick in WWE) among the wrestlers competing for a contract, and Hulk Hogan and English legend Mark "Rollerball" Rocco in mentorship roles — helped fuel the league's popularity in the UK. In India, *Ra Ka King*, a TNA-backed promotion, ran on The Colors Network for one season in 2012.

Talent included Sonjay Dutt, Nick Aldis — then wrestling as Sir Brutus Magnus — Davey Boy Smith Jr. and Gurv and Harv Sihra — the

Singh brothers in WWE. Jeff Jarrett was placed in charge of the project. "When I look back on my career, it's one of the proudest things I've done," he said. "At least in the top five. We put together a great roster, and India, as a population, is astronomically bigger than the U.S. The entertainment — the Bollywood influence, kushti, which is their form of wrestling — and the culture — much like Mexican culture — is very compatible with professional wrestling. It's built on sports and entertainment.

"But as always happens in entertainment, there was a regime change [at the network]. We were successful in the ratings, but then they switched us to a weekend time slot. And then, with the new leadership, we were not renewed. We weren't the only program that wasn't. But 10 years from now, we're going to be talking again, and we'll be talking about the explosion of wrestling in India."

As for North America, TNA's storylines seemed too erratic to ever gain traction with a large audience. In 2014, the promotion lost its deal with Spike TV, contributing to TNA's decline. For a period, both wrestlers and production people were complaining about delayed payments.

After 14 years in charge, Dixie Carter resigned in 2017, after Anthem Sports & Entertainment, a Canadian broadcasting and production company, purchased an 85 percent majority in the promotion. Despite its relatively low visibility, the group — now rebranded Impact Wrestling — embarked on one of its most inspired periods, with the incisive Scott D'Amore and Don Callis heading the creative team, overseeing compelling performers like Rosemary, Scarlett Bordeaux, Eddie Edwards, the Lucha Brothers, LAX and Sami Callihan.

In the summer of 2019, just as WWE and All Elite Wrestling (AEW) were poised for battle, Anthem announced that it had acquired a majority stake in AXS TV, which had run the English-language edition of New Japan Pro Wrestling's TV show, and secured a new home for Impact on North American cable systems.

Six-time TNA Knockouts champion Angelina Love had been with the organization four separate times before debuting with Ring of Honor in 2019. "I have nothing but admiration for Impact Wrestling," she said. "There's always a talented roster, and there's always an eleventh hour reprieve."

10
CHAPTER

It's no coincidence that Ring of Honor came into existence at approximately the same time as TNA, within a year of WWE's consumption of WCW and ECW. Co-owner Rob Feinstein had been bootlegging and selling wrestling videos for years. In 1995, he started RF Video, a distribution company whose biggest sellers would become tapes of ECW matches. When ECW folded, he first attempted to become involved with CZW. After the overture was rejected, he cofounded Ring of Honor, staging a 2002 card in Philadelphia that featured Eddie Guerrero — on hiatus from WWE — Super Crazy, Low Ki, Christopher Daniels and Bryan Danielson — later Daniel Bryan in WWE. Feinstein, who was a pioneer in marketing "shoot interviews" of wrestlers breaking kayfabe, hoped to fill the void created by the death of ECW with a tape catalog featuring Ring of Honor's high-intensity roster.

Very quickly, the promotion branched out of Philly, holding shows in Maryland, New Jersey, New York, Connecticut, Massachusetts, Ohio and Florida. In 2003, Ring of Honor co-promoted a card with the Frontier Wrestling Alliance (FWA) in London.

Ring of Honor was different than other indies in that there were very few green guys incapable of doing much beyond the basics or brawlers who were lost when they weren't required to punch, kick or assault with foreign objects. The large quantity of technical wrestlers enabled the league to develop a "Code of Honor" to match its name. Competitors were initially required to shake hands before and after every match. Outside interference and sneak attacks were banned. Generally, the bouts ended via pinfall or submission, with announcers perpetuating the fiction that disqualifications would lead to banishment. On the rare occasion that some type of deviousness occurred after a referee was knocked down, crowds pelted the ring with boos.

Although the Code of Honor would be phased out, aspects remained. In 2019, Ring of Honor presented a "pure rules match" in which grapplers were penalized for not following the referee's order to break against the ropes. One rule violation would result in a warning, the second a disqualification.

Paul Carboni, the ECW fan who hated TNA, embraced the Ring of Honor product. "It didn't have the blood and guts of ECW, but it had the great scientific matches I was used to seeing from Dean Malenko and Chris Benoit and those kinds of guys. Year after year, Ring of Honor brought in wrestlers like Davey Richards, Eddie Edwards, Bryan Danielson, Samoa Joe, CM Punk and Austin Aries. It seemed to have legs. I remember saying, 'This could be my ECW replacement.'"

Referee and CZW producer Derek Sabato saw the timing of Ring of Honor as fortuitous. "RF Video already had a base. The internet was new and got behind the company, since there was nothing else to get behind at that time. CZW definitely felt the pressure because they told some of the wrestlers, 'One or the other.' And they ended up losing guys because Ring of Honor was the better place to go for money and exposure."

Ticket broker Cary Silkin was among the early investors. Cary had begun his career hustling concert tickets outside Madison Square Garden and other music venues in New York City, then worked at a ticket agency before starting his own venture, Rave Review. But Silkin always imagined himself in the wrestling business and would talk about various schemes with his cousin Mike Greenblatt, a columnist for a New Jersey rock publication, *The Aquarian Weekly*, as well as a writer for a chain of low-budget magazines, including *Wrestling World*.

In the late 1990s, Greenblatt was running *Wrestling World* and had made numerous contacts around the industry. During a vacation in Puerto Rico, the cousins contacted Victor Quiñones, a wrestling manager who at one point owned a percentage of the most popular promotion on the island, the World Wrestling Council (WWC). When the pair returned to New York, they pitched an idea to launch a Spanish-language magazine, *Lucha Libre de Puerto Rico*, to Greenblatt's publisher.

The two regularly visited the island, with Greenblatt conducting interviews while Silkin worked as a ringside photographer. But it was a paranoid environment. Some 10 years earlier, WWC booker Jose Gonzalez, who wrestled as the masked Invader #1, stabbed renegade wrestler Bruiser Brody to death during a backstage confrontation. Citing self-defense, Gonzalez was acquitted of murder, amid rumors that the promotion had called in favors with the Puerto Rican authorities. Silkin always felt that he was being watched with a wary eye.

Still, the cousins managed to publish four issues, and everybody appeared happy with the arrangement. Then, one night at a small show, Silkin looked away from the ring to see Greenblatt gesturing in an effort to make a point to a disapproving Victor Jovica, WWC's Croatian-born cofounder. When he attempted to assist, Silkin heard Jovica scold, "You two Jews from New York think you can just come down here and do whatever the fuck you want. Fuera!"

Silkin knew enough Spanish to understand that Jovica was exiling them from the island.

After ECW's formation, Silkin became a regular attendee, spending time at the merchandise table where Feinstein sold videotapes. When Ring of Honor began, Silkin let it be known he wouldn't mind becoming involved. Around 2003, Feinstein and his associates Doug Gentry and Syd Euick reached out to Silkin and asked for financial help. "I go talk to them, and we negotiate whatever," Silkin remembered. "From a business sense, I'm probably throwing money away. But I liked wrestling and thought, potentially, maybe I'd make some money down the road. But I also thought I might lose money. My ticket business was doing well. The hell with it.

"It was a vanity project to say the least."

One of the first issues he raised with booker and cofounder Gabe Sapolsky was the quality of the lighting. "He said, 'Cary, this is an indie. We don't need lighting.' And I said, 'Dude, you're a rock guy. You love Pantera. You love Rush. Imagine seeing Rush with no lighting?'"

For a show at Philadelphia's decaying Murphy Rec Center, a lighting company set up four stands, each adorned with six ring lights. "We got a little half-assed entrance way with some spinning lights you could probably get at a Kmart." Silkin said. "As soon as we did that, it just brought us out of the dark ages."

The small changes continued. While watching *Raw* one night, Silkin noticed the black barricades surrounding the WWE ring. "So instead of showing the steel bike rack barricades, we ordered a black drape with a Ring of Honor logo. It looks better on TV and the people bang on it and you can hear it. It's something no one ever speaks about, but it gave us a bigger feel. We already had the great in-ring product. But this helped us become more of a show."

No one could anticipate that the company was about to become ensnared in a sex scandal. In 2004, the Perverted Justice website, in conjunction with WCAU-TV, Philadelphia's NBC affiliate, cast a net, hoping to catch pedophiles. According to news reports, an adult posing as a 14-year-old boy ended up messaging with Feinstein. The person allegedly claimed that his parents were away and invited the promoter over to his house. When Feinstein turned up, he was greeted by news cameras and swiftly drove away.

Feinstein was quickly identified, and his association with Ring of Honor was covered in the media. Feinstein insisted that the news reports were inaccurate, and he believed that he was communicating with an adult. He also said that sex was never discussed. Nonetheless, in the hailstorm that followed, he ended up selling his stake in the company to Doug Gentry, while partner promotions distanced themselves from Ring of Honor. TNA refused to let its contracted talent appear on the group's cards, depriving Ring of Honor fans of seeing stars like AJ Styles and Christopher Daniels.

Silkin, who'd already become a majority investor in January 2004, now acquired Gentry's shares to become 100 percent owner. "I basically said, 'Look, man, there are three options,'" he said. "'A) You give me my money back. I'll go away, and you can have your Ring of Honor. B) I'll buy you out, and you go the hell away. Or C) I'll sue you.' So we took B."

Jay Briscoe started with the company in 2002, and although he would end up wrestling for Ring of Honor for most of his career, there were a lot of unknowns at the time. "When Cary first bought the company, nobody was sure what was going to happen," Briscoe said. "He was either going to save our ass or drive us into the ground."

At that point, Silkin recalled, many were expecting the company to fail. "We were on such shaky ground. It took about three months of turbulence while I tried to do crisis management. There were rumors that Feinstein was still involved. People were accusing me of doing things. Then, Samoa Joe versus CM Punk happened."

Ring of Honor World champion Samoa Joe's one hour draw with CM Punk took place on June 12, 2004. Both wrestlers were still building their legends. But anyone who witnessed the confrontation — either live at the Montgomery County Fairgrounds in Dayton, Ohio, or on DVD — immediately understood that they were watching two future greats. "The match, and the buzz from that match," recalled Silkin, "gave us the attention we needed."

As ECW had done with its shows at Lost Battalion Hall in Queens, the promotion hoped to establish a presence in New York City. The group's cards in nearby Elizabeth, New Jersey, drew a sizable amount of New York fans. The day before *WrestleMania XX* in 2004, a Ring of Honor card pulled in hundreds of spectators who'd come to town to witness WWE's premier event at Madison Square Garden. "We even had a write-up in the *Newark Star-Ledger*," Silkin said. "When our building in Elizabeth closed, we booked a show in a beautiful building all the way uptown in Manhattan, above Harlem. We weren't sure if everyone would go because it was out of the way, but, by now, our fans were pretty loyal."

At the time, Japan's NOAH promotion had established a relationship with Ring of Honor and was sending its star Kenta Kobashi to main-event against Samoa Joe. The clash was scheduled for October 1, 2005, but two weeks before the match, Silkin learned that there was a problem with the building permits. "We'd sold quite a few tickets. *Fuck!* Syd and I are looking all over the place for buildings. But you'd never imagine who came to the rescue."

Manager Prince Nana had been trained by WWE Hall of Famer, "The Unpredictable" Johnny Rodz in Brooklyn. Although born in the United States, Nana had spent part of his childhood in his parents' native Ghana and joined Ring of Honor at the start, playing the role of Ashanti royalty, using riches plundered from Africa to bankroll a heel stable. When he wasn't wrestling, though, Nana worked in sales and understood the New York real estate landscape.

On a whim, he cold called the Hotel New Yorker, one block from Madison Square Garden and connected by a walkway to the Manhattan Center, where the first *Monday Night Raw* had taken place in 1993. It also had a ballroom large enough to fit a ring and hundreds of wrestling fans. Through Nana, Ring of Honor and the hotel — run by the Reverend Sun Myung Moon's Unification Church — quickly came to terms.

"You talk about being in the shadow of Madison Square Garden," Silkin said. "We were *literally* in the shadow of the Garden. We also were next to Penn Station, so people could get there from Jersey, from Long Island, any subway in the city. And now, we're in fuckin' New York City."

He claims that the promotion jammed 700 fans into the 400-capacity ballroom. "If there was a fire marshal there, the show would have been shut down. The chairs were butt to butt. There was no egress, as they say. No one could get up to go to the bathroom. But people still talk about Kobashi and Joe. And eventually, we were able to go next door to the Hammerstein Ballroom in the Manhattan Center, where we still run shows today.

"So these things started happening." Through NOAH as well as the Japanese promotion Dragon Gate, Ring of Honor toured Japan. In 2007, in fact, the company would become the first American wrestling group to have all its titles held by athletes from other countries, with Takeshi Morishima holding the Ring of Honor World Championship while Naruki Doi and Shingo had the tag team straps. "So we went from being a small indie based in Philly to something that people wanted to see internationally."

Around this time, Ken Gelman, WWE's former director of marketing, pitched Ring of Honor on the possibility of supplementing its DVD sales with delayed pay-per-views. Remembered Silkin, "He took us to a meeting somewhere in Manhattan with some guy who said, 'You're doing it backwards. You need to be on TV first before you put on a pay-per-view.' And I said, 'You're right, but we don't have that option.' We were talking about content, and another guy in the office said, 'In a couple of years, the kids are going to be watching everything on their phones.' We leave the office, and I'm like, 'This guy's fuckin' nuts.'"

The company's initial pay-per-view, dubbed *Respect Is Earned*, featured a main event of Morishima and Bryan Danielson versus Nigel McGuinness and KENTA (later Hideo Itami in NXT). The show was taped on May 12, 2007, at the Manhattan Center, then edited and broadcast on July 1. Still, the company opted to improve its production values. "Our cameras were junk," Silkin said, "so we upgraded to better junk."

By the end of 2008, the promotion had presented nine pay-per-views, with between 9,000 and 15,000 fans ordering each show over a period of several weeks. "We showed people we were interested in expanding our business," Silkin said, "and got new fans watching. But not only did I not make money, I was always losing money. Ring of Honor was being financed by Rave Review tickets. We were flying in talent. We had to hire crews, lighting. Even though we were trying to do it on the cheap, these guys were very good and it was expensive."

During this period, Sapolsky consistently received credit for his creative acumen, winning the *Wrestling Observer*'s best booker award from 2004 to 2007. But Silkin said Sapolsky was also adroit at handling attrition, as Ring of Honor's stars moved on to more lucrative gigs in TNA or WWE. "He had an eye for younger talent. Wherever we traveled, he'd get away with not having to fly a lot of guys in by putting great local wrestlers on our shows, and help turn them into stars."

In 2008, Sapolsky left and was replaced as booker by Adam Pearce, a five-time NWA World Heavyweight champion after the organization's affiliation with TNA ended. A veteran of the Southern California indie circuit, Pearce introduced Joey Ryan and the Young Bucks, Nick and Matt Jackson, to Ring of Honor. Very quickly, the Bucks transformed fan tastes with their high-paced style of tag team wrestling. "You get a reputation for something and people begin to watch you with higher expectations," Matt Jackson told the website *Ring Psychology*. "Even the wrestlers expect a certain quality from you. In the end, you just want to do your best and hope it lives up to the hype."

Pearce allowed the Bucks the freedom to come up with their own ideas for their matches and work out the details with their foes. "The best matches happen because you don't put any thought into them," Nick told *SPORTbible* in the UK. "Sometimes, you overthink things. Every wrestler in the world overthinks things."

Backstage, the Bucks formed the nucleus of a group of wrestlers who rejected the pastime's hard-partying lifestyle: Danielson, Tyler Black (Seth Rollins in WWE), Jimmy Jacobs, El Generico and Kevin Steen. "We'd order pizza and just talk about the business for seven hours," Matt told *Talk Is Jericho*.

Yet the company continued to struggle. "We were a great indie brand, a critical success and a financial nothing," Silkin said. "Between 2008 and 2010, I wanted to sell it, but there were no buyers."

In 2009, HDNet, the cable and satellite television network later rebranded AXS TV, began financing a weekly Ring of Honor television show. "My thought was always that if people got their eyes on the product, they'd watch," Silkin said. "But now, there was pressure to do TV every week. I don't want to be negative, because HDNet gave us an opportunity, but little did I know that they barely had penetration in the cable world."

Nor did anyone backstage really understand what to do with an hour of television. Through Pearce, the company hired former WWE producer Dave Lagana to format the show, among other tasks.

Then, on September 26, 2009, Danielson and Nigel McGuinness main-evented the company's *Glory by Honor* show at the Manhattan Center, only to depart for WWE immediately afterwards. But Ring of Honor clandestinely brought in legendary manager Jim Cornette, who'd just been fired from TNA, and former Ring of Honor champion Homicide to make surprise appearances. Not only was the night salvaged, the fans were ecstatic.

"Instead of putting a fork in us," Silkin told Ring of Honor's website, "it was like an oxygen tank was attached to us."

Even more valuable was the range of behind-the-scenes talents Cornette brought to Ring of Honor. Despite a personality that has politely been called divisive, Cornette was a scholar of the industry and a virtuoso at writing a creative TV show. Nonetheless, the relationship with HDNet only endured for two years. Said Silkin, "Unfortunately, we were writing something no one was watching."

Silkin was desperate to find a buyer. At one stage, Luke Williams of the Bushwackers arranged for Silkin to speak to TNA founder Jerry Jarrett, but nothing came of the discussions. "Another time, CM Punk texts me," Silkin said. "*A text!* 'What would you want for Ring of Honor?' He'd met some people. As if I'm going to do this by text."

Cornette suggested a conversation with Gary Juster, a well-regarded executive who'd worked for the old NWA and WCW and, most importantly, knew Joe Koff, the vice president of training and development for Sinclair Broadcast Group, the largest television station operator in the United States.

By providence, Koff loved wrestling. He'd grown up in the New York area, watching Capitol Wrestling, the forerunner of the WWWF, two nights a week on local TV. He also followed *All-Star Wrestling with Antonino Rocca*, Jim Crockett Sr.'s effort to raid the territory. "You could tell there was something different about the Rocca group," Koff said. "I was a kid and didn't know what an outlaw or an indie was, but I knew it was something less. They were at Sunnyside Gardens in Queens, and the WWWF played Madison Square Garden.

"I saw such amazing shows at Madison Square Garden. I was there when Gorilla Monsoon made his debut. I saw an unbelievable match between Hans Mortier and Edouard Carpentier. I saw Dory Dixon and Bobo Brazil tag team there, the Kangaroos, Brute Bernard and Skull Murphy."

Koff attended the University of Miami, where he continued to read wrestling magazines — despite the worked storylines created by the editors, these were among the few places to track the North American wrestling scene — and follow *Championship Wrestling from Florida*. Upon graduation, he was hired at WTOP, the independent Tampa station where the promotion's show was posted. And it was there in 1985 that he produced the first *Battle of the Belts*, at which the local Florida titles, as well as those recognized by the AWA and NWA, were defended.

Some five months earlier, the WWF had presented the inaugural *WrestleMania* at Madison Square Garden, and various promotions decided it was in their best interest to unite behind an event with a major league feel. "This was prime-time television," Koff said. "We'd do it live and syndicate it out to stations all across the network."

While the house was a disappointing 7,600 fans at the University of South Florida's Sun Dome, the broadcast was enough of a success for Koff to produce a second *Battle of the Belts* in 1986. But the WWF was becoming a juggernaut that was impossible to eclipse. A final version of the event took place in 1987, the year Jim Crockett Jr. absorbed the Florida territory. By then, Koff had left the company.

The *Battle of the Belts* "fell back in the hands of people who thought that, because it looked so easy, it was so easy," Koff said. "Wrestling requires a trust between the talent and the office. That trust doesn't come easy. You have to earn it. You have to be bilingual, speak the lexicon of the talent and the lexicon of the public. It takes conviction. It takes that love. This is a business that a lot of people don't understand. But people who are in it love being in it. Once you're inside of it, it's your community."

In 2010, Koff approached Sinclair president David Smith, whose Baltimore station previously posted WWF shows. "I told him, 'I think we have an opportunity to go back into the professional wrestling business, at least on the regional level,'" Koff said. "At that time, Sinclair owned stations in at least 30 percent of the country. So we had a network of stations right off the bat, and television stations need content. I thought Ring of Honor had a lot of integrity to it. I knew I was watching skilled athletes who believed in what they were doing, and the fans believed in them. And David Smith said, 'Go see what you can find out.'"

It took months for Silkin and Koff to meet. "It wasn't that Joe Koff was so busy," Silkin said, "but that he wanted to get the other people from Sinclair on board and didn't want to waste our time. But after that first meeting, I walked out and said, 'Wow, maybe we can sell the company *and* keep Ring of Honor alive.'"

On May 21, 2011, after lengthy negotiations, Sinclair announced that it had purchased Ring of Honor. Koff would become the COO, while Silkin retained an executive role. The promotion's show would run on Sinclair's owned or operated stations, as well as the company's CW and MyNetworkTV affiliates. "You say you can't keep a secret in wrestling," Silkin said, "but you can if you have the right people working together. We kept it a secret until it was a fact."

Ultimately, Sinclair's stations expanded to cover 40 percent of the United States, and Ring of Honor's touring schedule changed — with cards held in Alabama, Tennessee, Louisiana, Texas, Minnesota and other places the network reached. In 2018, the company also developed a streaming service, Honor Club. It was not a scenario Silkin would have envisioned. "I think about this all the time," he said. "If it wasn't for Jim Cornette introducing us to Gary Juster, who brought us to Joe Koff, we'd be out of business."

Because of its corporate backing, Ring of Honor's stature as an indie became a source of debate. "We don't consider ourselves an indie," Koff said. "We're not even a super-indie. We're a distributed wrestling pro-gram with a weekly hour of television, touring 40 events a year, with talent coveted by all the other promotions. That's not an indie. But we're always labeled an indie because, if you're not WWE, you're an indie. And that's fine."

Given its augmented position, Ring of Honor formed a partner-ship with New Japan Pro Wrestling, Asia's most prominent promotion, in 2014, and Mexico's Consejo Mundial de Lucha Libre (CMLL) — World Council of Wrestling — the world's oldest continuous wrestling organization, two years later. The international axis took on a European partner in 2017 when Revolution Pro Wrestling in the UK aligned itself with Ring of Honor.

Yet, none of this prevented certain talent from departing for WWE and AEW. The launch of AEW, in particular, featuring some of the wrestlers who had been among Ring of Honor's biggest draws, resulted in diminished houses. "I can't blame people for shooting for the stars," Koff said. "The day I came here, Christopher Daniels left [for TNA]. A year later, Kevin Steen and El Generico left. Adam Cole left. It's a transactional business. I only want people who want to be in Ring of Honor and give their all and live up to the fans' and their colleagues' expectations. When they're gone, you hope everyone has good memories. But they're always welcome back. And someone else will come in to create a different kind of excitement."

11
CHAPTER

I wasn't sure if Mike Quackenbush would want to talk to me. Known for esoteric storylines that whirl in his head for years, Quackenbush is a conceptual artist as much as a wrestling personality. Although its following might be small compared to other wrestling organizations, the promotion he founded, CHIKARA, attracts a breed of fan that can be discriminatory toward more pedestrian patrons of sports entertainment. If you haven't been following CHIKARA's byzantine narratives from the beginning, Quackenbush's disciples might suggest you get yourself a foam hand and work on your "This is awesome!" chants.

Yet, when Quackenbush and I finally connected, he apologized for being elusive and invited me to CHIKARA's training facility, the Wrestle Factory, in Philadelphia that week. When I arrived, I made note of the fact that I hadn't been the only one pursuing him. On numerous occasions, he'd been flown down to the WWE Performance Center in Florida to work as a guest trainer and production consultant.

"The irony isn't lost on me," he said. "Do you remember when the Cure put out the album, *Wish*? [Singer] Robert Smith did an interview and said the band had made up their minds a long time ago that they would not change their sound to fit the mainstream. If they were going to have a hit, the mainstream was going to have to change to suit them. I feel a little kinship with that remark."

On the wall facing Quackenbush hung a gold-framed, velvet painting of Max Moon, a futuristic wrestling character who wore a powder blue bodysuit, jetpack and firework-shooting wrist devices in the early '90s — the period in between the WWF's Hulkamania and Attitude eras. Initially, Konnan, a Florida-born performer who'd attained superstar status in Mexico, was slotted for the role. But after a number of backstage disagreements, Konnan left, and Paul Diamond — who'd wrestled as a masked member of the Orient Express — was handed the gimmick, supposedly because he fit into the already-tailored suit.

Quackenbush had the painting specifically commissioned for his office. "The artist said, 'I only paint Elvis or panthers. I've never been asked to do this.' I just got Paul Diamond's phone number last night. So I'll get to connect with this character who I love. That gives me such weird joy. I'm going to ask him, 'Do you still have the blue tights? And if so, can I convince you to come and play?'"

These types of vanity endeavors were important, Quackenbush pointed out, since the daily responsibilities of running an indie can deplete the vivacity of even the most besotted mat watchers. "None of the things I do to keep CHIKARA operating were on my list of reasons for getting into professional wrestling. Dealing with insurance premiums and the bureaucracy of the state athletic commission, renewing music licenses, building contracts, travel logistics. So, for me, I have to ask, 'Where is the joy? How do I rediscover the joy in my work so it's not just work?' This is my livelihood and my business, but I don't want it to be just that. I have to remember this is my passion. I don't want to lose what seduced me about wrestling."

A self-described geek, Quackenbush grew up in Reading, Pennsylvania, reading Bronze Age comics and science fiction. On television, he watched reruns of the 1960s *Batman* series, starring Adam West, and *The Amazing Spider-Man*, a live action program that ran from 1977 to 1979. "Seeing real live action superheroes, not animation, and the fisticuffs and the feats of derring-do, that resonates really powerfully with me."

Of course, he was a wrestling fan. "I could not name another art form that captured my imagination as entirely as professional wrestling. If you have this relationship with wrestling, then you know it has this funny way of corrupting every other element of your life. So all the things I wanted to express, I found a way to express them through this medium. Once it got its fangs in me, it went deep and it felt very real to me."

That didn't mean that entering the wrestling business reduced his excitement for other stimuli, notably serialized dramas like *Dexter* and *Lost*. But now, everything got channeled into the sport of kings. "I steal from the things I love. 'This is something interesting for a character to do. This is interesting as a storyline.' I try to look outside the normal tropes that professional wrestling tends to visit. There are a lot of obvious soap opera tropes in wrestling. 'What's this, another betrayal story?' So I thought, 'Let's steal from other genres. And can we jam that into professional wrestling and make it work?' Sometimes it does. Sometimes it doesn't. But the idea that I could get together with a group of people who are similarly impassioned, and we could make this into something, was appealing.

"We couldn't make our own Adam West *Batman* show. We couldn't make our own Bill Bixby/Lou Ferigno *Incredible Hulk* show. We don't have the budget for that. But we can make this on a ham sandwich and a Coke."

The name CHIKARA is inspired by a Japanese term meaning force, strength, proficiency and influence. In addition to Japanese wrestling, Mexico's lucha libre culture enlivened Quackenbush's thoughts while he was molding the promotion. Many performers wore masks, and the roster was divided between tecnicos, or babyfaces, and villainous rudos.

Originally an outgrowth of the school Quackenbush ran with "Reckless Youth" Tom Carter, CHIKARA's inaugural shows — like TNA and Ring of Honor, the group *also* happened to launch in 2002 — featured Wrestle Factory students like UltraMantis, Hallowicked and Ichabod Slayne, along with such indie names as CM Punk, Colt Cabana and Chris Hero (Kassius Ohno in NXT). By the end of the year, Quackenbush and Youth participated in a memorable tag match against student Master Zero and Mexican star La Parka, later known as L.A. Park following a copyright dispute with Mexico City's AAA promotion.

"I feel fortunate that I need not be consigned to the front row," Quackenbush said of his skill at wrestling as well as coming up with story themes. "I can be close to the mat. I can be between the ropes. When the time comes that my body does not allow me to do it anymore as a creative outlet, I will probably do improv comedy or some other stage act to be able to flex those muscles."

Although CHIKARA did not initially have a television outlet, the promotion's schedule was segmented into seasons, with stories arcing and climaxing over the course of several months, and the league creating cliffhangers before going on hiatus. In order to follow the elaborate plot twists, followers either ordered the group's DVDs or made it a point to attend the promotion's eastern Pennsylvania cards.

As technology developed, fans were able to catch up on old episodes by watching shows on YouTube, as well as a streaming service called Chikaratopia.

AEW referee Bryce Remsburg began working for CHIKARA in 2002, when he was a freshman at Temple University. "When my roommates were having keg parties," he said, "I was driving through snow storms to referee in front of 40 people. The CHIKARA wrestlers had an open mind, a little bit of silliness, a different sensibility. They were not a bunch of jocks. There were comic book nerds and punk rockers. These were my people.

"The whole thing was off-brand sketch comedy: guys in ice cream suits, hand outfits, gender breakdowns. I mean, CHIKARA was having intergender matches in 2002. If WWE was painting with six colors, CHIKARA was a giant box with 64 crayons."

In 2005, after WWE acquired ECW's assets, WWE staged a massive reunion show at New York's Hammerstein Ballroom, and broadcast it on pay-per-view. Rather than rely on WWE's corps of writers, Paul Heyman and ECW stalwart Tommy Dreamer organized the event, infusing it with authenticity. The card, featuring Chris Jericho, Chris Benoit, Eddie Guerrero, Masato Tanaka, the Dudley Boyz, Sandman, Psicosis, Lance Storm and others responsible for ECW's allure, received a thunderous reaction. Fans, particularly in the Philadelphia area, now craved seeing former ECW talent again.

Because it regularly ran shows at the old ECW Arena, CZW seemed to be in the best position to capitalize on the enthusiasm. "They didn't take advantage of the situation, and CHIKARA did," said Derek Sabato, who refereed for both promotions. CHIKARA and CZW were already using the same training facility and production company, Smart Mark Video. "The big difference was that CHIKARA really put a lot of care into the booking and going over the matches. They didn't ask the guys for exclusives. The focus was on building the brand and getting guys to *want* to work there."

Crowd sizes continued to grow. More than 750 fans attended *Chikarasaurus Rex: King of Show*, featuring stars like Johnny Gargano, Tommy Dreamer and Claudio Castagnoli (later Antonio Cesaro in WWE) in 2010. Smart Mark Video made it a point to release the DVD within a day. Partnerships were formed with Japanese promotions. In 2011, 864 fans turned up for the company's first live internet pay-per-view, *High Noon*.

The same year, Quackenbush and Reckless Youth realized a fantasy when they brought in the 1-2-3 Kid. On May 17, 1993, 20-year-old Sean Waltman, a virtual unknown at the time, stunned fans by toppling highly heralded Razor Ramon on *Monday Night Raw*. "To a lot of us at a formative age, that was the moment when we said, 'I can do it,'" Quackenbush recalled. "That kid was me. He was the first guy I ever remember seeing in a WWF ring who didn't have wrestling boots on. He wore sneakers, just like I had. Then, there was his size, of course. And his young appearance. [Heel announcer] Bobby Heenan would make jokes like, 'He hasn't done his homework.'"

Quackenbush contacted Waltman with a special request: "Would you become the 1-2-3 Kid again? You've been all these other characters. You've been X-Pac and you've been Syxx, and I know you're not a kid anymore, but would you do it?"

The CHIKARA cofounder claimed that his primary goal was not even selling tickets. "I thought, 'It's great if it's something that the audience wants to see. But I have to do it for me.'"

Waltman ended up working for CHIKARA on and off until 2016. But to Quackenbush, few experiences compared to watching the 1-2-3's comeback. "To see him in the old ECW Arena with all his facial hair shaved off like he was 20 years old again — that was the magic I wanted to reconnect with. If it wasn't for those moments, I think I'd get really bitter and jaded."

Yet, even as Waltman was taking spectators back in time, Quackenbush was planning what may have been the most curious angle in the history of the business. It stemmed from a conversation he'd had in a Center City, Philadelphia, steak house with future WWE show writer Robert Evans, who played time-traveling, marching band leader Archibald Peck in CHIKARA, and comic book writer and editor Ruben Diaz.

"Because he'd worked at Marvel and DC Comics, Ruben knew about structuring these long-form stories," Quackenbush said. "There had been invasion stories in CHIKARA before, and every [raiding faction] had its own motive. They'd been disadvantaged or they were dark reflections of our most popular characters. The arc was always the same. These guys show up, they have a gripe, they win for a while, they are repelled."

As the three chatted, Quackenbush wondered what would happen if, at the conclusion of one of these storylines, the bad guys actually won.

"The question kind of tumbled out on the table. And the answer seemed to be, 'They would close us down. We go dark.' And we all kind of sat back and then we said, 'Well, you know we have to do that, right?'"

The culprits, it was decided, would be a group of corporate overlords who were fearful of secrets that might be exposed if the promotion stayed in business. At the center was Wink Vavasseur, the company's bizarrely named "director of fun," who, utilizing a perverse algorithm called Chikarametrics, had previously broken up tag teams and placed wrestlers in units for no rational reason. He was also supposed to be so incompetent that he didn't know the names of the wrestlers who worked for CHIKARA. But he'd secured his job through the intersession of his father, a powerful executive with CHIKARA's storyline owner, the Titor Conglomerate, founded by business titan John Titor. Like Archibald Peck, Titor possessed the facility to travel back and forth through time.

"It was the single largest project I ever worked on," Quackenbush said. "We were timelining it three-and-a-half to four years before it happened. And we started building all these related websites, so if you really dug into them, the conspiracy theory information would be there. People could go back and find these cryptic messages from three years earlier."

Observed Tassilo Jung, COO of Germany's wXw promotion, a sometime CHIKARA partner, "This was one time when Mike's OCD worked for him."

To prepare, Quackenbush surveyed the alternate reality scene, along with gaming and viral marketing campaigns. "I just started looking at these different methods of telling a story, and we would steal it and steal it and steal it."

A meeting was called, and 50 CHIKARA associates signed non-disclosure agreements under the penalty of a $35,000 fine for breaking kayfabe. "Everybody was in. But some people definitely felt that this was the worst idea I ever had in a long list of terrible ideas. But at least they respected me enough as a storyteller to let me tell the story."

On June 2, 2013, CHIKARA presented an internet pay-per-view called *Aniversario: Never Compromise* from Philadelphia's Trocadero Theatre. In the main event, Ronald "Icarus" Grams was on the verge of using his signature "CHIKARA special" submission to wrest the promotion's Grand Championship from Eddie Kingston, when Wink Vavasseur ordered an army of security personnel to flood the arena. Both wrestlers and referee Bryce Remsburg were removed from the ring, and the video stream suddenly went black.

Remarked Quackenbush, "The security team swarms in, they cut the pay-per-view feed; it's very last episode of *The Sopranos*."

In the Trocadero, security began dismantling the set and herding the fans outside. A fan who was infuriated by what he viewed as an unsatisfactory finish, smashed the venue's glass door. Remsburg was seen fleeing the scene in tears.

"I knew what was going to happen for a few months," Remsburg said. "Some of the wrestlers didn't know until a few hours before."

Pinkie Sanchez had worked as Carpenter Ant in CHIKARA, and been involved in these types of angles before. "Mike Quackenbush was very meticulous," he said. "He didn't always let you know *why* you were doing what you were doing. Sometimes you'd find out almost at the same time as the fans. But when you'd stand back and look at the whole picture, it made sense."

Within a day, CHIKARA cancelled all upcoming cards — although these events had been announced, in reality, not one ticket was ever sold

— and took down its website and Twitter accounts. According to online rumors, Quackenbush had lost the fiscally feeble company in an acrimonious divorce. Regardless, it appeared that CHIKARA had shut its doors for good.

"We pushed the boundaries of pro wrestling storytelling," Remsburg said. "It was an unparalleled rib."

In truth, CHIKARA's fans would still have access to their wrestlers at other local indies. "By this point in time, we were secretly running eight other wrestling organizations," Quackenbush said. "Wrestling Is Cool. Wrestling Is Hard. Wrestling Is Intense. When you combined the first letters of the last words, it spelled 'CHIKARA.' Since we were planning to go dark, the talent needed places to work during that period. The idea was the ship sinks, everybody gets into these lifeboats."

Among his confidants, Quackenbush referred to his experiment as the "ashes project." "In the nine months that CHIKARA was dark, I ran more live wrestling events than at any time of my career. I ran almost 80 different live events. I personally was hidden from view. I would see this wrestler once a month over here, but he and I were never together with this other guy. And that part became a little lonely."

After nearly capturing the CHIKARA Grand Championship at *Aniversario: Never Compromise,* Icarus appeared to be leading a group of wrestlers in urging fans to convince Wink Vavasseur and his cronies to bring the promotion back. The grapplers held a guerilla event, wrestling several matches at Philadelphia's Franklin Delano Roosevelt Park, and at a comic convention, Icarus handed out CHIKARA DVDs, which, along with the group's t-shirts, were no longer on sale at the usual outlets.

"It was a complex story," Quackenbush said. "You couldn't follow it in passing. This was not a three-panel *Peanuts* comic strip. Characters would show up at fans' houses. They'd ring doorbells — you'd open the doors and there they were. There were secret auctions to get information about where the next guerilla event was happening.

"It's going to sound stupid, but a lot of this came from a speech I heard about how the word 'nostalgia' came into the American vernacular. 'Nostalgia' is a Russian word — we haven't adapted it — and literally means 'an ache of the heart.' What is it when something you love is withheld? That was the whole underlying theme of it. Our fan base didn't attach to one character. They attached to us as an ensemble. Even though you could still see these characters in the lifeboat promotions, when CHIKARA went away, you felt the loss."

The second annual National Pro Wrestling Day — another event conceived in the brain of Mike Quackenbush — provided the opportunity to relieve the suffering. On February 1, 2014, at the Palmer Center in Easton, Pennsylvania, a group of CHIKARA-affiliated wrestlers were in the ring when they were assaulted by a legation of heels. Suddenly, a squad of CHIKARA veterans — tecnicos and rudos alike — stormed the ring. These included the tag team 3.0, who arrived in a DeLorean, the vehicle used by Michael J. Fox to time travel in *Back to the Future*. With them was Archibald Peck; the pair had clearly journeyed to another age to find him. As the villains were forced from the ring, Icarus took the microphone and made a long-awaited announcement. CHIKARA was back.

"Mike had the foresight to see the finish line," Remsburg said. "It did not feel fake at all that night. There was pride. There was emotion. Some people got off the bus when CHIKARA went dark. But a lot got on."

The promotion's return show, on May 25, 2014, at the Palmer Center, drew an unprecedented 1,600 spectators. "We sold out, we reorganized the floor, we sold it out again," Quackenbush said. "When we walked out there, we felt like, 'We've broken through.' There was more attention on us than any other period in our existence."

But the engine soon stalled. "Ninety days later, we had returned to the same level we'd been at two years prior," Quackenbush continued. "We burned hot and fast for a very short period of time. But once the ashes project was over, there was no alternate reality game for you to take part in. Fans were asking, 'What's the next thing like that?' And the answer was, 'There isn't.' We wanted to get back to doing what we did. It was lonely and depressing when we were away from each other. We needed to cleanse our personal palates. We were done with dark storytelling."

As with other indies, a number of future stars passed through CHIKARA, including Castagnoli, Punk, Chris Hero, Bryan Danielson, "The Right Stuff" Brodie Lee (Luke Harper in WWE) and Sara Del Rey, who, under her real name of Sara Amato, became one of the most influential trainers at the WWE Performance Center. CHIKARA's training school claimed to be the only one in the United States that taught lucha libre, puroresu (Japanese-style pro wrestling) and, from Britain, groundwork-centric Lancashire wrestling and catch submissions.

The Wrestle Factory looked as the name suggested, its location an industrial building in the northeast Philadelphia neighborhood of Torresdale, along the Delaware River, among body shops, plumbing and heating businesses and construction companies. Inside, metal bleachers flanked the ring on two sides and a small entrance ramp protruded from between a set of black curtains and a honeycomb-like stage design.

On a cold Tuesday night in January, students trickled in, with at least one taking the time to kayfabe me by putting on his mask in the car.

While others stretched before training began, Quackenbush sat in the ring and talked about a Maryland indie looking for fresh, inexpensive talent. "They actually have a manager in a wheelchair called Cripple H," he laughed.

The lesson plan that night revolved around comebacks. They were supposed to wake the crowd, Quackenbush lectured, and be delivered in a chain of electrifying moves. That's why, he cautioned, it wasn't wise to execute, say, a cross-body block in the middle of a sequence. It curbed momentum.

"Either put it at the end," he said, "or switch it out with something else."

He warned against other things that could force a match to lag. "If you have to hesitate before delivering a belly to belly, it slows the pace. I'm not sure it can't be used somewhere in the match, but if you have to stop, it doesn't belong there."

Likewise, he criticized wrestlers who bent to motion a foe forward during a string of fancy maneuvers. "Make an edit. Put something else there."

As for the victim in the match, it was important to figure out a way to register every blow. "Sell your back while setting yourself up for the next movement."

Only after ingesting this basic knowledge could a worker step through the ropes and portray a sewer-dwelling goblin, communist cow, break-dancing pharaoh or some other gimmick you likely wouldn't find anywhere but CHIKARA. "We're starting to fine tune these things," Quackenbush said, wrapping up the night. "We can't have comebacks that sputter, stop and start. We want it to explode right here before we put it in front of the paying customers."

He paused. "Good work, everybody."

The trainees applauded, the sound reverberating off the steel seating and warehouse walls. Quackenbush appeared satisfied, flashing the smile of a cinematic action hero posing on the red carpet — a role he likely envisioned for himself when he was reading Bronze Age comics, watching *Batman* and marveling at the antics of King Kong Bundy and the Junkyard Dog.

12
CHAPTER

Six years after putting on a wrestling show with his high school friends near Cleveland, John Thorne contacted the proprietor who'd initially rented him the ring. If 21-year-old Thorne was still willing to pay a few hundred dollars, the man said, the ring was his to use.

This time, Thorne looked beyond his social circle for talent. Over the years, Absolute Intense Wrestling (AIW) promoted cards featuring Icarus, Hallowicked and Green Ant from CHIKARA, along with future WWE wrestlers like Bryan Danielson, Johnny Gargano, Adam Cole, Cedric Alexander, Ethan Carter III (EC3), Heidi Lovelace (Ruby Riott) and Athena (Ember Moon). On the night Shayna Baszler won the group's women's championship, Ronda Rousey turned up in the audience to cheer on her fellow MMA fighter. "She actually drove here from California and ended up drinking with us backstage," Thorne recalled.

Yet, while a teenage John Thorne was able to book a church gym simply by opening the yellow pages, the adult version found securing a venue problematic. "Indie promoters didn't always have the greatest reputation," he said. "A lot of places were afraid to work with us after 20 years of being ripped off by different indies."

While social media had been a boon to most small promotions, AIW experienced its drawbacks. "We got kicked out of a Catholic elementary school because too many fans tagged the show on Instagram," Thorne said, "and the parents saw all these wrestling pictures. As much as people say wrestling is mainstream, it still has a stigma to a certain segment of society."

Shows involving meet and greets with the legends of yore presented their own challenges. Former WCW World Heavyweight Champion Vader, for instance, agreed to an appearance on the condition that he receive his payoff in cash stuffed inside a *Maxim* magazine. Thorne said that Kamala once cancelled because he claimed to have gone to the airport with the wrong pair of pants. "The other one must have had his proper ID."

Another legend almost didn't board a plane because he was arrested that day on an old warrant. "His brother had to bail him out," Thorne said, "and he managed to make his flight."

"Big Poppa Pump" Scott Steiner was prompt and agreeable — as long as one requirement was fulfilled. "He wanted to go to Cracker Barrel over and over. Same order. Six chicken breasts. And he didn't want to wait for the order. He'd tell the waitress, 'I know it's ready. Bring it out now.'"

Mark Pollesel, owner of Ottawa-based Capital City Championship Combat, or C4, recalled having a former star call him several times on the day of an event, insisting that he was switching flights at different airports. Pollesel suspected that the performer was trying to back out of his obligation after receiving a deposit. Still, C4 extended the length of its show on the hope that the attraction would turn up at the end of the card.

"He lands at 10:30," Pollesel said, "calls from the cab and asks, 'What do you want me to do in the match?' I had him in a tag team match. At about 11:00, he comes in and takes his time getting ready while the other guys are waiting around in the ring. The match starts without him. A few minutes in, his music hits. He runs out to the ring, delivers a DDT and goes right to his finisher. Then, as the fans are leaving, he sets up a table and starts selling merch for another hour.

"In the days and weeks after that, I'd be getting texts from him. 'Hey, that was great. I had a good time. When can we do something together again?'"

Since the crowd appeared to be happy, Pollesel couldn't dismiss the offer outright.

A former film major at Ottawa's Algonquin College of Applied Arts, Pollesel entered the wrestling business in 2004, doing odd jobs for a number of local indies, including the IWS, which ran shows just over the provincial border in Quebec. In November 2007, while working as a civil service clerk in the Canadian capital, he promoted his first C4 show. The company's inaugural champion was Kevin Steen.

"I still think about becoming a screenwriter," Pollesel admitted, "but this is a creative outlet." For four years, he tried balancing his artistic impulses with managing C4's finances. Eventually, he took on a business partner, who was content remaining silent while dealing "with the stress of making money."

Another source of anxiety was monitoring the online response to the cards. "I care about our reputation on social media," Pollesel said. "I want workers to come back and tell other workers it's worth driving eight hours from wherever you live to work for C4. Really, it doesn't make any sense to run shows and fuck people over. All people have to do is go online, and nobody good will ever work for you again."

Traditionally, with Montreal and Toronto serving as wrestling epicenters, Pollesel regarded Ottawa as a city that the industry missed. The indie revolution changed that. "Anyone has the right to come here and run a show, and a lot of people do. But it's not like there's a huge, huge fan base. Look, it's great that indie wrestling is so popular. But I'm always scared of burning everyone out."

Tom Green was hardly considering these same big picture dynamics when he fell into the wrestling business in December 2006.

At the time, Green was a broadcasting major at Indiana's Vincennes University. In those months before the launch of the first iPhone, his dorm room telephone largely served as a lifeline to the outside world.

When it rang one night, his friend Mikey Blanton — the future owner of Chicago-area indie Black Label Pro — was on the other end. Blanton had figured out a way to book ex-WCW wrestlers Scott Norton, Raven and Disco Inferno. Could Green help promote a show?

"I was 18 and had no concept of time or sleep, so I agreed," Green said. "That's how Fight Sports Midwest was born."

What made Green qualified for his position was that he had something Blanton didn't: a computer. So when wrestlers reached out to him via email, he was able to lend a professional air to the operation by replying with a Fight Sports Midwest address.

"Looking back, the wrestlers could clearly tell that we were jokers that would blow some money and disappear, so they wanted to cash in on us before we went *kaboom*."

The group's formula was uncomplicated: book every cool name they could from larger promotions like CZW, TNA, Ring of Honor and IWA-Mid-South. "We were using all sorts of talent with whatever 'name recognition' meant on the indies in 2007," Green said. "We spent every dime we had, and thousands we didn't."

Samoa Joe was in the midst of his TNA feud with Kurt Angle, exhibiting signs of superstardom, and Green and Blanton were overjoyed to have him on one of their shows. They mentioned a number of prospective opponents, and Joe demurred until Eddie Kingston's name came up. The two had worked together before, and Joe was convinced that they'd have an entertaining match. But when Kingston broke his ankle, and internet pundits began speculating that he'd be out of commission for six months, Green was nervous.

Shortly after being released from the hospital, Kingston cut a promo on a primitive digital camera, transferred the footage to DVD and sent it to Green in the mail. Said Green, "That's how we knew he wasn't going to no-show."

Interestingly, this now-forgotten promotion played a role in reshaping the long, proud lineage of the NWA. In the spring of 2007, Tiger Mask IV, the NWA World Junior Heavyweight champion, had flown to the U.S. for a two-week tour, working mainly with TNA talent. The plan was for the championship to change hands, Green noted, "but the relationship with TNA was breaking up, so none of the TNA guys could win the belt. We were told to book Tiger Mask IV with someone safe who wouldn't hurt him."

Green and Blanton chose Mike Quackenbush.

The match took place in an indoor soccer stadium connected to a bowling alley in Green's hometown of Portage, Indiana. "I remember Tiger Mask IV bowling in a suit and his mask before the show, and all these Midwestern families just watching him," Green said.

The encounter ended when Quackenbush appeared to shock his rival by yanking off his mask, then pinning his shoulders to the mat. "I guess I didn't have your attention before," the new titlist boasted, while tapping the belt. "Do I have it now?"

The admission for Fight Sports Midwest was $15 per ticket. "The first show did alright, about 260 fans," said Green, who'd later work with another Indiana group called School of Roc. "The second show not so much. We were done after two events. But I learned a lot of skills that I kept with me: how to format and time out a show and boring details like how many hot dog buns to order."

He also discovered that a single promoter's decisions could impact the rest of the industry. For one event, Green booked Low Ki into a Marriott near the arena. A few weeks later, another local promoter sent the same performer to a less high-end facility a few miles away. "I think Low Ki told them, 'You know, these other guys put me up at the Marriott,'" Green recalled. "The next day, we got an angry email from the promoter, telling us that if we kept putting wrestlers up at the Marriott, pretty soon, everybody would expect it."

In the same way that Fight Sports Midwest enabled fans in some distant reaches of the Hoosier state to partake in a small piece of pro wrestling history, the aptly named Pro Wrestling Phoenix (PWP) spent much of the 2010s trying to revive Omaha, Nebraska, where the "Nebraska Tiger Man" Joe Pesek had headlined some 100 years earlier.

The old Omaha territory stretched into sections of Kansas, Iowa and South Dakota. Max Clayton began promoting out of Omaha in the

1920s and was a founding member of the NWA. When Clayton passed away in 1957, Joe Dusek — of the "Dirty Duseks" wrestling clan with his brothers Ernie, Rudy and Emil — claimed the spot.

On June 14, 1957, a two-out-out-three fall match in Chicago between NWA World Heavyweight champion Lou Thesz and Edouard Carpentier ended indecisively when — after each grappler took a fall — the referee ruled that the titlist could no longer continue. While the NWA ultimately ruled that the circumstances did not warrant a title change, Carpentier was billed as champion in other places, including Omaha. On August 9, 1958, he dropped his version of the title to Verne Gagne. As previously mentioned, Gagne also crowned himself champion of his new Minneapolis-based American Wrestling Association (AWA) in 1960. The Minnesota and Nebraska titles were defended separately until they were unified under the AWA banner in 1963.

Crowds of between 8,000 and 9,000 people regularly attended the Omaha Civic Auditorium for AWA cards, while summer shows were held at the home of the annual College World Series, Johnny Rosenblatt Stadium. When one of these events was bombarded by a rain storm, fans retreated to the auditorium, which had set up a ring just in case.

But, in 2004, Verne Gagne's AWA had been defunct for 13 years when PWP promoter Chris Metry began training in Omaha at age 21. The first sessions occurred in a backyard, where Metry learned the basics: hitting the ropes, bumping, some chain wrestling, very simple crowd psychology. He gained a far better education by traveling to seminars conducted by name wrestlers, including Samoa Joe, Steve Corino, Abyss, AJ Styles and Christopher Daniels.

"Somewhere between 10 and 25 guys who wanted to be wrestlers would show up," Metry said. "The cost was something like $60, and that included a ticket to the show that night. We were all just trying to grab whatever training and knowledge we could. I don't recommend training without going to a proper wrestling school. But these seminars worked for me."

On the East Coast, Joey Janela had a nearly parallel experience, attending classes run by, among others, Terry Funk, Samoa Joe, Dean

Malenko, Matt Hardy, Nigel McGuinness, Lance Storm and the Great Muta. "Even if the seminar was a money grab," Janela said, "I always took something away to bring on my journey."

At 5:30 p.m. on a Saturday, an hour and a half before doors were scheduled to open to the paying public, I stepped into the gym at St. Finbar, a Catholic church in Bath Beach, Brooklyn, serving the neighborhood's Irish, Italian, Hispanic and, more recently, Chinese residents. While a number of former performers, including Tammy "Sunny" Sytch, Norman Smiley and Barry Horowitz, set up eight-by-tens and other merchandise at tables on the side of the room, 66-year-old Ricky "The Dragon" Steamboat — a former NWA World Heavyweight champion and WWE Hall of Famer — stood in the center of the ring, addressing approximately 30 younger wrestlers seated on folding chairs on the gym floor.

The topic was selling with believability.

"It's hard for the audience to see you selling if you're on the mat," he pointed out. "It's much easier for the people to understand what's going on if you're standing up. If your wheels are good, sell upright."

When going blow for blow with a foe, he continued, it was foolish to turn around and sell an injury for the benefit of the crowd. "Don't sell with your back to your opponent. You wouldn't do that in a street fight. Everybody knows it's entertainment, but it comes down to basic logic."

The same reasoning should be applied, he said, when performing a spot that involved both participants falling to the canvas. After slinging your adversary, chest-first, into the turnbuckles, he counseled, run up behind him and attempt a clothesline. Then, the first wrestler could turn around and lurch forward. "You bang heads," he said. "But it looks like a mistake that would happen naturally. There should be a reason why you're both on the mat."

Although he never worked as a heel, Steamboat had wrestled enough of them to understand the art of drawing heat to yourself. He quoted Dave "Fit" Finlay, the former British Mid-Heavyweight champion and WCW United States titlist: "I'm so stingy, I don't want to share my heat with anybody, even the referee."

As an example, Steamboat painted a scenario in which a heel was cheap-shotting his rival in the corner. "The referee comes over. '*Back off.*' You hit your opponent with two more shots. '*I said, back off.*' You throw three more cheap shots. The referee begins to count. '*One . . .*' Now, you back off to the center of the ring, raise your arms, taunt the crowd. What happens? Instead of booing the referee for not being able to control the match, the heat's on *you.*"

As Steamboat spoke, Horowitz left his table, wandered over to the last row of ringside seats and listened. "That's an education you can't afford," he told me, motioning at The Dragon. "In the old days, you'd have to hope you'd end up in a car with him to get his wisdom."

After attending a number of these seminars, the six-foot-four, 280-pound Metry developed a persona, Chris Havius, a brooding emo character with black eyeliner. While also going to culinary school, Metry worked small shows in Sioux City, Des Moines and Joliet, Illinois. But he noted that a lot of these shots were seven to eight hours away. One day, while chatting with some wrestling friends, he had an idea:

"What would it take to do this ourselves?"

In 2005, the group found a ring once used by a non-operational indie in a garage and rented out a middle school gym for $250, 10 minutes outside of Omaha in Council Bluffs, Iowa. Word went out to workers as far away as Kansas City. Omaha had a new wrestling league. The pay sucked — Metry couldn't afford to give anyone more than $25 — but this was the chance to be there at the beginning of something.

After a disappointing house, Metry tried again a few months later, this time without partners. Buddies in the wrestling business set up the ring and sold concessions. Attendance was slightly better: 75 fans, as opposed to the 30 who showed up for the first card.

PWP kept going. Venues changed. Outside names came in. Before his death in 2013, Mad Dog Vachon, who began the first of his five AWA World Heavyweight Championship reigns in Omaha in 1964, signed autographs and cut a scowling promo. "Since that first show, I don't know if we ever drew less than 40," Metry said. "And on a good night, we've had upwards of 300. It's definitely been sustainable."

In 2015, the group moved into the Waiting Room Lounge, a concert venue in Omaha's trendy Benson neighborhood. As Metry interacted with spectators before and after the matches, he noted that many weren't WWE supporters. Some never watched wrestling at all. "A lot of these people just look at us as another show, something that's fun to do on a night out. It's a different experience than watching wrestling on TV, or even attending a WWE event. I mean, you can reach out and touch the apron. You can hang out with the wrestlers after the show."

It's an atmosphere Baron Von Raschke and Mad Dog Vachon might not have understood. No one was waiting outside the building, trying to vandalize the heels' cars. And even with the prevalence of alcohol, few, if any, fans came to the building to challenge the performers to a shoot. "Does the indie wrestling of broken-down VFW Halls still exist?" Metry asked. "Absolutely. But I see a lot of hipsters in fedoras and suspenders, even at our level."

13
CHAPTER

Shortly after I arrived Los Angeles for a series of shows in the winter of 2019, a friend in the business told me that I needed to interview Southern California's biggest wrestling fan.

Around 2016, Shawn Scoville, aka DaShawn2Cents, became known for hanging out at indie shows and inviting the wrestlers back to his home for web interviews in a hot tub. Shirtless and rotund, with water bubbling against his body creases, Scoville's interview style was uninhibited. "I give zero fucks," he said of his corpulence. "I'm a large guy. That's who I am."

He also knew the Southern California indies, impressing his subjects with his appreciation of their craft and awareness of their respective careers. To some, a segment on Scoville's channel came to be perceived as the modern equivalent of an appearance on *Piper's Pit*. When Matt Riddle was passing through town, he apologized for not having the time to make it to the host's Bellflower, California, home, but agreed to be interviewed in the hotel bathtub instead.

The renown elevated Scoville to a different status, something slightly above working press. Before a series of death matches during a Game

Changer Wrestling (GCW) swing through Los Angeles, I saw Scoville backstage, assisting in organizing the light tubes.

"I have ADD, Asperger's and depression," he told me. "I was kicked out of school. They had me on so many pills, I couldn't figure out what was going on. I have so many mental health issues, I can't hold a job. My dad said I'd grow out of it. I never did. You know what helps me? Wrestling."

According to Steve Bryant, who runs the SoCalUncensored website, as of 2019, there were approximately 50 indie cards in Southern California each month. Scoville tried to attend as many as possible, relying on the many friends he'd made on the circuit to drive him to the various venues.

"If I miss a wrestling show, I go into a depression."

A lot of Southern California fans felt the same way.

"There's a wrestling style that's very unique to Southern California," noted Pete Trerice, the cameraman and editor for Scoville's hot tub series. "We draw on lucha, obviously, because we're so close to Mexico." But unlike traditional Mexican wrestling, the SoCal luchadores work on the left side of their opponent's bodies, allowing them to use the right hand when mounting a comeback. "It's harder hitting than lucha. And with New Japan having a dojo in Los Angeles, there's a lot of Japanese influence too."

Said Brody King, who debuted in New Japan in 2019 in addition to working for Ring of Honor, "Everything I am essentially came from the mixed Japanese strong style and lucha I learned on the Southern California indie scene."

In the territory days, the Los Angeles promotion centered on the storied Olympic Auditorium at 18th and Grand in East L.A. and extended from the Mexican border to south of San Francisco. The rights to promote at the Olympic were held by Aileen Easton — the first woman inducted into the International Boxing Hall of Fame — while her son Mike Lebell ran the business end of the territory. Her other son, notorious shooter "Judo" Gene Lebell, was the promotion's enforcer, putting on the trunks when necessary to punish a wrestler who didn't want to do business the way the family wanted.

Although a member of the NWA for most of its existence, the territory broke away in 1961, creating its own title, the Worldwide Wrestling Associates (WWA) Heavyweight Championship. Unlike other belts, which were regional, the WWA championship had international cachet, with the title changing hands in both Japan and South Korea. In 1968, the group rejoined the NWA and flourished, broadcasting in both Spanish and English, with Mexican stars like Black Gordman, Great Goliath, Rey Mendoza and Mil Mascaras supplementing cards featuring The Destroyer, Pampero Firpo, Killer Kowalski and Rocky Johnson. A 1971 grudge match between the territory's biggest name, Freddie Blassie — then known as "El Rubio de Oro," or "The Golden Blond," to his Mexican devotees — and "Maniac" John Tolos was held outdoors at the Los Angeles Coliseum. Officially, the card drew 25,847 fans. Both Tolos and Blassie suspected that the attendance was significantly higher, but Mike Lebell downplayed the numbers to siphon off a larger share of the proceeds for himself.

Even during its waning days, the territory was a showcase for future headliners like Chris Adams, Chavo Guerrero and Roddy Piper. Officially, the promotion held its last show in December 1982. As Vincent Kennedy McMahon began his national expansion, Lebell affiliated himself with the World Wrestling Federation, allowing WWF to claim beachheads in both Los Angeles and New York.

In the aftermath, a few small promoters attempted to run shows with former Olympic Auditorium names and luchadores who'd come up from Tijuana for the day. But California State Athletic Commission requirements were costly. When the authority stopped regulating wrestling in 1989, previously reticent promoters reconsidered. The same year, the Slammers Wrestling Gym opened in Sun Valley, recruiting the Fabulous Moolah as a trainer, with the goal of producing the next generation of SoCal wrestlers.

Lucha always hovered above the scene. After Mexico's AAA promotion attempted a U.S. incursion, selling out the Los Angeles Sports Arena for the *When Worlds Collide* pay-per-view in 1994, a number of promoters attempted to gain traction with lucha-oriented cards. World Power Wrestling (WPW), based in Santa Ana in suburban Orange County, started in 1996, sometimes drawing 1,000 spectators for shows featuring wrestlers from Mexico.

By contrast, Bill Anderson and Jesse Hernandez began operating the Empire Wrestling Federation (EWF) in Covina the same year, primarily using students from their wrestling school, offering a presentation based on what fans had seen in the WWF in the '80s.

"California felt disconnected from the rest of the wrestling world," said Kevin Gill, a West coast–based commentator for GCW. "Everything seemed to be focused on the East Coast. You had these hard-working wrestlers on the other side of the country, but how many people knew they were there? Some of these guys had to actually travel to New York or Philadelphia to get people to pay attention to them."

Recalled Joey Ryan, "You didn't have these super-indies, like ECW, that everyone knew about. So there weren't these shows with all-stars from all over the country. At the same time, there was something starting to happen. The people were less jaded and more appreciative of the talent they saw. They started going to indies and kept coming back again."

In the late '90s, Fred Olen Ray, a director, writer and producer who worked on more than 150 low-budget movies, including *The Brain Leeches, Attack of the 50-Foot Centerfold* and *Hollywood Chainsaw Hookers*, created All-Star Championship Wrestling (ACW). Using ECW as an inspiration, Ray, who wrestled under the name "Fabulous" Freddie Valentine, went out of his way to feature a hardcore match on virtually every card. He brought in celebrated bloodletters like Terry Funk and Abdullah the Butcher, and staged title matches that involved stunts like placing the championship in a box of rattlesnakes or on the back of an alligator. "I think the alligator was drugged," said Steve Bryant. "He really didn't do anything."

By the early 2000s, upcoming SoCal talent like Ricky Reyes, Super Dragon, Rocky Romero and Messiah could find work at a growing number of indies, including Revolution Pro Wrestling — not to be confused with the British group of the same name — and Xtreme Pro Wrestling (XPW). Founded in 1999 by Rob Zicari, aka Rob Black, the owner of L.A. porn company Extreme Associates, and his wife, Janet Romano (adult actress Lizzy Borden), XPW ran matches featuring porn stars and an annual death match tournament called *Baptized in Blood*.

Provocative by nature — Extreme Associates would later face obscenity charges for sex scenes featuring an adult actress pretending to be a young girl, Jesus Christ coming down from the cross and having sex with an angel and a gang rape led by Osama bin Laden — Zicari's troupe attended ECW's *Heatwave* pay-per-view at the Olympic Auditorium, the company's Los Angeles debut. Before the action started, security had warned the visitors to turn their XPW shirts inside out. Although they complied, tensions in the arena remained high.

Throughout the night, porn star Kristi Myst was seated in the front row and feigned removing her top, riling up the crowd. Just prior to the main event, featuring Justin Credible defending his ECW World Championship against Tommy Dreamer, Myst turned to the audience and took off her shirt, exposing a black leather bra. This infuriated Dreamer's valet, Francine, who was supposed to lose *her* top in the match. She rushed over to the front row, berating the X-rated performer for drawing the heat to herself. Hoping that the cameras were catching the confrontation, XPW wrestler Supreme then tried to show off his XPW shirt, as security swarmed him. In the fracas, Supreme accidentally bumped into Myst, who fell to the ground.

The pushing and shoving caused much of the ECW locker room to charge down to the ring, throwing punches at the intruders. Security removed the XPW posse to the parking lot, where they were again confronted by the ECW contingent. Outnumbered, members of the XPW ring crew were allegedly punched and kicked several times — reportedly by Paul Heyman, among others — before escaping the scene.

Yet, XPW was able to use the altercation to their advantage. *Why was ECW so defensive? Was it because XPW really was more extreme?* Playing off the incident's notoriety, XPW staged a show at the Olympic on April 21, 2001, called *Scene of the Crime.* Much had changed in professional wrestling at this point. Most notably, ECW was out of business, its resources now owned by the WWF. Indeed, the invasion angle that pitted ECW and WCW wrestlers against the WWF involved a ringside melee that conjured up memories of the Olympic Auditorium incident.

By sheer circumstance, *Scene of the Crime* happened to take place on the same night as the first and only championship game of the first incarnation of Vince McMahon's XFL — six miles away at the L.A. Coliseum. Not only was the football league's acronym similar to XPW, the team that ultimately won was named the Los Angeles *Xtreme.*

To most observers. *Scene of the Crime* was a disappointing show. But a match between Rising Sun and Super Dragon left the fans awestruck. Despite their masks, the combatants were not luchadores from south of the border. They were Californians wrestling the new SoCal style. When a tape of the match was shown on XPW's broadcast on KJLA, thousands of viewers suddenly realized that the local indies were worth checking out.

"It was a great time," recalled B-Boy, a future Pro Wrestling Guerrilla (PWG) World Tag Team champion. "There was fan intensity. People were loyal and started coming to every show. There was a familiarity between all the top talent. There was still a lot of tape trading going on, so we'd study moves and recommend opponents for the promoters to bring in. Every time we toured somewhere, the people would learn what we did in Southern California — how it was a hybrid of styles, how nobody here knew just one genre."

Growing up in a military family, B-Boy — the real-life Benny Cuntapay — followed different wrestling territories as he moved from base to base. But it was the Randy Savage–Ricky Steamboat match at *WrestleMania III* in 1987, when Benny was eight years old, that solidified his love for wrestling. "Even at a young age, I thought talent was more important than whatever character you were playing," he said. "I knew these were two of the greats."

Attending high school in San Diego, Cuntapay made bad choices, falling in with a Filipino gang. Still, the craving for wrestling endured. "I was a thug. I was always getting into fights. The other guys would make fun of me because they said wrestling was fake. But I didn't care. It gave me direction. I knew what passion was."

He began training at the Palace of Pain in San Diego in 1997. When Rick Bassman, the man credited with discovering Sting and the Ultimate Warrior, opened a gym in Mission Viejo in 1999, B-Boy switched there. Bassman's Ultimate Pro Wrestling (UPW) group eventually became a developmental league for WWE and included John Cena, Samoa Joe and The Miz among its rotating roster. Coached by Tom Howard and

Christopher Daniels, B-Boy learned how to structure a match and tell a story.

Around this time, B-Boy received a piece of advice he'd impart to every young wrestler who'd ask him for guidance. "You just have to make the drives." In B-Boy's case, that meant commuting, when necessary, as far away as Sacramento, more than 500 miles from his hometown.

In 2003, he flew to Philadelphia and won CZW's third annual Best of the Best tournament, beating Sonjay Dutt in the finals. With his reputation authenticated, he went from being an aspirant to an indie attraction, receiving dates in Europe, Asia and Australia.

While others moved beyond the indies, B-Boy never received the call, instead starting the Level Up Pro Wrestling school in La Mesa, as well as the Ground Zero promotion in the Imperial Beach section of San Diego. "I'm one of the boys first, but business is business," he said of running a promotion. "I have to tell my students when they're not ready to be on the show. It's never easy but, hopefully, it motivates them to work harder."

For his trainees, a glance at the careers of arguably the most ostentatious duo to arise from the modern Southern California indies was a reminder that Golden State fans did not suffer mediocrity.

Although their surname is Massie, the Young Bucks have been calling themselves "Jackson" since an indie promoter gifted them the moniker around 2005. The sons of a part-time minister and full-time general contractor from Rancho Cucamonga, Matt and Nick and a younger brother, Malachi, were wrestling obsessed. Matt's annual birthday celebration was centered on screening the latest *WrestleMania* while eating pizza with his friends and family.

Of all the wrestlers they idolized — Edge and Christian, The Rock, Matt and Jeff Hardy — Shawn Michaels would have the greatest impact on the Bucks. Their preferred attire was spandex, conjuring up memories of Michaels and his partner in The Rockers, Marty Jannetty. Their specialty would be the Heartbreak Kid's finisher, the superkick. When Michaels headed the WWF's D-Generation X faction, he and his partners taunted foes with crotch chops. Later, Matt would march the entire length of the ring, crotch chopping the whole way, before delivering a clothesline.

Nick compared a Young Bucks match to a visit to Disneyland. "Our act is pretty much your routine tag team wrestling, but you're on cocaine," joked the straight-edged Matt to *Vice Sports*.

In exchange for working for their father, the boys were allowed to build a ring — hammering down the wood frame and setting the posts in concrete — in the backyard. It was unveiled on Matt's 16th birthday. "Nick was 12 and Malachi was 10 years old," Matt told the *Ring Psychology* website. "We taught ourselves how to do flips and impersonated what we saw on television, We fell in love at first bump."

When the family relocated to Hesperia in San Bernardino County, they began staging a wrestling event every Thursday at a local skating rink that would occasionally feature known indie wrestlers en route to their weekend SoCal dates.

Early on, the brothers wrestled as single performers. But at an Olympic Auditorium show, they were booked as a duo. When the promoter had them come out to the Twisted Sister song "We're Not Gonna Take It," they complained about having the "whitest" presentation in the business. Converting an embarrassment into an asset, they flippantly referred to themselves as the "Young Bucks."

At the time, Malachi was part of the act. Before he retired in 2010, citing travel fatigue, the siblings periodically billed themselves as the "Jackson 3."

They accumulated fans as well as detractors. Their synchronized gymnastic style was derided as hackneyed, while their propensity for leaving their feet caused certain blocs to label them "spot monkeys." After other wrestlers diminished their matches as one long "superkick party," the siblings plastered the slogan on t-shirts, bracelets and stickers. In 2015, in a naked effort to go viral, they helped a kid celebrate his ninth birthday by superkicking him during an event in Baldwin Park, California.

The plan worked.

It wasn't the first time that a child got involved in a wrestling match. During the days of Les As De La Lutte, 13-year-old Jacques Rougeau participated in an angle in which Tarzan Tyler bodyslammed him in the

Montreal Forum. In 1996 in ECW, the Sandman's six-and-a-half-year-old son, Tyler Fullington, berated his father as a drunk and blamed him for divorcing the boy's mother. At the "Natural Born Killaz" event at the ECW Arena, tow-headed Tyler — who'd begun dressing like Sandman's enemy, Raven — blasted his father with Sandman's Singapore cane. Twenty-two years later, at *WrestleMania 34* in 2018, Braun Strowman seemed to randomly pick a fourth grader from the crowd to team with him against Sheamus and Cesaro. Although Strowman and his teammate, Nicholas — the real-life son of referee John Cone — were successful, capturing the tag team title recognized on *Monday Night Raw*, the two relinquished the championship the next night, due to the youngster's demanding school schedule.

It was all fun, as long as a kid didn't get hurt.

In the Bucks' case, they took pride in being "light" performers who could make a move look believable while barely grazing an opponent and were confident working with an amateur. They also enjoyed boasting about having the most exciting match on every card. Hoping to consistently achieve a five star rating in the *Wrestling Observer*, the Bucks named their finisher the Meltzer Driver. During those times when Dave Meltzer happened to be in the audience, Matt and Nick blew him a kiss before executing the maneuver.

In reality, the *Wrestling Observer* rating system benefited not just the Bucks, but the entire SoCal scene. "After all those years of Southern California not having the bigger promotions, like you saw on the East Coast, the fans were less jaded and really appreciative of what our wrestlers could do," said Joey Ryan.

Ryan first discovered the indies when he attended a WWF card in Anaheim with his brothers, and someone handed them tickets to a local show. In 1999, he began training with the EWF but switched to Rick Bassman's UPW a year later. Although he was working regularly on the SoCal indie scene, he continued his apprenticeship under Bryan Danielson in 2004 at the dojo opened by Japanese legend Antonio Inoki.

He soon developed a character patterned after Tom Selleck's 1980s *Magnum P.I.* television persona, coming to the ring in tight trunks, his body oiled, a lollipop jutting from below a well-trimmed mustache. In both promos and in-ring action, he secreted sexual innuendo. Indie fans grew accustomed to seeing Ryan grab an opponent while positioned on the turnbuckles, facing the ringside area. Taking his rival along on a drive to the floor, Ryan's catchphrase became, "Who wants a mustache ride?"

After working for TNA and its India-based affiliate, Ra Ka King, between 2011 and 2013, Ryan developed the gimmick for which he'd become best known. During a confrontation with Danshoku Dino in Japan's DDT promotion in 2015, he seemed to develop prodigious strength in his penis, using it to win a test of strength. Video of the exchange received international attention, prompting Ryan to name a new signature move the YouPorn-plex, in honor of the online video company YouPorn. In the course of a match, he'd somehow manage to get an opponent to grab his crotch, then flip the victim to the mat.

"I've been wrestling a long time and tried stuff that worked and stuff that didn't work," he said of his penis routine. "It's the evolution of me as a wrestler or as an artist."

At the end of 2015, Ryan was signed to *Lucha Underground*, then a year-old television series that mixed American indie wrestlers with standouts from Mexico's AAA promotion. The hour-long program was divided into seasons, broadcast in Spanish and English and featured storylines with supernatural and science fiction themes. Ultimately, conflicts were resolved in the ring, located not in an arena or a television studio, but in an intimate, darkened warehouse in L.A.'s Boyle Heights neighborhood — in 2018, the location was moved to an old cold storage facility in downtown Los Angeles — known as "The Temple." Seen primarily on the El Rey Network, founded by film director Robert Rodriguez for a Hispanic-American audience, *Lucha Underground* was the first television show to screen theatrically, using 4DX technology, allowing the audience to experience environmental effects like seat motion, wind and scents.

For the first few years, *Lucha Underground* appeared to be yet another option for the plethora of indie talent trained in the SoCal style, including Brody King, Eli Everfly and Jake Atlas, who were also all graduates of the Santino Brothers Wrestling Academy.

"When you look at the quality of the wrestlers who've gone through Santino Brothers, you realize why they've made such a big difference out here," said SoCalUncensored's Steve Bryant.

Founded by Mongol Santino and his in-ring "brother" Joey "Kaos" Muñoz — the team that battled the Young Bucks in their Olympic Auditorium debut — in 2007 in Norwalk, California, the school dedicated itself to teaching submission grappling, lucha libre and SoCal strong style, along with cardiovascular training, mental endurance, character development and even ring crew set-up.

The wrestling seminary's establishment corresponded with a time when interest in even the fringes of the industry had been revitalized. In 2008, Mickey Rourke starred in *The Wrestler*, portraying Randy "The Ram" Robinson, an '80s wrestling star still hanging on in the New Jersey indies. Necro Butcher, Ron "R-Truth" Killings, Johnny Valiant, Claudio Castagnoli (Cesaro), Robbie E, Austin Aries and the Blue Meanie all had roles in the movie. Although the mood of the Darren Aronofsky film was hopelessly dreary, the excitement that Randy and his fellow indie performers engendered was conveyed. At one point, Rourke's character is going through some papers when he finds a photo of Afa the Wild Samoan, at whose Allentown, Pennsylvania, school, the actor trained. Even the fans in the film were legitimate indie followers.

Journalist Kenny Herzog noted that, by the turn of the 2010s, anyone who attended an indie show was aware that not just one, but numerous wrestlers on the card had the potential to become top talent. "These guys weren't waiting for anyone to make it happen for them. They were making it happen."

No place was this philosophy expressed as purposefully than at Santino Brothers, which moved to the city of Bell Gardens in 2010. Jake Atlas was one of about 30 students when he began training. In a typical Santino Brothers class, he said, only one to two graduate. "If you can make it to that level," he said, "you're ready to start generating a buzz wherever you go."

At GCW's *To Live and Die in L.A.* show, on a rainy Saturday night a half block away from a homeless encampment in downtown Los Angeles, I stood with Steve Bryant watching Santino Brothers graduate Matt Vandagriff wrestling New Jersey native KTB. While I scribbled on a notepad, Bryant held his phone in his palm, glancing down to monitor fan reaction to the newcomer on Twitter. As Vandagriff executed a sky twister, Bryant pointed out that the comments were intensifying.

Until Vandagriff was picked up by WWE, AEW or Ring of Honor, Bryant speculated, this kid was going to help reconceive the Southern California indies. "It's kind of cool," he said, "to see the world discovering this guy."

14
CHAPTER

The premium promotion in North America, in terms of consistent match quality, was founded only because another Southern California indie pissed off the boys.

I met Gary Yap years ago when he was running the EPIC promotion out of his home. Yap, an artist who worked on *The Simpsons* and *King of the Hill*, was a nice guy and passionate wrestling fan. If I ever became a wrestling promoter, I thought, I'd want to be as respectful of the business as Gary Yap.

But here's the thing. I *wouldn't* become a wrestling promoter. I'm a writer. And just because I *like* wrestling more than most people doesn't mean that qualifies me to be a businessman. I simply don't have the skills.

Apparently, neither did Gary Yap.

"He had very big ambitions and good intentions," said Excalibur, cofounder of Pro Wrestling Guerrilla (PWG). "He wanted to pay everybody fairly. He was paying everybody out of his own pocket. He ended up spending a lot more money than he should have."

In November 2002, Yap had scheduled a show at an L.A. entertainment center. The night before, he graciously threw a party for the participants at a strip club. It was sparsely attended, but Excalibur didn't have the sense that anything was amiss. Yoshihiro Asai, aka Ultimo Dragon — who melded the traditions of his native Japan with those of lucha libre and is credited with popularizing the Asai moonsault — was coming back after an injury that nearly ended a career that once saw him hold a record 10 championships simultaneously from various parts of the globe. "There was going to be all this stuff," Excalibur said. "It was going to be Ultimo Dragon and Super Dragon and American Dragon [Bryan Danielson] all on the same show."

The next afternoon, a group of wrestlers gathered in the entertainment center's parking lot to get ready for the night's event. In addition to the SoCal regulars, several CZW performers had flown in, along with ECW legends Sabu and Jerry Lynn, who was supposed to be a surprise guest on the card. But the building was locked. "Maybe a hundred fans are there, standing with the wrestlers," Excalibur recalled. "The ring truck is there. Nobody knows what's going on. Everybody had the same amount of information, which is a terrible place to be as a wrestler. Luckily, I have an average white guy face without my mask, so the fans didn't know I was supposed to be wrestling that night. Nobody can get Gary on the phone."

The assumption was that some unanticipated expense had arisen that Yap couldn't pay, or he was delinquent for a variety of past costs. Since no one arrived to open the door, both wrestlers and fans had hours to get to know one another while they speculated. Eventually, Yap drove up. "He doesn't get out of the car," Excalibur said. "He's on his phone. He's trying to book another venue. He'd pleading. '*You don't understand. I need to book the show for tonight. I need it right now.*' And [future NWA World Heavyweight champion, Ring of Honor booker and WWE Performance Center coach] Adam Pearce is irate. He has a very old school mentality. It was just an embarrassment that he would be involved in something like this. And he's pounding on the window, cursing Gary out as Gary's sinking into the seat."

Finally, Yap looked out the window and addressed the small crowd. "Sorry. There's no show," he said sheepishly before driving away.

If there was an upside to the calamity, it was what occurred in the aftermath. Six wrestlers who were booked on Yap's show and had been waiting in that parking lot, Excalibur, Disco Machine, Super Dragon, Scott Lost, Joey Ryan and Top Gun Talwar, would go on to create PWG.

"We were just tired of dealing with promoters — money marks whose money would dry up after two or three shows," said Ryan. "We're breaking our backs and some big name star would fly in and eat [the promoter] out of all his money, and we'd have to settle for whatever was left over. We knew what constituted a good show. And we were working so much ourselves that we knew the guys we could get to put on elite matches."

With or without his mask, Excalibur couldn't have agreed more.

Before he first donned the hood, Excalibur had what he called a "prototypical wrestling childhood." Growing up in the Detroit area, he was just short of seven when Andre the Giant wrestled Hulk Hogan in the main event of *WrestleMania III*, at the nearby Pontiac Silverdome in 1987. "I remember some of my classmates went," he said, "and I was insanely jealous." But by the early '90s, when the WWF roster featured names like Sid Justice, Skinner, Tatanka and Irwin R. Schyster, he'd lost interest.

He was perusing through an AOL chatroom around 1996 when he made a friend who rekindled the intrigue. "He lived two towns over, but his dad had a satellite dish in the backyard. So they got shows from Mexico, and it blew my mind." Reaching into his VHS collection, the kid showed Excalibur a broadcast of AAA's *When Worlds Collide* pay-per-view from Los Angeles in 1994. In the semi-final, La Pareja de Terror (The Terror Pair), Art Barr and Eddie Guerrero, had their heads shaved after losing a hair versus mask match to Octagon and El Hijo del Santo. In the main event, Perro Aguayo vanquished Konnan in a wild brawl in the cage, following a double stomp from the top of the enclosure.

"I'd only seen the WWF," Excalibur said. "I had no idea wrestling could be something else. I just went down a rabbit hole of, first, Mexican wrestling and then, Japanese wrestling. And really, with the Attitude Era, I'm aware of some of the stuff, but I missed a lot. When people talk about Limp Bizkit performing the theme song for *WrestleMania XIX*, which was probably the coolest theme music of all time, I never saw it. I watched [WCW's Monday night broadcast] *Nitro* because *Nitro* had luchadores."

While studying art in junior college — after creating a persona as a masked wrestler called El Scorpio Diablo in a backyard wrestling league — he connected with people involved on the SoCal indie circuit, notably Super Dragon, who'd actually wrestled in Mexico and was part of the "New Generation" of California's version of Revolution Pro Wrestling. One night, Excalibur had an epiphany: he'd move to L.A., work as a professional designer and train to be a wrestler.

In L.A., Excalibur took on his current moniker and began training with Super Dragon. By coincidence, Disco Machine was another student at the dojo and happened to be working in design. As the pair became familiar with each other, Disco Machine helped his fellow trainee find day work. "I was extremely lucky," Excalibur said. "If it hadn't been for him, I would have been back in Detroit within a year."

When Excalibur finally made his in-ring debut, he was prepared to electrify the arena. Executing a dive from the top rope onto the arena floor, he overshot his fellow wrestlers and knocked himself out. "One of the guys we trained with, his mom was in the crowd, and she said, 'You have to go to the hospital.' I went to the hospital, they charged me $800 for two ibuprofen and sent me on my way. That was my introduction to professional wrestling.

"My dad hated me moving to L.A. He was a teacher, born in Latvia and raised in Germany. He could put up with me being an artist because that was a semi-viable career. But he hated wrestling. He thought I was making the biggest mistake of my life. We were a very Teutonic family, where it was hard to say 'I love you.' He once came to see me at a show in Detroit where I wrestled Bryan Danielson. When I asked him after the show, 'What did you think?' He went, 'That guy was really good.' Well, yes, he was the best wrestler in the world. But what did he think of me?"

PWG scheduled its first show on July 26, 2003, at Frank & Son, a large space generally dedicated to collectible shows in City of Industry, California. The partners pooled their money for the venue and airline tickets for the guest talent. In the main event, AJ Styles, then coholder of the Ring of Honor World Tag Team Championship with Amazing Red, defeated Frankie Kazarian.

"We paid the wrestlers up front, so everyone knew we were on the up and up," Excalibur said. "Unfortunately, we couldn't pay what Gary was paying. All the guys knew they could work a swap meet on Friday for $25, and Gary would give them $300 the next night for the same match. But they understood that they were just getting lucky. We were pretty forthright with people: 'Hey, this is us. We're just as poor as you are.'"

Because of his graphic background, Excalibur was responsible for designing fliers, the website and, eventually, t-shirts and DVD covers. "Art gave me some built-in viability, besides what I could do in the ring. Today, people barely need a website. But there was a time when that was what you had to do to communicate to your audience, and I could do it in a way that made us seem a lot bigger than we were. When you're running in a little Jewish community center, drawing 125 people, you need a website to make it seem like a professional operation."

PWG moved to the Hollywood/Los Feliz Jewish Community Center in July 2004, presenting a card that included Styles, Danielson, Kazerian, Pearce, Christopher Daniels, CM Punk and Samoa Joe. "The thing about indie wrestling in L.A. is that everyone's charging you L.A. prices," Excalibur said. "So this was the one place that we could afford. If we'd been in Harrisburg, Pennsylvania, we might have gotten a building for $300 a night. In L.A., the cheapest buildings were usually three grand. We were charging $20 a ticket. There are a lot of tickets you have to sell to cover the rent. We needed every advantage we could get."

Within a two year span, PWG started to grow, sometimes drawing as many as 500 spectators. Excalibur attributed Super Dragon's eye for detecting marketable performers to the company's success. "He has this ability to spot talent early, guys with insane natural ability. It's such an intangible thing, but in his mind he understands a good match. If you ask the average fan, or even the average wrestler, to lay out a good match in words, it would be hard to do. Super Dragon could do it off the cuff."

After a time, the country's best indie workers were sharing stories about the caliber of matches and performers at PWG. In some ways, the small promotion became the equivalent of St. Louis in the territory days — a city that drew the top wrestlers in the NWA, AWA and WWF, along with a discerning fan who took the in-ring product seriously. "If you got booked there once and had a good showing, you could get booked everywhere," said B-Boy.

GCW commentator Kevin Gill would marvel at the capacity of the wrestlers he saw: "I'm sitting there thinking that the highest form of this art is being practiced five feet away from me."

What also made PWG different was the fact that the owners never sought a TV deal, relying on the DVD market instead. This allowed PWG to form cooperative agreements with promotions that barred talent from appearing on rival broadcasts.

The DVD market may have saved PWG from folding within a few years, since the distributor, High Spots, was paying the company a licensing fee that helped subsidize airline tickets and other charges.

In 2006, PWG expanded its exposure by journeying to Europe, presenting cards in Essen, Germany, and Kent, England, supplementing the promotion's regulars with local performers.

The same year, the company shifted its base to American Legion Post No. 308 in Reseda, a building that became known as the "PWG Clubhouse." Although fans would grow to sentimentalize the tumble-down facility, Excalibur remembered his exasperating exchanges with Larry, the cantankerous veteran who ran the post. "If the chairs showed up before 3 p.m., Larry would make them drop the chairs outside. Even after we'd been there 10 years and made the Legion a fortune in alcohol sales, everything was a struggle. We'd ask, 'Larry, could we go backstage? We're going to open up the doors in about five minutes.' He'd kind of exhale, go, 'Hold on,' and finish his game of video poker. Then he'd say, 'Alright, now you can come backstage.' And we'd say, 'Alright, this is 10 minutes after we wanted to, but thank you for letting us, Larry.'"

Whatever anxiety the owners felt, the fans didn't notice. When PWG began selling tickets online — announcing details generally a month before each show via Twitter — the building would sell out in less than two minutes. To secure the best seats, fans would start lining up outside the PWG Clubhouse at 11 a.m.

Few, if any, ever complained about time spent languishing in the sun. "PWG had an aura," said SoCal Uncensored's Steve Bryant. "Most promoters would say, 'It's the opening match. You don't have to go all out.' Super Dragon, who never does interviews, would tell the opening match guys, 'Let the wrestlers in the other matches prove they're as good as you. If the fans like your opening match, maybe you guys belong in the main event next time.'

"So you'd see wrestlers trying harder, breaking out new moves up and down the card. Guys did things on a PWG show you wouldn't see them doing anywhere else. It became the place to be discovered." Wrestlers would soar so high that they regularly collided with the lights hanging from the legion's low ceilings. When that occurred, fans chanted, "Fuck that light."

"It's a different kind of art, mate," "The Villain" Marty Scurll, winner of the 2016 annual Battle of Los Angeles tournament, told *L.A. Weekly*. "There's no silly storylines, just pure in-ring action where we're telling stories with our bodies."

In 2007, Danielson, El Generico (Sami Zayn), Kevin Steen (Kevin Owens), Tyler Black (Seth Rollins) and Roderick Strong were among the future WWE performers who were regulars in PWG. Owens would cite PWG as the reason he was summoned to WWE, noting that WWE's head of global recruiting, William Regal, regularly attended the events in Reseda. "There was one NXT show I watched in 2018," said Excalibur, "where it seemed like the only person who hadn't been in PWG was Velveteen Dream."

In 2010, a year after forfeiting his PWG World Championship to join WWE, Daniel Bryan was fired by his new company after an angle in which he appeared to strangle ring announcer Justin Roberts with his necktie. Although Bryan said that the company was apologetic, the sponsors were apparently uncomfortable with that degree of violence. Although he was eventually rehired, he first returned to the indies.

In PWG, he was given a massive ovation, which included fans lobbing neckties from all directions (he received the same reception at CHIKARA). "That was how they showed they were happy to have him back," Excalibur said.

As the years progressed, Super Dragon became PWG's booker and edited the company's DVDs, while Excalibur continued creating the graphics. That left four other partners with limited responsibilities.

"What were the other guys going to do?" Excalibur asked. "Set up chairs and stuff? Little by little, people drifted off. Top Gun Talwar got a real job. He was like an engineer or something. He had a *really* real job. Scott Lost retired. Disco Machine retired. And Joey Ryan, as you all know, started doing his thing."

Ryan's contract with TNA ended his co-ownership of PWG. When the TNA stint ended, Ryan returned, but only as a performer. With Candice LeRae, Ryan formed an intergender duo that twice challenged the Young Bucks for the PWG World Tag Team Championship. As with the necktie incident, it was the type of confrontation WWE was wary of presenting, since the company's stockholders and sponsors were uncomfortable with imagery of men overpowering women. "I think an important difference between domestic violence and professional wrestling is consent," Ryan said on an IMPACT! Wrestling media call, after he resumed working with the company formerly known as TNA." The wrestlers have agreed to wrestle each other. There is a split as to if pro wrestling is a sport or if it's theater. I lean toward the theatrical part."

As the 2010s progressed, people on the indie circuit could sense that their scene was morphing into a phenomenon. "You could feel a movement starting around 2013, even 2012," said the Young Bucks' Nick Jackson. "At that point, PWG had become so hot."

In fact, at one stage, a Bucks' losing streak in PWG helped expand the team's following. "Sometimes, people get tired when it's like, 'The Bucks won again. Another title,'" Matt told the UK's *SPORTbible*.

Nick added that PWG left it to the Bucks to proceed in that direction: "It was our choice. We were like, 'Let's lose. Screw it.'"

Backstage, the Bucks had begun helping Super Dragon with the booking and were so content with their PWG situation that they were willing to demand a clause in their contracts with other companies that allowed them to continuously return to Reseda. "In 2014, Michael Elgin was the Ring of Honor champion and he lost in the first round in the Battle of Los Angeles," Excalibur explained. "The championship wasn't on the line but still, [Ring of Honor] were very upset about that. Then

Adam Cole ended up getting hurt on a PWG show and had to pull out of a Ring of Honor gig. And I understand how Ring of Honor felt. They were like, 'You're working twice as hard for them, and we're the company you have a contract with. That's bullshit. That has to stop.'"

But when Ring of Honor asked the Bucks to sign a North American exclusive contract, the brothers demanded a provision that made an exemption for PWG. Said Excalibur, "They were ready to walk. But there were some negotiations and, finally, Ring of Honor said, 'Fine.' So when Cole, Kyle O'Reilly and Roddy [Roderick Strong] were up for renewal, they said, 'Okay, we want the Young Bucks deal.' Ring of Honor acquiesced, so then, Jeff Cobb, Bandido and Jonathan Gresham also got the Young Bucks deal."

Cobb, who was the flag bearer for Guam in the 2004 Olympics and won the PWG World Championship in 2019, claimed that the PWG clause allowed him "to do my thing. The PWG type of atmosphere molded me. I'd hate to leave it. I don't want to ever leave it."

Excalibur described a PWG event as "a completely different form of self-expression. These guys need to scratch that itch. We're never coming to Philadelphia to run a show the same night as Ring of Honor. We're never going to take their talent away. I mean, if we wanted to run the Staples Center [in Los Angeles], that would be cool. But it would be an awful pain in the ass. It's just me and Super Dragon. That would be a lot of chairs to set up."

When Cody Rhodes became a free agent after leaving WWE, he tweeted out his wrestling goals. Among the priorities was working for PWG and competing in the Battle of Los Angeles. When he finally realized this ambition, his wife, Brandi, introduced him as "the grandson of a plumber," a reference to Dusty Rhodes' habit of characterizing himself as "the son of a plumber," and "the star that left them in the dust."

It was one of the many times Cody flaunted his liberation to his former employer.

Even then, no one at PWG took it for granted that Cody would remain there as a permanent fixture. Situations changed and performers moved on. "Guys get taken away," said Bryant. "But PWG finds ways to bring new people in. If they're not from the U.S. or Canada, they're from Mexico. Or they're from the UK. Or they're from Australia."

And in the social media age, those workers became easier to find. "We share things with the speed of a retweet," said Mike Quackenbush. "Some guy who does a hot move in Auckland, New Zealand, can be in PWG the next weekend."

It's an opportunity a newcomer never takes lightly. "To get that email [inviting you to PWG] means you are on your way," said Jake Atlas.

In May 2018, PWG held its final card at the Clubhouse and moved to the Beaux Arts-style Globe Theater, built in 1913 in downtown L.A. for full-scale stage productions. Because the building was bigger than the now-romanticized American Legion post, fans could actually acquire tickets the day of the show, rather than having to scramble to score the ducats the moment an event was announced. But much of the mood stayed the same. With no barricades surrounding the squared circle, spectators could easily approach the wrestlers standing at ringside, their t-shirts draped over the ropes, merch spread out on the apron. During a 2019 show, I saw Bandido selling masks and chatting with Dave Meltzer, while Ortiz from the Latin American Xchange (LAX) tag team signed a fan's Mexican flag and spoke with me about PWG's appeal.

"The atmosphere," he said, "the legacy. You're always bringing your A-game, not just because of the caliber of the talent, but the caliber of the fans."

Added his partner, Santana, "The fans expect to see the best pro wrestling possible, and they've seen it before, so they know what it's like."

Jeff Cobb compared a PWG event to the episode of *Monday Night Raw* that follows *WrestleMania*, when followers who've come from all over the world crowd into the arena, chanting, singing and becoming as big a part of the show as the performers. "No matter how many times you're here, the feeling doesn't change. The fans are rabid every time you're in front of them."

To Bandido, the fervor was rooted in an unspoken pact between the wrestlers and the crowd. "They feel the way we feel," he told me in Spanish. "They love wrestling. They *live* wrestling, like we do."

As I circulated, I was assured that I didn't have to worry about leaving my general admission seat unattended. Apparently, there was an honor system at PWG. If you placed your ticket stub on your chair, no one else would sit down.

Indeed, there was much about PWG that didn't exist in other promotions. "By modern standards, we're still a dinosaur," Excalibur said. "We don't have live streaming. Our shows go up on the High Spots wrestling network after the DVDs have been out for a year. We don't book big venues. If you can come, great. If not, we have a DVD for you."

The show began with fans pounding on the ring apron as Excalibur addressed the crowd: "Fifteen and a half years ago, this was an experiment, and here we are, 200 shows later."

The crowd applauded loudly and respectfully. This was definitely something everyone had done together.

He set down some ground rules. No one was to record the matches. Photos were okay. As fans packed themselves tight near the ring, they were urged to make room for the official photographers. And during those moments when the action spilled onto the arena floor, spectators were urged to pull their fellow audience members out of the way. "Save a life," Excalibur urged.

Just as importantly, all bottles and cans were to be carried to the back and deposited in the proper receptacles. "Here at Pro Wrestling Guerrilla, every week is Earth Week because . . ."

Excalibur let the words hang in the air, as the crowd responded with a mantra they'd shouted many times before: "We re-cy-cle!"

The first match was a Triple Threat, involving Jungle Boy, Trey Miguel and Jake Atlas. When Atlas entered the ring, I noticed him give the finger to someone at ringside, which I thought was odd, since most of the 550 people in attendance were applauding him. Then, Jungle Boy rolled out of the ring and seemed to get in a fan's face about something. Once the entrance music stopped, though, the incident appeared to be forgotten and the three had a fast-paced, fun bout.

When I saw Atlas the next day, he asked, "Did you see what happened last night?"

At that point, I barely remembered.

"One of the fans called me a faggot."

Save for the rainbow-colored bracelets Atlas wore to the ring, there was little else to indicate any type of sexuality. But he wasn't in the closet, either, and one asshole had blurted out something that cut the performer close. That's why Jungle Boy had left the ring. He later told me that he simply went up to the fan and said, "Shut the fuck up."

He'd come to the arena preoccupied, since his father, actor Luke Perry, had recently suffered a stroke that would claim his life several days later. "If I had known how bad it was," Jungle Boy said, "I'm not sure if I would have been there. But my father always encouraged me, and I know he would have wanted me to go. It was such a strange night. PWG has always freaked me out because you have to perform at such a high level. But on that night, with everything that was going on, being there and wrestling, being with the fans, it just grounded me."

That's why he was so rattled by the swipe at Jake Atlas, particularly in front of an audience that tends to be open-minded. "Jake's one of my best friends and also one of the best independent wrestlers there is," he said. "I thought about saying something to the guy afterwards, but we had such a good match that I got caught up in it."

Months later, he reflected, it was probably better that he didn't give the fan attention he obviously didn't deserve.

"Wrestling has become more progressive," Atlas said, "but you can never change everyone in the world."

I noted that it seemed like the majority of the people in attendance were indifferent to whether he was gay, straight or asexual. In fact, when the match was over, the fans followed a lucha tradition of showering the apron with money.

"When I publicly came out," he said, "I was a heel. They booed me because I was supposed to be an arrogant jerk. But they didn't boo me because I was gay. And that was very reassuring."

By and large, Atlas' attitude is that there is a time and place for advocacy. "We can be loud and proud," he said, "but be a wrestler first."

For David Starr, though, wrestling seemed to be a vehicle to trumpet his political views. Before his match with Jonathan Gresham, the ring announcer introduced Starr as, "The cream in your coffee, your favorite wrestler's favorite wrestler, the Jewish cannon, the physical embodiment of charisma, the most entertaining man in professional wrestling, the Bernie Sanders of professional wrestling, the best of the best, Mr. Americana, Davey Wrestling, the 104-minute man, the main event, 'he's really good at Twitter,' the king of taunts, 'The Product' David Starr."

When I mentioned that the Bernie Sanders reference might not have gotten the same babyface pop in other parts of the U.S., Starr offered a different opinion. "Most people — it doesn't matter where — cheer. In America, most people are working class or middle class. And so the Democratic-socialist message comes through."

Since the 2020 election season had barely begun, I resolved to ponder the merits of that statement another time.

The main event, a PWG title defense between Cobb and Bandido, told a good story. Despite a weight difference of about 90 pounds, the two appeared capable of executing the other's moves. Cobb, the powerhouse, frequently left his feet. The more diminutive Bandido delivered a vertical suplex and piledriver to his more ample foe. After Cobb retained the championship, helping Bandido to his feet and shaking hands after the bell, fans beat rhythmically on the ring while hurling streamers at the competitors.

There were many skilled wrestlers in the world, but to watch guys who were *this* good in such a cozy setting felt like a rarity. With the industry evolving so quickly, it was natural to wonder how soon it would be before fans could only view Jeff Cobb and Bandido from the other side of a barricade — and the intertwined arms of a security brigade.

15
CHAPTER

Although a number of fighting styles are particular to the UK, the early days of what became British professional wrestling has some parallels to its American counterpart. Before the turn of the 20th century, a Michigan-born wrestler named Jack Carkeek traveled to England, issuing challenges to anyone there who wished to engage in a shoot — not unlike the carnival wrestlers who barnstormed the U.S. heartland. Carkeek's parents were British, and he'd been trained in Cornish wrestling, in which competitors gripped onto each other's jackets in order to gain an advantage. But he also was proficient at catch, a British discipline that was modified in America as "catch-as-catch-can."

In 1903, "The Russian Lion" George Hackenschmidt arrived in London after winning championships in Moscow, St. Petersburg, Vienna and Paris. In addition to being a strongman, Hackenschmidt was a fitness author, philosopher and public speaker proficient in seven languages. In the UK, he was regarded as a celebrity, but his fame extended to the United States, particularly after he pinned American champion Tom Jenkins in two straight falls during a 1905 Greco-Roman rules bout at Royal Albert Hall. Before Hackenschmidt dropped his title to Frank

Gotch in Chicago, Theodore Roosevelt commented, "If I wasn't president of the United States, I would like to be George Hackenschmidt."

As wrestlers traveled back and forth over the Atlantic Ocean, the influence spread in both directions. By 1930, though, the styles started to diverge. English wrestlers combined the rules of a number of wrestling forms, including catch and Greco-Roman, to create what was called "all-in" (given the historical knowledge of its organizers, it's hardly a coincidence that this became the name of the pay-per-view that helped trigger the indie revolution). In 1930, the British Wrestling Association (BWA) was founded by Henry Irslinger and Sir Atholl Oakeley, who somehow managed to win the group's national championship. If that wasn't suspicious enough, a number of other incidents occurred that suggested that the BWA was not presenting legitimate contests. Women appeared on shows, more to titillate the men in the crowd than display athleticism, and competitors resorted to badgering foes with chairs and other weapons. Even so, by the onset of World War II, fans had largely lost interest, and wrestling was relegated to the backrooms of pubs.

In 1947, troubled by reports that professional wrestling had become "fake," a committee headed by Antarctic explorer Admiral-Lord Mountevans created a set of rules that was supposed to restore the sport's integrity. Women were no longer permitted to participate — leading to the elimination of mud matches and other related attractions — weight classes were defined and matches divided into six five-minute rounds with 30-second breaks in between. Victory could be achieved via two pinfalls, two submissions, or one of each, as well as a knockout.

As a result of these rule changes, the city of London, along with other jurisdictions, lifted its ban on professional wrestling.

More than 95 percent of the promoters in the UK agreed to adhere to Mountevans' "modern freestyle wrestling" boundaries. But the truth was that British wrestling was still primarily a work. That didn't mean that wrestlers didn't take the art seriously. Karl Gotch, Bert Assirati, John Foley, Billy Robinson and the Dynamite Kid were among the treacherous "hookers" — guys who could hook your body into crippling holds you'd never see in an amateur match — who passed through Billy Riley's Snake Pit gym, located in the Lancashire mining town of Wigan.

Although doing business constrained them from maiming most rivals with less daunting credentials, the threat was always there.

Generally, the average British wrestling promoter presented shows with "blue eyes," or babyfaces, "baddies" and theatrical storylines. By and large, everyone cooperated. Hence, the inspiration for the title of Jackie "Mr. TV" Pallo's 1985 tell-all, *You Grunt, I'll Groan*.

As with the NWA, a syndicate of British promoters banded together in 1952, forming Joint Promotions, consisting of operations based in London, Yorkshire, Manchester, Liverpool and Scotland. Their efforts were aided by the introduction of Joint Promotions' segments on ITV's *World of Sport* series, starting in 1964, adding names like Pallo, Mick McManus, Tony St. Clair, Big Daddy, Giant Haystacks, Les Kellett, Jim Breaks, Johnny Saint, Marty Jones and Mark "Rollerball" Rocco into the British cultural vernacular.

The system worked for a long time. As the years passed, though, the group was criticized for its reliance on older wrestlers whose matches had become routine, notably Big Daddy, whose brother, Max Crabtree, happened to head Joint Promotions. In 1980, British World Heavyweight champion "Mighty" John Quinn, a Canadian who'd appeared in the WWWF as the Kentucky Butcher, left for rival All Star Wrestling (ASW), taking the belt with him. Quinn's chief adversary, Wayne Bridges, eventually joined him in ASW to continue the feud.

Then, in 1986, ITV cancelled *World of Sport*. For a few more years, wrestling remained on British television but with no consistent time slot. Having lost its exclusive with ITV, Joint Promotions tapes were rotated with those of ASW and the World Wrestling Federation. Finally, in 1988, the same year Ted Turner was forced to step in and bail out what remained of the old NWA, ITV cancelled wrestling for good.

Before folding in 1995, Joint Promotions became little more than a touring vehicle for Big Daddy and later, British Bulldog Davey Boy Smith, during a period when he was estranged from the WWF. By contrast, ASW — started in 1970 by Brian Dixon, who'd first become acquainted with the business as president of the Jim Breaks Fan Club — used the cliffhangers from the cancelled wrestling broadcasts to continue plotlines at live events, developing stories from show to show.

ASW also thrived in the summer, touring holiday camps, collections of bungalows, chalets and campers in country settings where families vacationed. "Hundreds of people would come to the holiday camp shows," said Will Cooling, a writer for *Fighting Spirit Magazine*, a highly respected British wrestling and MMA publication that closed in 2019. "Even if they didn't see it on TV, fans still needed that wrestling fix."

For those unfamiliar with current storylines, and for those who'd never watched at all, an announcer would describe the details of the various feuds on the public address system. "He'd say, 'Look what this awful guy is doing,' letting you know who to cheer and who to boo," Cooling said. "That way, everyone could enjoy themselves. The holiday camps are one part of the British wrestling industry that gets no coverage. You'd do these shows once a year — no more. And then, people would come back the next year."

For a period, ASW formed an alliance with the UK Hammerlock promotion, founded in Kent in 1993 by Andre "Sledgehammer" Baker. "Hammerlock was taken very seriously," said former *Fighting Spirit* editor Brian Elliott." Andre Baker insisted that his students knew mat wrestling. You had to know how to shoot before you took your first bump class. It wasn't like today, when people go to a wrestling school as a hobby. There were only guys who really wanted to be wrestlers. You started out by putting up and taking down the ring. It might be months before they'd let you in the ring to train."

Eventually, the group split with ASW, becoming a member of the NWA. Perhaps the biggest event in the history of the renamed NWA UK Hammerlock occurred in 1999, when the promotion's top star, submission specialist Gary Steele, won the NWA Heavyweight Championship from Naoya Ogawa in a three-way match with Brian Anthony in Charlotte, North Carolina.

Steele had become the first Brit to hold the crown, but ASW seemed to barely notice. While running a wrestling school in Birkenhead, Merseyside, the company was busy, developing relationships with promoters in Canada, France, Germany and Japan and even sending wrestlers Robbie Dynamite, Frankie Sloan, James Mason and Dean Allmark, Brian Dixon's son-in-law, to TNA as Team UK in 2004.

By then, though, ASW had created bad feelings among some followers. They presented what became known as "WWE tribute shows," advertising characters like a "UK Undertaker" and "British Doink." In at least one instance, a poster hyping the appearance of the "Big Red Machine" included a promotional photo of WWE's Kane. After 580-pound, former WWF World Heavyweight champion Yokozuna died of pulmonary edema in his Liverpool hotel room before a 2000 show, ASW is said to have continued to use his image to publicize upcoming events.

"You'd see posters with all the WWE guys," said Dann Read, cofounder of Pro-Wrestling: EVE, "then, you'd go to the show and The Rock would have a Welsh accent. I remember my friend telling me, 'We're going to see WWE in Colchester" — in Essex, about 90 minutes from London — "and I'd think, 'If WWE is coming to England, they're not going to an 1,100-capacity building in Colchester.' That really killed a lot of towns."

In 2002, Scott Conway, a disaffected member of the ASW roster, cut his ties with the Dixon family and started The Wrestling Alliance (TWA). Doing away with the British system of breaking a wrestling match into rounds, Conway was still enough of a traditionalist to present many of the company's bouts as two out of three falls. But with no exclusive contracts, TWA's wrestlers often worked for ASW on off days. Said Read, "You could work every day of the week, mainly outside of London. London wasn't a thing. But the Corn Exchange in Ipswich could draw 1,000 fans on a Tuesday night. There were shows in town halls. And both groups had different holiday camps."

Then, in 2004, Conway left the UK and moved to Thailand, with hopes of setting up a wrestling league — a decision, incidentally, that didn't go very well. "It opened the door to other promoters," Read said. "Dixon never gave a shit. He was too focused on his own stuff to try to block someone else from getting started. That's when the British wrestling model started to change. Instead of bringing in old WWF guys like Greg Valentine or Earthquake or the Honky Tonk Man, promoters were looking at wrestlers who'd been in ECW or Ring of Honor, more indie-type wrestlers."

Among the new English promotions were Kent's International Pro Wrestling: United Kingdom (IPW: UK) and Manchester's FutureShock, formed in 2004; Newcastle's Main Event Wrestling (MEW) and London's Lucha Britannia, formed in 2006; Hull's New Generation

Wrestling (NGW), created in 2008; and Wolverhampton's Fight Club: Pro, launched in 2009. In Scotland, the Scottish Wrestling Alliance (SWA) started in 2002, while Insane Championship Wrestling (ICW) began two years later. Many of the wrestlers working for these groups also appeared on cards promoted by Irish Whip Wrestling (IWW), founded in 2002 — one of its biggest stars, two-time champ Sheamus O'Shaunnessy, would dispense with the last name when he joined WWE's main roster in 2009 — and Northern Ireland's Pro Wrestling Ulster, which held its first event in 2007.

In 2003, Dann Read began working with the Frontier Wrestling Alliance (FWA), originally named the Fratton Wrestling Association when it was created by wrestler Mark Sloan 10 years earlier. Like NWA UK Hammerlock, FWA was gravely earnest about the *sport* of wrestling. The piledriver was banned because, in a real fight, a person would likely be paralyzed if his neck were driven into a hard surface. As in professional soccer, a penalty card system was implemented, with a yellow serving as a warning and a red as a disqualification.

"I didn't want to be involved with these old school shows anymore because, by the 2000s, that's not what the audience was wanting," Read said. "We began using wrestlers like Robbie Brookside, Jody Fleisch and Alex Shane." These were modern athletes who fans believed could handle themselves in an actual shoot. At the FWA Academy in Sloan's hometown of Portsmouth, he trained a number of performers who'd later appear in WWE, including Paul and Katie Lea Burchill and Drew McIntyre.

The group gained an international reputation after Americans Sabu and Dan Severn appeared on FWA shows and Christopher Daniels defended the promotion's British Heavyweight Championship in Ring of Honor.

"You'd get indie bookings because you were an FWA student," Read said. "I think one of the reasons Mark shut down the academy was because people would come in, do one session and then contact promoters and say, 'Oh, I'm an FWA trainee.'"

In Leicester, though, Brookside was in the process of opening his own school. Brookside was unique in British wrestling because he managed to span several eras. He first received national exposure by appearing on ITV during the period when it televised ASW; although Robbie's real surname was Brooks, Brian Dixon thought a moniker inspired by the British soap opera *Brookside* would be more memorable. In ASW, Brookside formed a team with Steve Regal — later William Regal in WWE. During a broadcast in 1988, Brookside unmasked Kendo Nagasaki — the real-life Peter Thornley from Stoke-on-Trent, Staffordshire, not Kazuo Sakurada, who played the character in Japan and North America. In retribution, Nagasaki hypnotized Brookside into turning on the other blue eyes, an angle that continued after ASW was no longer televised.

Even after winning FWA's version of the world championship, Brookside remained an ASW wrestler, making appearances in both promotions. But his scope extended well beyond the British Isles. He performed in Germany and Austria, particularly for Otto Wanz's Catch Wrestling Association (CWA), and for WCW and WWE. Nearly 30 years after his career started, he was working as a WWE talent scout and, later, an NXT coach.

But while Brookside was able to transition from one league to another, pro wrestling's limited UK exposure caused British performers to struggle. At one point, Doug Williams, one of the country's most respected grafters, as the Brits called their workers, relocated to Florida to become a regular in TNA, whose UK broadcasts led to sold-out tours.

With American companies commanding the curiosity of casual fans, wrestlers like Jonny Storm, Martin Kirby and Kris Travis kept their dedicated supporters interested. Still, the opportunities outside of Great Britain seemed limited. "El Ligero probably wrestled more dates over the period of two years than anyone on the planet," said Elliott. "Twelve to 14 matches a week. Very rarely injured. An excellent worker, entirely proficient, knew how to time his spots, not do too much in one match. But his gimmick was a Mexican luchador. He was really from Leeds and had a heavy accent like the British Bulldogs. I remember he had a really excellent match against Akira Tozawa in Preston City Wrestling (PCW) in 2012. I mentioned it to Konnan [then an international liaison for AAA], and he said, 'There's nothing you can do with the guy because he's a British wrestler with a Mexican gimmick, and the Mexicans would never believe in him.' Of course, when WWE signed him [in 2018], everything changed."

It was 2010 when Elliott began writing for *Fighting Spirit*. As a wrestling fan with mainstream tastes, he was more intrigued by WWE, TNA and Ring of Honor than anything distinctly British. But once he started exploring the indies, he realized that the momentum was shifting in the UK.

Within a year, Steven Fludder started PCW in Lancashire, and future WWE United Kingdom champion Pete Dunne and ring announcer Jimmy Lee opened ATTACK! Pro Wrestling in Wales. With a rotating roster that included Mark Andrews and Chris Brookes, ATTACK! resembled CHIKARA in both the intimacy it established with its fans and unorthodox storylines. One show, labeled *Press Start*, had a video game theme. An affectionate French mouse was called Love Making Demon. Referees and stuffed animals won championships. "They would do Christmas shows where people would dress up outside their gimmick, and the fans would find it hilarious," Elliott said. "There would be a lot of talking on the shows, not interview segments, but wrestlers shouting out something during their matches to make the crowd laugh. The wrestling itself was very high spot–oriented. Tremendously entertaining, even for someone who wasn't a fan of that type of wrestling.

"Pete Dunne, who was very young then, had possibly the ugliest ring gear I ever saw. The talent was always there, of course, but in some ways, he was unrecognizable compared to what he became later on."

Glasgow-based ICW also stood out for presenting an unabashedly Scottish product, with a tartan-sporting YouTuber known as the Wee Man working as a manager and commentator and references to the country's preferred soft drink, Irn-Bru. "They never made any bones about it," Elliott said. "Nobody tried to dull their accent. Wrestlers who were dealing with the promoter, Mark Dallas, would joke that they needed a translator. I'm Irish and even I can tell you that a thick Scottish accent is a lot to deal with on occasion."

By 2012, the promotion started to break out, exporting shows to Newcastle, Leeds, Liverpool, London and other UK cities. But the center point of ICW was Barrowland — officially the Barrowland Ballroom in Glasgow, a nightclub where the Clash, U2, Oasis, the Smiths and Foo Fighters had all performed. "This was a big thing for ICW," Elliott said. "The wrestlers would say, 'We're going to Barrowland,' which was something special. The kind of people who came to see them tended to be goth people or emo people. The fans were integral to the promotion. You know how, in ECW, they had Hat Guy and Sign Guy who all the people knew? There weren't singular fans like that in ICW but, collectively, they were behind the local talent, and the local talent were busting a gut to do well.

"It was almost like a little club, a little ICW club that you had — a community. If you can create that indie vibe, whether it's for music or for wrestling, people will gather toward it."

Much like TNA, Ring of Honor and CHIKARA rose from the aftershocks of WCW and ECW, Revolution Pro Wrestling and PROGRESS, Britain's two best-known indies, were founded as ICW and other UK companies were creating a scene that had little to do with the *World of Sport* days.

RevPro, as fans would grow to call it, was the brainchild of Andy Quidlan, the former booker for IPW: UK, who took that group's British Heavyweight, Tag Team and Cruiserweight titles to the new league. The inaugural show, in August 2012, featured Fergal Devitt (Finn Balor in WWE), Marty Scurll and Zack Sabre Jr. — as well as stalwart American babyface Johnny Gargano. While the groundwork was there, the company's turning point arguably occurred in 2015 when it formed an allegiance with New Japan, along with the Nipponese organization's other allies, Ring of Honor and Mexico's oldest promotion, CMLL.

The union gave RevPro international credibility. In 2015, AJ Styles captured the group's British Heavyweight crown while he was already the IWGP Heavyweight champion in New Japan. Two years later, the promotion started a British J-Cup tournament, patterned after New Japan's Super J-Cup competition that drew cruiserweights from all over the world.

As its reputation increased, RevPro came to be associated with York Hall, an edgy, former Turkish bathhouse in London's Bethnal Green section, catering to Jewish immigrants from Russia and Poland until the 1970s. It was later converted into an arena, hosting boxing events and concerts.

Unlike the American promoters who lived and died by television, Quidlan made little effort to secure a deal. "It only takes one person to turn it down and you're back to square one," he told *SE Scoops*. "It's a very long process and it becomes very time-draining. I remember when I was producing the IPW show, the money we were getting paid wasn't worth the effort that was going into it because our ticket sales didn't increase as a result." In the digital age, he continued, he felt more comfortable offering RevPro shows on YouTube and through On Demand.

The same year RevPro held its debut card, PROGRESS presented *Chapter 1: In the Beginning* in March 2012, an event that showcased Sabre, Scurll and future WWE performers Noam Dar and Zack Gibson.

What made PROGRESS unusual was its origins outside the traditional wrestling universe. Cofounder Jim Smallman was a comedian fixated on Japanese wrestling. Teaming up with his agent Jon Briley, Smallman eventually brought in actor Glen Joseph as another owner. Devoting themselves to creating a punk rock ambiance in a big city setting, the three tried using primarily British wrestlers, rather than relying on fly-ins.

"One of the reasons PROGRESS worked was they ran central London when no one else wanted to take a chance on central London," said Dann Read. "It was convenient by rail. You didn't have to drive and sit in massive amounts of traffic, and then get to central London and not be able to park. It helped that the owners were Londoners themselves, and they reaped the rewards."

Yet, despite their connection to England's largest city, the trio showed concern for the commuters who came from elsewhere. Shows generally started on Sundays at 4 p.m. and ended by 8 p.m. "That meant that if you were a traveling fan, you could get a train home before all the trains stopped running," Cooling said. "That's the difference between Britain and America. Britain is more densely populated and connected by the train lines. I live in Northampton in the East Midlands. It takes me about two hours by train to go to London. I'm literally traveling half the country, but I can do it as a day trip. Most successful British promotions had fans willing to travel three hours to a show."

Certainly, PROGRESS did. Following 11 consecutive sellouts at The Garage in East London, the company drew 2,400 fans to the Brixton Academy in 2016. Two years later, after branching into Birmingham and Manchester, the group attracted more than 4,700 spectators to its *Hello Wembley* event at the SSE Arena.

One testament to PROGRESS' popularity: its ability to sell season ticket packages to its shows at London's Electric Ballroom.

"We covered them from the very start," said Elliott. "I know we wrote about their first DVD release because they were quite sensitive about what we said in our review. We gave them a glowing review, but we said that, in front of the hard cam, you could see the computer screens that the guys were working on, and it was distracting. The PROGRESS guys weren't very happy about that, and I wonder if they noticed the same thing and didn't want us reminding everyone."

But there were few criticisms of the actual shows. Jimmy Havoc attributes this to the promotion allowing its performers to fashion their own characters. In his case, "I found elements in my life, my film taste, my music taste that I brought to the person you saw in the ring. All my promos in PROGRESS were my own. My friends helped me shoot and edit my promos [and vignettes]. The storyline was a collaborative effort between me and PROGRESS. When you write and create your own stuff, people can tell. It's more you."

When they weren't working for PROGRESS, many of the same wrestlers could be seen in RevPro. Still, there was virtually no crossover of storylines. "You can't say they had a fractious relationship," Elliott said. "It seemed like they didn't have any kind of relationship. They had different philosophies. RevPro was more traditional wrestling, and PROGRESS was more modern.

"What I will say is that fans of PROGRESS and RevPro didn't like each other. PROGRESS fans were the sort of fans who'd come up with funny chants. In some ways, it could be that kind of ironic, *wink, wink, nudge, nudge* wrestling. And RevPro drew an audience that liked British strong style."

ABOVE: Joey Janela pours beer into the mouth of a grateful aficionado.

LEFT: A young Sami Zayn looks on excitedly at an International Wrestling Syndicate show in Montreal.

BELOW: The Bullet Club (left to right): Tama Tonga, Adam Page, Matt Jackson, Kenny Omega, Marty Scurll, Haku, Tanga Loa, Nick Jackson and Cody.

ABOVE: Chuck Taylor vs. Ricochet.

RIGHT: Hiroshi Tanahashi vs. Jay "Switchblade" White.

BELOW: Cody crowd-surfs at one of Joey Ryan's Bar Wrestling shows.

ABOVE: A Darby Allin coffin drop from the balcony.

LEFT: David Starr.

ABOVE: Jeff Cobb vs. Jonah Rock.

LEFT: Jimmy Havoc displays his crimson mask.

Luchasaurus carries Jungle Boy on his shoulders.

Keith Lee vs. Donovan Dijak, who'd adopt the name Dominik Dijakovic after both started in NXT.

Kenny Omega and Kota Ibushi.

Dragon Lee launches himself onto Bandido.

ABOVE LEFT: Kyle O'Reilly.

ABOVE RIGHT: Lio Rush.

LEFT: The Lucha Brothers, Fenix and Pentagon Jr., with the Pro Wrestling Guerrilla Tag Team titles.

Maxwell Jacob Friedman, aka MJF.

Marty Scurll shows off his signature umbrella and the 2016 Battle of Los Angeles trophy.

Johnny Gargano and Oney Lorcan.

LEFT: PCO.

Nick Gage cracks David Arquette with a collection of light tubes.

Puma King with Hollywood's Roosevelt Hotel as a backdrop.

RIGHT: PWG
co-founder
Super Dragon.

BELOW: Proud and
Powerful, Santana
and Ortiz.

BELOW: Frankie Kazarian
and Scorpio Sky of SoCal
Uncensored.

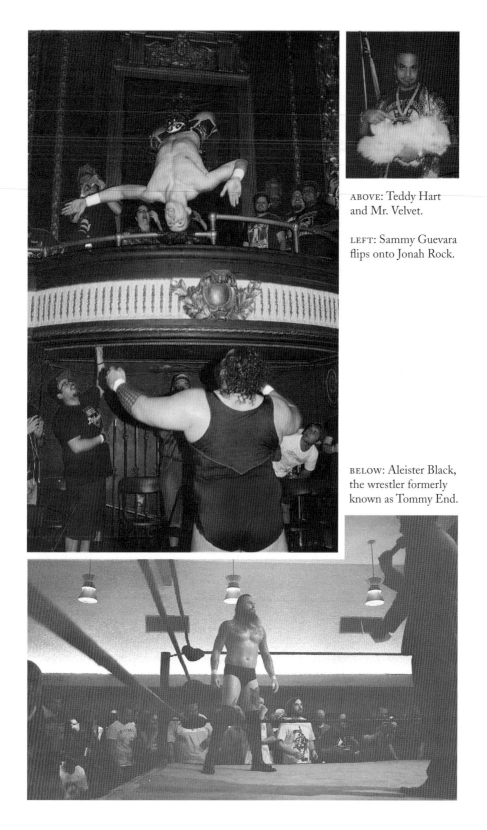

ABOVE: Teddy Hart
and Mr. Velvet.

LEFT: Sammy Guevara
flips onto Jonah Rock.

BELOW: Aleister Black,
the wrestler formerly
known as Tommy End.

WALTER with the PROGRESS Atlas
Championship.

Tetsuya Naito.

Kota Ibushi stands in with the Elite (from left to right): Cody, Adam Page, Ibushi, Kenny
Omega, the Young Bucks, and Marty Scurll.

ABOVE: Will Ospreay vs. El Phantasmo.

LEFT: Indie phenom Orange Cassidy.

BELOW: "Le Champion" Chris Jericho weighs in for an AEW title defense.

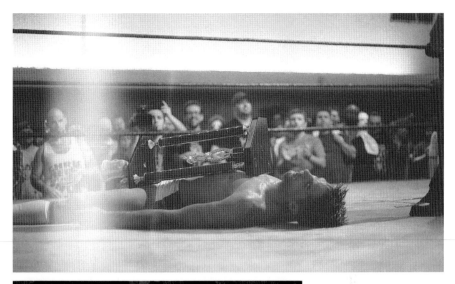

ABOVE: Zack Sabre Jr. with the 2015 Battle of Los Angeles trophy.

LEFT: Jon Moxley enters through the AEW crowd.

BELOW: The Inner Circle attacks Mox.

Joey Ryan.

Joey Janela in an epic encounter.

Yet, Quidlan told the British music monthly, *VultureHound*, that even if the companies didn't cooperate, there was an effort to coexist. "The basic rule, to borrow from PROGRESS, is don't be a dick," he said in 2015. "Don't tread on anyone's toes if you can help it, and respect other promoters if you want to be respected yourself. I'm too busy with my own promotion to worry about sabotaging anyone else, and everyone else should be too."

Where PROGRESS, RevPro and the other British promotions could find common ground was the satisfaction in knowing that the grafters in the UK were no longer going into forced exile to support themselves. Now they could venture to L.A. or Sydney or Nagoya and evangelize on the merits of their homegrown scene not with words, but their exploits between the ropes. "For a long time after the *World of Sport* era of British wrestling, everything was based on international wrestlers coming in," Sabre told New Japan's website in 2017. "Now we're at a point where the most popular matches feature British wrestlers. [We] want as many British wrestlers traveling around the world as possible. People watch us and then want to watch more British wrestling. So I'm proud to be a part of this generation."

16
CHAPTER

"I want to say a few bits," Emily Read, cofounder of British women's company, Pro Wrestling: EVE, said as she addressed the crowd from center ring at London's Resistance Gallery. She'd been ill, she confessed. In fact, she'd been "insane." Feeling debilitated and defeated, she'd ended up in a mental hospital, forced to walk away from her dream of presenting wrestling with a ballsy, third wave feminist attitude. But the dark days were over, she assured the fans. Emily Read was back. And that meant Pro Wrestling: EVE was back.

"I wanted to stand up and say that I could beat mental health," she declared, "with the help of my family," she paused, "and with the help of prescription drugs."

The audience rocked with laughter, shouting out their love for Emily and the promotion she regarded as a dear but sometimes troubled child.

Mentally ill gimmicks have been a staple of wrestling. "Crazy" Luke Graham, Bugsy McGraw and Norman the Lunatic are three names of emotionally impaired characters I was able to list without the help of Google. And then, there was Roughhouse Fargo who, as the storyline went, would only appear in the Memphis territory when his "brother"

Jackie, desperate for assistance against a pack of heels, checked him out of the state hospital. But Emily wasn't bulging her eyes or sticking her tongue out of the side of her mouth. She was shooting, not working.

It was 2013, three years after Emily and her husband, Dann, launched their company, that she started to fall apart. "I had a nervous breakdown," she said, "a really big one. There was just so much stress in running the promotion, and there was always the fear that rivals were going to do something to put us out of business. It was too much for me. We lost EVE, we lost our savings, we lost our house."

Racked with guilt, she despaired about the wrestlers who weren't getting bookings and the fans who'd come to believe that EVE represented them. "The thing I wanted to do, to give power to women, had stopped. I was crushed. This was supposed to be something to inspire my daughter, and I thought that I'd let her down and everyone else."

It was while Emily was hospitalized that she was able to view her circumstances with clarity. After an initial diagnosis of depression, it was determined that she was suffering from bipolar disorder, accounting for her mood swings and anxiety. She also learned how to treat the condition with medication.

"I'm very public about this," she said. "It happens to a lot of people. When I was healing, I thought about all the things people like me don't say and keep hidden. When other people don't understand you, it's easier for them to judge you. And I decided that I was going to put myself back together and, when I did, there was going to be nothing I was going to hide."

These were not the grandiose thoughts of a person in the throes of some chemically altered mania, but a measured strategy of a woman who believed in her mission. When Pro Wrestling: EVE returned in 2016, she made it clear that the company had not gone on sabbatical because the combatants were lacking in talent or the fans were indifferent. Rather, Emily admitted, she'd been struggling with issues that others might find relatable. Now, she was ready to come back "swinging and fighting."

Branching out of the company's home base in Sudbury, Suffolk, Pro Wrestling: EVE made London the nexus of their operation, challenging the wrestling media to cover them. "If we were in Sudbury, and they weren't writing about us, we could say it was because of the distance," Emily explained. "If we were in London and they weren't coming, we could say, 'It's because you are sexist.'"

As it turned out, the group's return show was covered by *Kerang!*, the British magazine normally dedicated to metal, punk and hardcore. When Emily stepped into the ring to address the obstacles she'd faced, she was unaware that her words would find allies in quarters where wrestling had been viewed with either apathy or condescension. "I told the crowd that I was bipolar, bisexual, a vegan and a mum of two. Non-wrestling fans read about us, and they wanted to hear more. So we began targeting our advertising to them too — anybody who wanted a good night out, people who wanted a good form of entertainment with strong women."

By 2019, Pro Wrestling: EVE was running about 35 cards a year. There was a definite social agenda — one t-shirt sold at the group's shows proclaimed, "Piledrive a Fascist" — but also a feeling like you were being invited into someone's home. "When I was working in hotels, I loved welcoming guests and making them feel comfortable in a strange place," Emily said. "I wanted people to come to EVE — vegans, people in the LGBTQ community and wrestling fans too — and know they were safe. These are your people. We are the weirdos. And, as long as you're not hateful, we won't judge you."

Through its many conquests and setbacks, Pro Wrestling: EVE operated on the premise that it was serving a different type of demographic. Said Emily, "Indie wrestling is a niche. Women's wrestling is a niche within a niche."

During the final days of FWA's first incarnation in 2007 — the company would attempt a comeback before finally closing again in 2012 — Dann Read, who'd been a member of the management team, became involved with a promotion called Chick Fight. "It was a horrible brand name," he said. "But they were using top level women. What the name Chick Fight conjures up and the presentation were two totally different things.

"We were trying to build a scene. I was a massive All-Japan Women's fan and was getting tapes from Japan in the mid-'90s. So I always knew women could wrestle. In the UK, there were a lot of women who wanted to do more than what they were expected to do in a match: an X-Factor, hair-mare or tombstone where you had your face in the other girl's crotch. But they hadn't had the chance."

Shows were expected to stretch three hours, which meant that, with a limited roster, the cards were primarily tournaments. "You had to use people multiple times," said Emily, who also helped organize events. "And we had to bring girls over from the U.S. and parts of Europe to work with the British girls."

Despite their athleticism and training, most participants were unaccustomed to the demands being placed on them. "They had to change their style from what they were used to because they weren't just the girls match on the show," Dann said. "They *were* the show. They couldn't just do a hip toss or snap suplex in every match because everybody was doing those moves."

Finding venues was an issue. "People would see the poster that said 'chick fight' and think it was a sex show," Emily said. "They'd contact the town council and the show would be cancelled."

To remedy the dilemma, Chick Fight cards were presented at night clubs where only adults were admitted, placing wrestling in the same category as a cabaret act. "We later discovered there really was a market for adult only shows," Dann said. "It was just a few years too early."

When the pair started Pro Wrestling: EVE in 2010, they circumvented resistance by holding events in their hometown of Sudbury, where the authorities knew them and understood their intentions. "We had this little daughter and we were looking around, and there were no strong female role models," Emily said of the company's motivations. "*Buffy*'s gone. *Twilight*'s out. We wanted to do a wrestling promotion and do it right, with kickass women."

The name Pro Wrestling: EVE had been inspired by Pro Wrestling NOAH in Japan. "I liked how the words 'pro wrestling' came first," Emily recalled. "We thought about using the name of Noah's wife. But when we went through the Bible, we discovered that Noah's wife was just called Noah's wife. So we went with Eve."

Historically, female wrestlers had frequently been subjects of sexual harassment, dating back to the days of Mildred Burke, America's premier female performer from the 1930s to the 1950s. Despite Burke doing the heavy labor in the ring, her husband, Billy Wolfe, was the official owner of their women's troupe and, for a period, a member of the NWA. On the road, Wolfe was said to not only take liberties with some of the 30 or so wrestlers in his stable, but pimp some out to promoters with whom he hoped to ingratiate himself.

More than a half century later, the abusive mentality lingered. "Your trainer would touch you and say, 'My hand slipped,'" Emily said. "It was bullshit, and it wasn't going to happen with us."

The group's first breakout star was Jenny Sjödin, who had a political science degree and served on her town council in Sweden. "She was the first real feminist we knew in wrestling," Emily said. "She was unique and a great wrestler who understood the European style and the Japanese style. Jenny was the person we wanted as a role model for our fans. She represented what we were trying to do."

Sjödin won the Pro Wrestling: EVE title in 2011, the year the promotion formed a partnership with the World Association of Wrestling (WAW), based in Norwich, Norfolk. WAW was run by Ricky and "Sweet" Saraya Knight, parents of WWE's Paige, along with *World of Sport* alum Jimmy Ocean. On the surface, a chemistry existed between the two groups, since the Knights had operated their own women's promotion. But while the Reads attempted to convey a global barrier-breaking worldview, the tone of WAW was nostalgic and stubbornly British.

Yet, the Knights intimately understood their audience. "Their fans were always loyal," said former *Fighting Spirit* editor Brian Elliott. "A lot of companies were happy to get 250 fans. They'd draw 1,000." In 2019, WAW attracted 4,000 spectators to Carrow Road, home of the Norwich City Premier League team, for the debut of the squad's former forward, Grant Holt. Still, Elliott pointed out, the promotion "didn't reach people outside their group. If you were on the internet and found something about PROGRESS, that might lead you to RevPro and that might lead you to ICW. But you'd have to really go down the line to find the Knights' promotion.

"Even though the shows had excellent production values, the feeling was sort of old school. We did cover their shows now and again, but not often because very few people asked about it. They sort of lived on an island."

Still, the allegiance with WAW added to Pro Wrestling: EVE's cachet. The two promotions organized a two-day tour, with one show in Norwich and the other in Sudbury.

At their home arena, Pro Wrestling: EVE kept their pricing reasonable and emphasized in their promotional material that the shows were family-friendly. Parents brought their daughters to the events. "At first, the little boys would ask when the men were coming on," Emily said. "Then it changed. They were waiting for the main event like everybody else. I was really pleased that the audience didn't see it as 'women's wrestling' anymore."

Still, the British indie scene could be treacherous. "We were told that other promoters were trying to put us out of business," Dann said, "calling the town councils when we performed in different places and complaining about us. We knew it had to be other promoters because they'd ask about the licenses, and the fans wouldn't know about that. In one case, when the council shut us out of one venue, we were fortunate to have a friend who'd taken over a nightclub, so we moved the show there. Another time, we had to move to a gym, literally a gym, and move the equipment around. We had to call up every single person who bought a ticket and tell them. But the good news was that we were having a show anyway."

It would be Emily who'd be charged with contacting the local media to explain the promotion's predicament. "It had to be me," she said, "so if the reporters had any questions when they saw the words 'women' and 'wrestling,' you had a woman who could explain what we were doing."

But it was this type of pressure that led to Emily's breakdown, and it was also what strengthened her resolve when she returned. The couple deliberately chose to center its shows at the Resistance Gallery, in Bethnal Green, because of its underground vibe. On days when Pro Wrestling: EVE wasn't running, the Resistance Gallery offered art and comedy shows and fetish nights, among other events. "People spend thousands and thousands of pounds to make venues look dingy, like something people just put together," said Dann. "But this was what the Resistance Gallery looked like anyway."

It was the type of spot that the Reads imagined potential EVE fans gathering. "There were a lot of odd and different types of people there," Emily said. "You'd see a teddy bear wrapped up in bondage and tied to the rafters. It's like a place you'd think would only exist in fiction. But it was authentic."

Whatever misunderstandings occurred during Emily's hiatus vaporized when she delivered her in-ring speech about her mental health travails. Jordynne Grace, Mercedes Martinez and Su Yung were among the talented American performers who regularly appeared in EVE. Relations were established with Japanese promotions like Pure-J, Stardom and Ice Ribbon, as wrestlers from those groups traveled to the UK, and Pro Wrestling: EVE was invited to tour Japan.

The Resistance Gallery was selling out. "At one show," Dann said, "I saw fans carrying in a sofa from downstairs because there were no more chairs."

Proceeds from these events went to mental health charities like Turn2Me and The 888 Collective, along with Bloody Good Period, which provided tampons and sanitary pads to those who couldn't afford them. In keeping with its progressive mandate, in 2019, EVE arranged with Equity UK, the country's trade union for professional performers, to provide accident insurance and other benefits. According to Dann, it was the first time that a professional wrestling company ever unionized. "EVE sees the unionization of independent performers as extremely important in this ever-changing and fast-developing wrestling scene," the company said in a statement.

The gesture was meant to send a message that professional wrestling, known for so long for ethnic and homophobic stereotypes, as well as reactionary politics, could move society forward and provide a forum for women to express themselves and support each other. "People think that when women get together, they're going to be bitchy," Emily said. "At EVE, when people go into the dressing room, the thing they're most shocked about is everyone building each other up."

17

CHAPTER

Six years after the end of World War II, boxer Joe Louis led a contingent of boxers and wrestlers to Japan to stage exhibitions for the American military personnel still stationed there. No one remembers if the boxing matches had any impact. Wrestling was a different story. Perhaps it was the country's fighting arts traditions. Perhaps it was something genetic. But within a month of the tour, Japanese athletes from the judo and sumo worlds began changing their lifestyle choices and training instead to become professional wrestlers.

Among them was a former sumo wrestler named Rikidozan, who made his debut in October 1951, wrestling American Bobby Bruns to a 10-minute draw. After more training in Hawaii, he began wrestling on the islands, then in San Francisco. Rikidozan returned home in 1953, starting his own promotion and positioning himself as the country's top babyface, avenging the country's wartime losses by taking on a succession of American heels.

It was precisely what the Japanese needed to lift their spirits. What no one bothered to mention was that Rikidozan wasn't even Japanese, but a member of the country's marginalized Korean community.

Nonetheless, Rikidozan remains a national hero to this day, a status he also enjoys in North Korea, where he was born. In a country that takes its history seriously, Rikidozan's matches with Freddie Blassie, The Destroyer and Lou Thesz are remembered fondly. So are Rikidozan's escapades outside the ring. In addition to building his own arena, he owned nightclubs, apartment buildings, hotels and golf courses. He was also known to travel in the same circles as members of the yakuza, or Japanese mob, and thrived in this precarious environment until December 1963, when he was stabbed by a mobster in the restroom of a Tokyo nightclub. According to folklore, he made it to the stage and cut a profane promo on his assailant before being carted off to the hospital.

An initial surgery was successful. But then, Rikidozan made some bad choices. He began gorging himself on sushi and sake, developed peritonitis and died.

Still, the 39-year-old father of puroresu — the expression is based on the way the Japanese pronounce "pro wrestling" — had prepared for the future and was already grooming his successors: Shohei "Giant" Baba and Antonio Inoki, who started All Japan and New Japan Pro Wrestling, respectively, in 1972. The two promotions would dominate Japanese wrestling until 1999, when Baba died from complications of colon cancer, a month and a half after his final match.

Inoki was retired at this point, but, in a nation populated with death match promotions, women's promotions, lucha promotions and other companies tailored for fans with very specific tastes, he'd transformed New Japan into the country's best-known wrestling organization, primarily due to his flair for self-promotion. In addition to battling Muhammad Ali in a well publicized but disappointing boxer versus wrestler match in 1976, Inoki staged numerous bouts against other combat sports figures, combined with WCW to pack more than 150,000 spectators into a stadium in the hermit kingdom of North Korea on two consecutive nights and was elected to the Japanese *Diet,* or parliament. Along with showcasing high-flying junior heavyweights like Tiger Mask, Black Tiger and Dynamite Kid, New Japan became the promotion most associated with the believable martial arts strikes and submissions that distinguish Japanese strong style.

But in the early 2000s, as MMA became more popular, New Japan's presentation didn't always match up. For the first few years of the century, the company's revenue markedly dropped off. In 2005, Inoki sold his stake in New Japan to video game developer Yuke's. Eventually, Hiroshi Tanahashi, who set the record for the most IWGP Heavyweight Championships when he won his eighth title in 2019, removed Inoki's portrait from the group's dojo in Tokyo's Kaminoge neighborhood.

"It was weird to have a photo of Inoki on the wall, even though he is no longer associated with New Japan Pro Wrestling," he told the *Japan Times.* "Many of the current fans haven't heard of Rikidozan and didn't grow up watching Inoki or Baba. We shouldn't get distracted by old memories."

Although it took several years, Inoki's absence allowed the newer generation of fans to appreciate a different breed of New Japan wrestler: Tanahashi, Kazuchika Okada, Tetsuya Naito, Kota Ibushi and others who'd help export New Japan to the rest of the world.

New Japan's turnaround occurred at the same time that the indie revolution was starting in North America and Europe. In 2012, collectible and trading card company, Bushiroad, purchased the company and began using On Demand and video streaming to stimulate interest. Downplaying the traditional good versus evil formula, New Japan placed greater emphasis on clashes between strong personalities or factions. The blueprint led to more females watching the promotion and, with the hiring of Dutch-born Harold Mejj as president in 2018, New Japan declared that it was no longer an insular Japanese operation.

What made Mejj qualified for the position was that, despite his western background, he'd moved to Japan at age eight and understood and respected the culture. Yet, he maintained a global worldview. Over the years, Mejj would also live in Indonesia and the United States and learn to speak six languages. Prior to entering the wrestling business, he worked for Heineken, Unilever Tea and Coca-Cola, among other companies in Japan. While Mejj was president and CEO of Takara Tomy, he was touted for turning the children's toy and merchandise company around, achieving record profits.

Among the philosophies he preached was that Takara Tomy's products should be viewed as borderless and timeless. "When the product doesn't sell anymore, Japanese companies throw it away, but they also throw away the brand," he told *Kyodo News*. "Whereas, in the west, we think totally that a brand is forever, and the product can change and update."

While he believed that the same was true for New Japan, he viewed his mission differently: "At Takara Tomy, I was in charge of a company. Here, I'm almost in charge of an industry."

On May 3, 2013, Prince Fergal Devitt, the future Finn Balor, came down the aisle on the shoulders of his "bodyguard," rugged Tongan wrestler Bad Luck Fale, at New Japan's annual *Wrestling Dontaku* event. Between the ropes, the "Ace" of the company, Hiroshi Tanahashi, had just defeated Karl Anderson, who'd trained with Devitt in New Japan's L.A. dojo five years earlier. Suddenly, Devitt and Fale attacked Tanahashi. After some hesitation, Anderson joined in. They were soon assisted in the beatdown by another Tongan star, Tama Tonga, stepson of former WWE wrestler Haku.

A new faction was born. Like the Four Horsemen and NWO, the Bullet Club would be a unit for the ages. Over the next several years, some 30 men and three women would attain Bullet Club membership.

"We were given a chance to start something, and we embraced it," Fale told New Japan's website. "I think really it's a credit to how smart we were in bringing in the right people at the right time and changing with the times. [With the NWO], it was a case of throwing everyone in together. It was super hot and exploded, but it couldn't last long."

Almost as soon as the Bullet Club began, he continued, "We knew we were onto something."

At the center of the Bullet Club was Devitt, who based the group's handle on his "real shooter" nickname — a rib on Minoru Suzuki, who actually was an authentic shooter — and finger gun hand gesture, along with Anderson's "Machine Gun" sobriquet. Devitt had wavered over names, contemplating Bullet Parade and Bullet League, before settling on the classic moniker.

The Bullet Club soon began using the "Too Sweet," sometimes

known as a "Turkish Wolf," hand gesture popularized by the NWO in WCW, a greeting Devitt and Anderson exercised when they'd shake hands at the New Japan dojo. After one victory in Tokyo, as Anderson attempted to high-five his friend, Devitt replied with a "Too Sweet."

"I started to get chills," Anderson told *WWE.com*. "I said, 'Are you doing this to me right now?'"

"Yep," Devitt replied.

Anderson told the website that was the moment "it transferred from the locker room to the ring." From that point forward, the Bullet Club flashed the sign everywhere, a group of gaijin — or foreigners — changing the rituals in a regimented culture.

"In Japan, they still have weight classes: the juniors and the heavyweights," Anderson said on the *Sam Roberts Podcast*. "They still have those guys separated. And Ferg was getting this huge push as a junior. And so when we created the Bullet Club, he started beating heavyweights, which started rubbing some guys the wrong way backstage. But even that added more to the Bullet Club coolness because he was getting this badass push that was transcending what people had done in the past in New Japan."

Before the end of the Bullet Club's first year, Doc Gallows came in, specifically to partner with Anderson in tag team clashes. The Young Bucks showed up as well, relying on the rest of the faction to assist them in New Japan's Super Junior Tag Tournament. "The junior tag division really had no hype behind it," Fale said. "But them coming in helped us. They had a niche following on the American indie scene and, from there, we helped them get bigger in Japan, and they helped us get bigger in America."

More than any other collection of wrestlers, the Bullet Club would turn into agents of New Japan's expansion. Tonga aligned with Rey Bucanero, Terrible and La Comadante to form a Latino Bullet Club in Mexico's CMLL. The Bucks even represented the Bullet Club in a tournament in CHIKARA.

"There was an international aspect to the Bullet Club that was unprecedented," noted Jeff Jarrett, the only wrestler to appear in both the NWO and the Bullet Club. "With Fergal Devitt, you had a European wrestler who was partnering with American wrestlers working for a

Japanese organization. That, in and of itself, lent to a completely different set of circumstances than you'd seen before."

Even the way the matches were booked was a break from New Japan custom. American twists, like ref bumps and outside interference, were commonplace. Although Japanese fans previously scorned these types of devices, they seemed to accept them when the Bullet Club was in the ring.

"The Bullet Club was speaking for wrestling fans in a lot of ways," Marty Scurll, who joined the Bullet Club in 2017, told me. "The attitude was, 'Yes, I'm a wrestling fan, but I don't want to be spoon-fed what you give me.' It was punk rock. It was alternative."

At the *Wrestle Kingdom 8* pay-per-view in early 2014, Devitt dropped his Junior Heavyweight Championship to Kota Ibushi. The next night, he was attacked by Ryusuke Taguchi, his former tag team partner in a unit called Apollo 55. Prior to joining the Bullet Club, the Irishman had turned heel by betraying Taguchi. Now, it was time for retribution.

In April, the pair met in a "Loser Leaves New Japan" match that would lead to the conclusion of the Bullet Club's first chapter. During the bout, the Young Bucks continuously tried to interfere on Devitt's behalf, but Fergal appeared to be committed to earning the win on his own merits. When the Bullet Club leader finally lost, the Bucks attacked him. Devitt fought them off, then shook hands with Taguchi, leaving the company as a babyface.

There was a reason for this storyline. Devitt was headed to NXT. Without him, some wondered how the Bullet Club would continue. Those fears were allayed when AJ Styles — arguably the best wrestler in the world at the time — joined the faction, becoming only the fourth American to win the IWGP Heavyweight Championship a month later from Okada.

Jarrett came aboard the same year. "Our business is about the in-ring product, first and foremost, and everybody in the Bullet Club could deliver," he said. "From the beginning, it was a really in-ring dominant — and I mean, *dominant* — faction like none other. When I'm asked about the main difference between the Bullet Club and the NWO, it's that."

By the summer of 2014, Styles still held the title, while Gallows and Anderson were the IWGP Tag Team champions and Fale the promotion's

Intercontinental kingpin. "At that point, videos of our matches would go viral every time a show would happen," said Nick Jackson. "When AJ Styles came in, a lot of things went right from there."

This was the period when the Bullet Club's "bone soldier" t-shirt — a white design on a black background, featuring a skull biting down on two crossed rifles, with bullets lined on each side — became a symbol not only of the group's turbulent march through New Japan, but the indie revolution itself.

Then, in January 2016, a missile from faraway Stamford, Connecticut, landed in Japan. "It was a crazy thing to happen," Fale told New Japan's website. "Loyalty, money, family, friends, it was all in the balance. We knew about it a couple of days earlier. At that point, the first thing you think is, 'What's going to happen now?'"

Along with three-time IWGP Heavyweight champion Shinsuke Nakamura, Styles, Gallows and Anderson all departed for WWE. But the depletion to the Bullet Club could have been even worse. A month earlier, Styles had asked the Bucks about their contractual obligations and discovered that they'd recently signed an agreement with Ring of Honor, which had a working arrangement with New Japan. "If we had never signed," Matt Jackson told *Vice News*, "there's a great chance we could have been walking out on *Raw* with those guys."

There's also a possibility that, with the Bucks tied up in WWE, AEW might have never come into existence.

But that isn't what happened. For the time being, the Bucks remained interlaced into New Japan storylines, as the Bullet Club continued to take on new members.

"When you took Fergal Devitt out and inserted AJ Styles, the group took on a whole other dynamic," said Jarrett. "Every transition was intriguing and brought in more fans. It goes without saying there were no steps taken backwards. There was good planning, a lot of thought going into it, an aura that all these guys brought. So the momentum from Day One of the Bullet Club continued to build."

But the addition of Kenny Omega would take the Bullet Club to an elevation never ascended by any other faction, a period remembered for The Cleaner's capacity to reach across cultures and perform in some of the most absorbing matches in history.

18
CHAPTER

"*Goodbye! Goodnight! Bang!*"

While his name and catchphrase may have meant little to the WWE Universe, on the indies, Kenny Omega may have been the most "over" wrestler on earth.

"I'm not here to cash in checks," he boasted to New Japan's website in 2018. "I'm not in it for the money. I'm not here to do the classic style. I'm the greatest fuckin' showman in professional wrestling, maybe of all fuckin' time. Even if I'm not in the main event, I'm still going to have the best match because no one comes close to what I do."

Over the years, Omega had worked for Deep South Wrestling, a pre-NXT developmental league for WWE, held the IWGP Junior Heavyweight Tag Team Championship with Kota Ibushi — an alliance rife with homoerotic implications — and wrestled a nine-year-old girl and a blow-up doll for Japan's DDT promotion. While others might have felt humiliated, Omega embraced his navigation into places where others feared to venture, evolving into a bigger star each time.

Vern May, aka Vance Nevada, remembered training the Winnipeg native early in his career. "He was doing stuff that was beyond the conventions of what we do. He'd incorporate these exaggerated actions, like in a video game. The first time you showed him something, he'd ace it. But I wasn't sure how he'd fit in. I admit, on the record, I was wrong."

Omega told *The Two Man Power Trip of Wrestling* podcast that he viewed wrestling as something equivalent to ballroom dancing, "where the best dancers in the world can dance in sync with any partners that are professionally trained. Their body responds to every twitch of the muscle fiber and it almost becomes an animalistic response. Without sounding too egotistical, a five-star match to me is kind of an easy thing to do with almost anybody. I could rehash and recycle the same old formula because I know what works. But if I start doing that, then I'll stop growing, and I don't feel that I am finished yet in my process or evolution. But if someone had a gun to my head and said, 'Have a five-star match with this guy,' it is kind of light work."

Fluent in Japanese, Omega had resisted associating himself with the Bullet Club because he'd claimed to be different than the other gaijin. He finally joined in November 2014, branding himself "The Cleaner," since his goal was "cleaning up" New Japan's junior heavyweight division. Two months later, at *Wrestle Kingdom 9*, he dethroned Ryusuke Taguchi for the IWGP Junior Heavyweight Championship.

At New Japan's annual *New Year's Dash* event in 2016, Omega and AJ Styles teamed up against Shinsuke Nakamura and YOSHI-HASHI. Although fans were in the dark about Styles' and Nakamura's decisions to leave for WWE, the mechanisms were in place for the next phase of the Bullet Club to commence. After pinning Nakamura in a clean finish, Omega turned on Styles, who was then expelled from the Bullet Club by the other members, freeing Styles to make a surprise entrance at WWE's *Royal Rumble* less than three weeks later.

Proclaiming that he was no longer a junior heavyweight, "The Cleaner" quickly captured the IWGP Intercontinental title vacated by Nakamura's departure and hailed himself as the new leader of the Bullet Club.

"Prince Devitt, Nakamura, AJ Styles, Gallows, Anderson — you guys still praise these muthafuckas as heroes," he taunted New Japan's fans on the company's website. "They stabbed you in the fuckin' back!

Who raised this company up from the ashes? It was fuckin' me! I was piloting the ship. I was the captain."

Following his anointment, Omega became the first westerner to win the prestigious *G1 Climax* tournament, defeating Tetsuya Naito in the semis and Hirooki Goto in the finals in back-to-back thrillers that concluded the grueling, 19-night event. Upon receiving his trophy, rather than adhering to tradition by waving the New Japan flag, Omega tossed the banner to the canvas and brazenly flew the Bullet Club emblem.

What followed was a classic series of matches with Kazuchika Okada over the IWGP Heavyweight Championship. The fourth, a two-out-of-three fall battle in which Omega emerged as the first Canadian to ever win the belt, was so impressive that Dave Meltzer awarded the bout an unprecedented six stars, writing that it was the only time he'd witnessed "the two greatest individual performances" by different wrestlers in the same match (more about this later).

Yet, while I was researching this book, I found myself wondering about the aspect of Omega's career that fans of the next generation would recall first. Along with the Okada sequence, The Cleaner's uncommon partnership with Kota Ibushi was a powerful candidate.

"I don't know if [Ibushi] wants what I want," Omega told a reporter from *MEL Magazine* in 2018, stoking romantic rumors. "But if he does, we can do something amazing together."

The Golden☆Lovers were formed in the DDT promotion in 2009. Both were bleached blond, in peak condition and, at the very least, quite taken with each other's company. While other duos hugged after a victory or satisfying moment in the ring, Omega and Ibushi kissed. It was a time in which pro wrestling's social evolution was experiencing a reframing. In another age, the gesture would have established the tandem as heels and invited a bombardment of homophobic chants. In DDT, a comedy promotion, the Golden☆Lovers' open display of affection was generally met with laughter.

While describing Ibushi as his closest friend, Omega kept the specifics of their relationship just vague enough to leave observers questioning.

Asked on Twitter whether he was gay or bi, Omega responded, "I don't know what the hell I am."

At the same time that they were working for DDT, the Golden☆Lovers began appearing in New Japan, trading the IWGP Junior Heavyweight Tag Team Championship back and forth with Prince Devitt and Ryusuke Taguchi of Apollo 55. When Ibushi became an official member of the New Japan roster and transitioned to the heavyweight division, Omega appeared to be jealous. He then shifted his focus to the Bullet Club, and the pair stopped teaming together. Those who'd been following the two for several years viewed the parting as a breakup.

"People go through [heartbreak] in all walks of life, regardless of age, sex, religion or whatever," Omega told *MEL*. "You feel alone. It's a very easy feeling to understand — the feeling of loss, heartache and pain. So I've put myself in the position to feel pain, alongside the fans."

Through the various manifestations of the Bullet Club, as well as Omega's post–New Japan exploits, the name Kota Ibushi would remain intimately associated with The Cleaner. "Regardless of the sexual orientation, it's based on a profound camaraderie," Omega explained. "The type of camaraderie you see in the backstage area, in the locker room of the arena. There's a lot of deep emotional connections between wrestlers. Those are the types of relationships where the two wrestlers have each other's back and make sure they aren't going loony. It's strange that no one has ever decided to explore the depth behind why two people would tag together, why two people would hang out together. I never meant it to be something revolutionary. I just meant it to be real."

19
CHAPTER

Through its first few years, the Bullet Club widened its reputation through the deeds of stars like Devitt, a product of the European system who learned the New Japan method by studying in its dojo; Styles, a former TNA World Heavyweight champion who hadn't been given the platform he deserved in North America; and Omega, who became a cult idol on the international indie circuit. Yet, WWE appeared to hover above the whole scene. When the corporate monolith needed a new talent, it was all but understood, it could pluck from any tree on the planet. After all, the prevailing mentality went, for virtually every wrestler in the world, there was no greater honor than to be selected by the most successful wrestling company that ever existed.

That is until Chris Jericho decided to blow everything up.

During Omega's scorching series of matches with Kazuchika Okada, The Cleaner appeared on Y2J's *Talk Is Jericho* podcast. To listeners, the chemistry between the pair was instantaneous. Both grew up in Winnipeg, shared a mutual friend in New Japan English-language announcer Don Callis and worked with some of the same personalities on the way up. At one point, Callis joked to Jericho that the next time he chose to "reinvent" himself, he should forsake WWE and do an angle with Omega in New Japan.

"I guess Don sort of picked up that Chris seemed more intrigued rather than entertained by the thought," Omega told *Bleacher Report*. "He kind of went above Chris' head and messaged me directly. And he said, 'Hey Kenny, *what-if* scenario. What if you could wrestle Chris Jericho at the Tokyo Dome?'"

Callis knew that Omega would be receptive. Not only had every Winnipeg wrestler of his era been trained on Chris Jericho stories, but the "Ayatollah of Rock 'n' Rolla's" longtime affiliation with WWE would present an opportunity to break another boundary. In fact, Omega said, he and the Young Bucks had recently tried to orchestrate an angle in which they'd battle their friends, the New Day, in a WWE ring.

According to Omega, WWE exhibited little interest. What was the point of promoting a match between the company's most compelling trio and a group of outsiders? All three members of the New Day were under contract to WWE, the company apparently decreed, and would only wrestle others who'd been fortunate enough to receive the same status.

But Jericho was different than the New Day. Despite his association with WWE, he no longer had an exclusive contract with the company and was technically able to work wherever he wanted.

The distinction between Jericho and every other wrestler who'd been in that position was that he actually decided to do something about it.

On November 5, 2017, Jericho stunned the wrestling world by appearing in a New Japan vignette, calling out Omega, who'd been crowned the IWGP United States Heavyweight champion, following New Japan president Harold Mejj's mandate to expand beyond Japan. The next month, Jericho made a surprise appearance at a New Japan show, beating up and bloodying Omega, then attacking him again at a press conference a day later.

Their no-disqualification clash, dubbed "Alpha versus Omega" was set for *Wrestle Kingdom 12* in January 2018, Jericho's first battle outside WWE since 1999.

In the 24 hours before and after the show, subscriptions for New Japan's international streaming service, NJPW World, jumped 35 percent.

Jericho took full credit. "A lot of people that never watched it before might've heard of this New Japan," he told *Busted Open Radio*. "They might have even known some of the guys that were in it. And then, when Chris Jericho shows up there, they're like, 'Oh my god, Chris Jericho's there? Well, let me check this out.' And then they watch the show and they go, 'Oh my gosh. Well, Jericho's great. But look at this Kenny, and they've got Okada and Tanahashi and the Young Bucks.'"

In the ring, Jericho tended to build a tale slowly over the course of a match, while Omega could speed from one reckless move to another, taking the crowd along the bumpy path. Yet, the two worked well together in this confrontation, with Jericho defying his 47 years and Omega reinforcing his "Best Bout Machine" label. After 35 minutes, Omega, who'd describe their exchanges as "sort of cool, sort of surreal," used his One-Winged Angel finisher to slam Jericho across a steel chair and score the pin.

Omega compared the intensity to the Ric Flair NWA title matches both he and Jericho grew up appreciating and described the organic nature of the match as the antithesis of a micro-managed presentation — a volley no doubt lobbed in WWE's direction.

Jericho avoided this type of description, and with good reason, given his status as the only wrestler granted the latitude to appear in both New Japan *and* WWE. About two weeks after *Wrestle Kingdom 12*, the free agent participated in *Monday Night Raw*'s 25th anniversary program, but confined his role to a backstage segment. "I don't like wasting a surprise appearance," he told *Sportskeeda*. "It was just a backstage bit, and that's the way Vince and I discussed it to be. I didn't want to go out in front of the crowd because you're wasting one of those cash-in chips of a Jericho appearance, so to speak."

In April, Jericho was the final participant to enter in WWE's 50-man, *Greatest Royal Rumble*, held at King Abdullah International Stadium in Jeddah, Saudi Arabia, receiving a reported $100,000 for three minutes and 18 seconds of work before being eliminated by eventual winner Braun Strowman.

For a period, Jericho lent the impression that, because of his long relationship with WWE, he had no intention of working for a rival operation on American soil. But as the competition escalated, he chose sides, picking the indie revolution and signing with All-Elite Wrestling in 2019.

"I love the fact that in this day and age that there are guys who can make a living outside of [the WWE] system," he told *Busted Open Radio*. He elaborated, "[In WWE], it's Vince's world and that's great, and you don't argue it, you don't hassle it. But [in New Japan] it was a lot of fun to do what I think is best and not have to go through a producer, a cameraman and a director, and this guy and that guy and this guy, then go sit outside of Vince's office for an hour, waiting to talk to him, to convince him that this is the right way to go."

20
CHAPTER

Even while Vince McMahon was being tweaked for his stubborn eccentricities — among the mogul's many reported quirks were aversions to employees who nodded too vigorously or sneezed in his presence — his son-in-law, Triple H, was monitoring the indies with the devotion of a fan, selecting the best talent for NXT. Although the league was initially billed as a feeder system for WWE, the quality of the wrestlers was so high, and Triple H's directives so uninhibited that, by 2015, the action in NXT often exceeded the matches presented on the main roster.

So when AEW announced its plans to broadcast on TNT in the United States on Wednesdays, WWE countered by pulling NXT into the limelight and running it on the USA Network at the very same time, going head to head the way Vince McMahon did in the territory days. Back then, he had Hulk Hogan, Roddy Piper, Big John Studd and Andre the Giant. Now, he was responding to Kenny Omega, Nyla Rose, Cody and Jon Moxley with Matt Riddle, Keith Lee, Rhea Ripley and Shayna Baszler.

In an atmosphere saturated with tension and high expectations, the lyrics of Triple H's entrance music, a song about playing "the game" and taking control, had particular poignancy.

Even if Triple H had not won 14 world championships, helped form the D-X faction during the Attitude Era, nor continued in a much-remembered 2001 tag team battle after tearing his quad, the founding of NXT alone would qualify the Cerebral Assassin for every Hall of Fame in the industry.

CHIKARA's Mike Quackenbush remembered his first conversation with Triple H during a guest stint at the WWE Performance Center: "He was reading fan tweets and was actually upset by one accusing him of trying to kill independent wrestling. And he told me, 'We need the independents to be vibrant or there isn't the next Cesaro, there isn't the next Drew Gulak, there isn't the next Ruby Riott, there isn't the next Luke Harper.' Now, there's a reason why he mentioned these specific names. These are all people who worked for CHIKARA, and he knew it.

"He is not the corporate automoton that people want to make him out to be. In a weird way, he is to NXT what I am to CHIKARA, except if I make a misstep, I lose $1,000. If he makes a misstep, he loses a million."

Prior to the emergence of NXT, WWE had worked with a number of developmental territories, including Ohio Valley Wrestling in Jeffersonville, Indiana, and Deep South Wrestling in McDonough, Georgia. NXT, which grew out of Florida Championship Wrestling (FCW), became its own entity, operating out of Full Sail University in Winter Park, Florida, in 2012, the same year Bushiroad purchased New Japan; RevPro and PROGRESS started in the UK; and El Generico, Kevin Steen and Adam Cole held the PWG World Championship.

By 2015, the group was holding its *NXT TakeOver* shows at major arenas, generally on the same weekend as an important WWE pay-per-view. The special events, seen on the WWE Network, would turn into showcases for stars like Finn Balor, Bayley, Sasha Banks, Becky Lynch, Kevin Owens, Sami Zayn, Charlotte Flair, Samoa Joe, Shinsuke

Nakamura, Johnny Gargano, Tommaso Ciampa and the Undisputed Era (Adam Cole, Bobby Fish, Kyle O'Reilly and Roderick Strong).

Future AEW referee Bryce Remsburg was among the early supporters. "As someone who's been around the wrestling business, it's hard to watch a pay-per-view without getting distracted," he said. "But NXT had great characters and fantastic matches, with the high WWE production values. It was a major league production with an indie blueprint."

In fact, some fans who no longer watched WWE followed NXT, as if it were another indie.

"When WWE bought WCW, they wanted it to have a different identity, but it never happened," noted Shane "Hurricane" Helms, who, like Quackenbush, had been invited to the WWE Performance Center to coach NXT talent. "When you went to an NXT show, it *felt* different. And morale was high. Because — this never happened before — the guys were *paid* to train."

In many cases, the coaches were people whom the talent had already encountered on the indie circuit. Rather than requiring the NXT competitors to digest WWE's house style, NXT trainers Steve Corino, Sara Del Rey and Adam Pearce were among those who preached the lessons they absorbed while barnstorming on the indies.

In fact, it was Del Rey, a former CHIKARA performer, who initially approached Quackenbush about working at the WWE Performance Center. "I must say I went with a little trepidation," he said. "Was I going to get down there, and somebody was going to follow me around with a clip board saying, 'We don't say, "wrestling." We say, "sports-entertainment."'? But it wasn't like that at all.

"It's easy to cast them as the evil corporate overlord — mainstream radio while everyone else is the new sound at CBGB's. But they gave me unprecedented access to every meeting, every conversation. I sat there, I think on the third day, listening to them debate over whether to release this person. And I'm looking around the table, thinking, 'Am I even meant to be in this meeting?'"

When Quackenbush attempted to run topics he planned to discuss past WWE Performance Center head trainer Matt "A-Train" Bloom, the former wrestler told the guest coach to trust his instincts. "I was stunned by the freedom they gave me," Quackenbush said. "Nobody said, 'Hey,

Mike, don't do this. We heard you out there talking about this subject, and we don't talk about that, okay?' There was never one second of that. It was more like, 'Go up there, grab a ring, and do whatever you want.'"

Even Sami Callihan, a wrestler who tended to be critical of his time in the WWE system, claimed his sensibilities expanded at the WWE Performance Center. He praised the company for encouraging the talent to work with Howard Fine, an acting coach whose students included Brad Pitt, Salma Hayek, Jennifer Connelly, Jared Leto, Bradley Cooper, Kim Delaney and Sela Ward. "He taught me something called 'emotional recall,' It's about taking moments from your own life and being able to plug into that moment. At any given time, you plug into a sad moment, a happy moment, a moment when you needed resilience, a moment when you needed to stand up. Everyone has experienced those moments. But to find those moments and put them into your art, that was really valuable."

Unexpectedly, NXT drew attention to the indies. "You watch NXT on the WWE Network, and what do you do?" Helms asked. "You go back in time, find that wrestler's early work on YouTube. And you know what happens? All those cool little companies start getting internet traffic."

Said the Young Bucks' Matt Jackson, "Fans would look at NXT and say, 'Wait a second. This guy came from *where*? I'm going to seek that out because I *like* this style. I want more of that.' I don't think that was the intention of NXT, but it shined a bright spotlight on the independents. It helped independent wrestling."

John Thorne of Cleveland's Absolute Intense Wrestling (AIW) viewed the period just before Kevin Steen was signed to WWE in 2014 as a golden era on the indies characterized by a glut of talent doing everything to get noticed. "Once fans saw Kevin Owens in NXT, it became obvious that there were so many other great wrestlers out there," he said.

When David Fuller, owner of Fort Worth's Iconic Heroes of Wrestling Excellence (IHWE), booked Johnny Gargano and Kyle O'Reilly in 2015, he was certain that both would eventually reappear in NXT. "We just didn't know when," he said. "But we knew that when they did, we were going to get a lot of hits on YouTube."

As each indie talent received an offer, another wrestler, slogging away in some high school gym or grange hall, suddenly hustled his or her way into the spot left by the performer's departure. "Adam Cole gets signed by WWE and is off the market," Joey Ryan told *Talk Is Jericho.* "And then, all of a sudden, an MJF steps up. And maybe the opportunities are not as prevalent if Adam Cole is still around, taking bookings. There's a lot of talented guys out there who just need an opportunity."

At a certain point, Drew Cordeiro, owner of Rhode Island's Beyond Wrestling promotion, realized that people from WWE were scouting his group for potential NXT signees. In fact, in 2016, Keith Lee flew himself to a show to, in Cordeiro's words, "have a crazy, Beyond Wrestling match that would go up on YouTube." Before Lee signed with WWE, Cordeiro returned the favor, paying for Lee's airfare to another card.

As the clash between NXT, AEW and other indies escalated, Cordeiro, a former backyard wrestler who started his promotional career by presenting marathons that literally went on all day, set a goal of "trying to find the next wave of future stars. I get gratification when someone can make a living just as a professional wrestler. I want to create that moment in Beyond Wrestling when everything changed, when NXT took notice. That gives us purpose."

In a dressing room populated with former indie stars, it was easy for NXT performers to maintain their outsider mentality, including, in some cases, a creative condescension toward the larger WWE roster. Matt Riddle, an ex-MMA fighter whose indie credits included PWG, EVOLVE and PROGRESS, boasted to *TMZ Sports* in early 2019 that NXT was superior: "We're different, we're new, we're fresh and we're not the same watered-down, child's product that WWE has turned into a lot. When people watch us, it's more real. It's more believable."

There was also the perception that a graduation to the WWE roster might end up feeling more like a demotion. For every Samoa Joe, Seth Rollins or Charlotte Flair in WWE, there was Shinsuke Nakamura, Bobby Roode and No Way Jose — athletes who seemed to engender more fan fascination before they'd been "elevated" from NXT.

"People appreciated the subterranean grit of NXT," said Kenny Herzog, the writer whose wrestling stories have appeared in *Rolling Stone* and *The Ringer*, among others. "But then they expected it to be maintained under the hot lights of *Monday Night Raw.* But once you're on that kind of stage, everything changes."

Perhaps echoing the official WWE line, WWE competitor Baron Corbin told the *Not Sam Wrestling Podcast*, "What's crazy is when people say, 'I don't want these guys to be called up so that they can be misused.' Nobody is being misused. They're going to be given opportunities. It's on you. It's not on anybody else. If guys are being misused, it's not anybody's fault but their own."

Despite the company's position that any wrestler with initiative could rocket to the top in WWE, grabbing the proverbial "brass ring," Simon Gotch, who left the promotion in 2017, claimed, "The reality is that you're not able to do that because WWE is a machine. Like any machine, they can make you successful or not. All you have to do is go cool, and you're losing your match in 30 seconds."

Another issue cited by former WWE performers: a departure from the authenticity of NXT when the wrestlers were forced to read scripts crafted by committees of writers. "I'm a professional wrestler who can tell stories and come up with promos," Jon Moxley complained on *Talk Is Jericho* shortly after leaving the company. "I believe I have the capacity to talk people into buildings. I believe that I developed those skills years ago and wanted to bring them here to WWE, and you just want me to say your stupid lines. If you want somebody to say your stupid lines, hire an actor because they'd probably do a better job. I'm not interested in doing it."

But with competition from AEW looming, WWE announced it was changing the way it did business. Harking back to the Monday Night Wars, Vince McMahon appointed the former heads of ECW and WCW, Paul Heyman and Eric Bischoff, as executive directors of *Raw* and *SmackDown*, respectively (Bischoff would last four months before he was replaced by "Brother Love" Bruce Prichard). And once NXT was slotted into the USA Network's prime-time lineup, it ceased to be described as a developmental arm of WWE. Rather, the division that was consistently responsible for the company's most exciting pay-per-views would now be seen as a peer — albeit, one with the type of edge that might enable it to eclipse the opposition by showing that, when the pressure was on, WWE could out-indie the indies.

The depth of the NXT brand was apparent in November 2019 when a contingent of 175 WWE wrestlers, production members and other staff were stranded in Riyadh, Saudi Arabia, after the company's *Crown Jewel* pay-per-view there. There were a number of theories about why this might have occurred, but since I was unable to confirm any of the conspiracies, I'll simply cite the charter company's explanation that the flight was delayed "due to a mechanical issue."

Regardless, much of the roster was unable to get to a live *SmackDown* broadcast in Buffalo, New York. As a result, *NXT* was required to make the save, leading to a thrilling telecast that saw Matt Riddle and Keith Lee brutalize an obnoxious Sami Zayn; Tommaso Ciampa conquer The Miz; and Adam Cole retain his NXT Championship over Daniel Bryan.

The energy continued into the *Survivor Series* three weeks later, during which an NXT squad consisting of Bianca Belair, Io Shirai, Toni Storm, Rhea Ripley and Candice LeRae vanquished *Raw* and *SmackDown* teams in a three-way: NXT North American champion Roderick Strong bested United States champion AJ Styles and Intercontinental champion Shinsuke Nakamura, and NXT Women's titlist Shayna Baszler beat her respective counterparts from *Raw* and *SmackDown*, Becky Lynch and Bayley.

Riddle was among the NXT performers caught up in the intensity of combat. "I'm super stoked," he told *Sportskeeda* shortly before AEW began its weekly telecast. "It's the Wednesday Night Wars! I hope they push the envelope. I hope they push it hard, and I hope they get a lot of fans. And I hope they're very successful. Because the more successful they are, the more successful we'll be."

21
CHAPTER

During a WWE angle in 2010, CM Punk planned to come out on *SmackDown*, wearing a t-shirt announcing, "I Broke Big Show's Hand."

Punk contacted his close friend at the time and fellow Chicagoan, Colt Cabana, who knew about Ryan Barkan's One Hour Tees shop in the City of Big Shoulders. Barkan cranked the shirt out quickly, impressing Cabana so much that he offered to cut a deal with the proprietor. In exchange for a discount for a batch of "I ✡ Colt" gimmicks to sell on the indies, Cabana would hype the t-shirt and Barkan's business on his popular podcast.

Initially, Barkan wasn't sure if the arrangement would work for him. "I wasn't a huge fan of the independent scene," Barkan said. "My brother was a Ring of Honor fan and filled me in" on this untapped market.

Very quickly, Barkan realized that there was a whole aspect of the wrestling business that he'd never thought about before. The WWE machine might have been serving the merchandising needs of John Cena, The Miz and the Undertaker, but what about the guys who were running with Cabana? Through Colt's intercession, indie stars like Joey Ryan and the Young Bucks began ordering t-shirts from Barkan in bulk.

In many ways, the success of the Bucks as a commercial entity mirrored the success of the company that would become known as Pro Wrestling Tees.

Back in 2009, the brothers had signed a deal with TNA, where they were originally labeled Generation Me and rechristened Max and Jeremy Buck. But they soon concluded that they'd made a mistake. TNA split up the Bucks and programmed them to feud with each other. Few fans were interested, and apparently neither was TNA management. At a certain point, the company ran out of ideas for them, and the pair sat around for weeks at a stretch, earning nothing.

Before departing TNA in 2011, Matt Jackson remembered passing through an airport and attempting to buy a quick meal at Popeye's. When his credit card was declined, he asked Nick to dip into his pocket and purchase the $1.99 chicken biscuit sandwich.

Matt's wife, Dana, was pregnant at the time, and he knew that his life could no longer continue in this direction. For a moment, he considered getting a straight job. But the Bucks weren't ready to quit wrestling. "I actually had to be the guy to say, 'Hey, Matt, there's a reason why we're doing this,'" Nick told CBS' Miami affiliate. "I just had a gut feeling. I'm glad that we stuck with it."

As the brothers surveyed the indie scene, they focused on Colt Cabana. He'd had some of the same lousy breaks they did — playing a forgettable character, named Scotty Goldman and based on Cabana's Jewish heritage, in WWE in 2008 and 2009 — yet he managed to hold his head above water. As they examined his situation further, they realized that the difference between Cabana and the Bucks was that Colt made a concerted effort to promote himself via social media and merchandising.

In time, the Bucks followed the exact same pattern, setting their wrestling price low enough that they could work three or four times a week. On the road, they tried tapping into the level of excitement they felt in PWG, arguably their favorite promotion, and passing it on to the spectators, regardless of the location. They became such a draw that the 2CW promotion in upstate Oswego, New York, named one event, "We Booked This Show Because It Was Literally The Only Available Date For The Young Bucks."

Before and after each card, they'd set up at the merch table, spending one-on-one time with the fans and promoting the hell out of their t-shirts. Many times, those same fans would return to the next show, remember their pleasant exchanges and line up to buy something else.

"Selling merchandise and superkicking people," Nick Jackson joked to *USA Today*. "That's pretty much everything about us."

As she raised their family, Matt's wife, Dana, took on the task of managing the team's merchandising empire. Ultimately, the Bucks would hawk more than 80 varieties of t-shirts on Pro Wrestling Tees' website. Like Cabana before them, the Jackson brothers inspired other indie performers to earn a better living by taking the small stuff seriously. "They're the first people who opened up my eyes to seeing, 'Oh, you can be successful outside of WWE,'" Joey Ryan told *Vice Sports*. "'You can make a full-time living in wrestling without WWE. You can have a career in wrestling without WWE.'"

By 2013, following the format set by the Bucks, Kevin Steen, Christopher Daniels and Jimmy Jacobs were all working with Pro Wrestling Tees, which sold their merchandise online and shipped it around the world. After production and other costs, the company and the performers shared approximately a 50-50 split.

In time, a number of wrestlers told Barkan, they could earn enough from t-shirt sales to pay their essential bills.

Aware that his reputation was building, Barkan attempted to associate larger names with his business. When he discovered that a number of wrestling legends would be appearing at a comic convention, he created a specific design for Diamond Dallas Page, who was just starting his DDP Yoga program. Impressed, Page turned Barkan on to Jake "The Snake" Roberts, a DDPY student who'd credit the regimen with helping him treat his substance abuse issues.

"I started getting credibility with the legends," Barkan said. After meeting WWE Hall of Fame announcer Jim "J.R." Ross through Twitter, Barkan found himself introduced to "Stone Cold" Steve Austin in 2014.

"Steve was my favorite wrestler of all time," Barkan explained. "Growing up, I had his posters all over my wall. When we finally spoke on the phone, I was sweating. I sent him four shirts that he didn't like. So I sent a higher quality t-shirt, and he said, 'Let's do it.'"

Once Barkan had the ability to drop Austin's name to potential clients, Pro Wrestling Tees was instilled with authority not just on the indies, but everywhere in professional wrestling.

On a Tuesday in 2018, Teddy Hart contacted Pro Wrestling Tees, asking for 50 shirts to be shipped to his hotel room in California. In Australia, Cody glanced at his stock and realized that he was a hundred gimmicks short. "They don't realize what they need until they get somewhere and see that they're out of t-shirts," Barkan said.

With the exception of Bullet Club shirts, which Barkan said "sold like crazy," Pro Wrestling Tees housed very little inventory. But the items could be instantly printed.

"Gone are the days when you had to have a huge stock of merchandise with one design that you had to gamble on because you weren't sure if people would love it or hate it," Matt Jackson told me. "So you give the people an option. Customize it. What color do you want? Put it on a tank top. I put together a team of artists I trusted. I implemented my own ideas. And we came up with merchandise we respected. And that's why it sold."

Barkan estimated that the entire process, from the moment of contact until the wrestler received his merchandise, took a total of four days. "We print them and ship the next day, all colors, all sizes, all designs. There are 80,000 possibilities."

Interestingly, before his immersion into the indie scene, Barkan maintained that he'd pitched his on-demand idea to WWE. "We would have been able to print t-shirts for every member of their roster, but they didn't want to do it. I don't think they remember that. In fact, I'm not sure the guy I spoke to is even with the company anymore. But Pro Wrestling Tees wouldn't have happened if WWE had said yes."

Instead, New Japan signed a deal with the company as the Bullet Club heated up. Due largely to the faction's popularity, Pro Wrestling Tees more than doubled the size of its staff and made arrangements with the Hot Topic chain to stock Bullet Club shirts in malls all over the United States.

"There were Bullet Club shirts for AJ Styles, Bullet Club shirts for Tama Tonga, over 50 Bullet Club shirts," Barkan said. "It was a cool-looking shirt: just white ink on a black background, a simple design, like the nWo or Austin 3:16 shirts. Except you never had 50 different nWo t-shirts."

Noted Omaha promoter Chris Metry, "I see people wearing Bullet Club shirts in the mall and sometimes wonder if they even know what it is."

Hot Topic executives apparently also spotted the trend. According to one story, when WWE was approached about working with the retail chain, the wrestling giant had to concede that it had no connection to the Bullet Club. Either way, Pro Wrestling Tees sold 200,000 Bullet shirts within five years. "If you add in all the other indie shirts, that's 600,000 shirts in the same period," Barkan said.

The same year that the Hot Topic deal was signed, Pro Wrestling Tees created its own store next to its print shop in Chicago, a place for traveling fans to stop while passing through the city. "The fans will order a shirt, and we print while they wait," Barkan said.

As their acclaim spread, certain Bullet Club members and legends like Mick Foley, Road Warrior Animal, and Jake "The Snake" Roberts also made the effort to check out the facility. "CM Punk comes by once a month to pick up his [royalty] check," Barkan said.

By 2018, Pro Wrestling Tees was working with 1,200 different wrestlers and 300 different promotions. "In every city, there's one independent wrestling company," Barkan said. "I know because I do business with all of them."

Of Pro Wrestling Tees' 35 employees, approximately 30 were fans. "We're not just a business printing shirts," Barkan said. "Since we're wrestling fans, we know what wrestling fans like. We have our own little focus groups in the shop, where we throw around ideas and talk about angles we watched on wrestling — what worked, what didn't work. I could be wrong, but I'd guess that the people printing the NFL's t-shirts don't enjoy the same level of intimacy."

CHAPTER 22

As the Bullet Club expanded, certain members formed sub-groups within the larger faction. Tama Tonga and his real-life brother, Tanga Loa, started the Guerrillas of Destiny. While competing in Ring of Honor, the Young Bucks and Adam Cole became the Superkliq. After AJ Styles, Doc Gallows and Karl Anderson left for WWE in 2016, the Bucks and Kenny Omega branded themselves "The Elite" of the Bullet Club — a distinction based on the trio's ability not only to move merchandise but open new pathways for New Japan.

As they traversed the globe, Matt and Nick Jackson chronicled their exchanges with an iPhone. Using the device as an editing system, the pair then posted a web series they called *Being the Elite*. "It was sort of a documentary," Matt told me. "Essentially, it was just me and Nick on the show, and Kenny would pop up a little bit. It was just the three of us, so we said, 'Let's make this more interesting. Let's add some characters. Let's add some storylines.'

"Then we started putting in cliffhangers. That's what I liked about the old [WCW] *Nitro*s when I was a kid. You couldn't wait until the next week to see what would happen. And it built and built. Our meet and greet lines got longer. People started referencing the show's storylines and catchphrases."

On the indies in the U.S., the Jacksons noticed fans holding up signs related to specific incidents that occurred on *Being the Elite*, or *BTE*, as insiders began to say. Once again, they'd taken their careers to another phase. Now, they started to amp up the content. "At times, the show could be sci-fi, where we had superpowers," Matt said. "Or it could be comedy. Or it could be a murder mystery. It didn't have to take itself seriously. Because that's not what we are. We're lighthearted guys."

During autograph sessions, fans would occasionally offer suggestions for *BTE* plot twists. Rather than kayfabe their followers, the Bucks indulged them, periodically incorporating the proposals. "It was a simple way of booking," Nick said. "We knew what the fans wanted and gave it to them."

No one in pro wrestling had ever quite done this before. "The mentality had always been, 'Let's surprise the fans. Let's swerve them,'" Matt said. "No, no, no. If the fans want something to happen, make it happen. Make them feel good."

Remarkably, the promotions where the Elite appeared — New Japan, Ring of Honor and the various indies — also began taking their signals from *BTE*. While members had previously been uncertain about how they might be booked, *BTE* gave them an opportunity to take their characters and plots in specific directions.

"Nobody was telling us what we could and couldn't do," "Hangman" Adam Page told me. "And if anyone tried, we had the power to ignore them. Wrestling outside the machine, we answered to the fans, not to anybody else."

The emergence of Cody in the unit added to the visibility. While WWE largely relegated the former Stardust to a mid-card role, as a member of the Bullet Club's Elite division, Cody carried himself with the bearing of a main-eventer and a haughtiness that lent itself to storyline tensions within the faction.

As with the Bucks, Cody took satisfaction in knowing that the disappointments of the past were over. Utilizing a lifetime of wrestling knowledge, he now had the control to move himself to a place where his success could be assured.

When outside forces impacted the Elite's direction, members took it upon themselves to explain the real-life dramas. For example, after the Bucks learned that Adam Cole would be leaving the Bullet Club for NXT, they dealt with it by blaming him for an actual illness Nick Jackson had recently suffered. According to the *BTE* plot, Cole had poisoned Nick and, obviously, could no longer be in the group.

In the midst of the *War of the Worlds* tour, coproduced by Ring of Honor and New Japan, Cole was officially fired from the Bullet Club by Omega and replaced by "The Villain" Marty Scurll. Eventually, the fans learned the full story when Cole debuted at *NXT TakeOver: Brooklyn III* in 2017, but they appreciated the clever way that the departure was handled on *BTE*.

Noted Scurll, "The very core of wrestling is the relationship between the performers and the audience. Just being a good wrestler isn't enough. You have to be more. *Being the Elite* became a platform where the viewer could know us in a different way than watching a 10- or 15-minute match. Every week, it was like a *Monday Night Raw*. It was always spontaneous, and that's something people could tell. Anything authentic always stands out."

Even the campiest lines delivered by the various wrestlers on *BTE* seemed entertaining; the performers clearly were enjoying what they were doing. "It was a camaraderie," said Page. "The fans were seeing more genuineness than they'd seen in wrestling in a long time. Everyone was legitimately best friends and having fun together."

The compatibility existed despite sometimes contrasting views of the wrestling business. Cody told interviewer Kenny McIntosh during an *Inside the Ropes* Q&A in Dublin, "I like a very traditional, conservative wrestling. Nick Jackson wants to set himself on fire. The common thing is pleasing the audience, and that was shared amongst everybody."

But how long could it last? The two-year contract extension that the Bucks had signed with New Japan and Ring of Honor would expire at the end of 2018. As fans admiringly watched the Bullet Club, it was natural to wonder when the Young Bucks might be sharing the same dressing room again with AJ Styles and Finn Balor — this time in WWE. "A lot of our friends [in WWE] say we might find it troubling that our creativity would be pretty much gone, and we wouldn't like it, but we'd like the money," Nick Jackson told the *Sporting News*. "Right now, we have both of those, and that's always nice because we're our own boss."

Yet, Matt Jackson did not completely rule out the possibility. Since the time they were kids, the brothers fantasized about performing in Madison Square Garden, which, at the time, meant wrestling for Vince McMahon. "If we did go there, it would have to be creatively appealing for me. If we don't ever go there, I feel like we're going to be remembered more than if we went there and became a mid-card act."

As they deliberated the various possibilities, the Jacksons were enticed by the thought of standing out in history as one of the few tandems never to make the jump. "You never know what's going to happen tomorrow," Matt told *USA Today*. "Right now, we're so happy with what we're doing."

Happy enough, he emphasized, that his instincts told him to maintain authority over the Elite in a forum he could manage. "I'd rather have *WrestleMania* every time I wrestle," he emphasized.

23
CHAPTER

Even with all the enthrallment that the Bullet Club as a unit inspired, Kenny Omega's distinction as the "Best Bout Machine" gave the faction the type of reliability no group had enjoyed since Ric Flair was having 60-minute matches on a regular basis as a member of the Four Horsemen.

Given the large personalities sharing the stage with him in the Bullet Club, it was inevitable that Omega would eventually clash with one of his stablemates. The initial plan, proposed by the Young Bucks, was to pit him against Adam Cole. But when Cole left for WWE, recent Bullet Club member Cody seamlessly slid into the spot.

The Bucks began hinting at a collision on *BTE*, but they needed the cooperation of New Japan and Ring of Honor to take the angle further. So they ran their ideas by Ring of Honor booker Hunter Johnson, as well as his New Japan counterpart, Gedo.

"Do you know how difficult it is to sit in a room with Gedo, who only speaks Japanese, and I have to tell him an entire multi-layered, HBO-drama type, crazy story in broken English?" Matt Jackson asked the *Sporting News*.

Ultimately, Gedo agreed that the Bucks' proposal would benefit all parties involved. The friction between Cody and Omega began simmering during the second of the Best Bout Machine's spectacular sequence of matches with IWGP Heavyweight champion Kazuchika Okada in June 2017. Omega and Okada were trading big moves, but neither could put the other away. Before the match was declared a draw, though, Cody did something bewildering. He attempted to throw in the towel for Omega, claiming that he was trying to protect a fellow Elite member from injury.

But fans wondered if his goal had been undermining Omega before he could capture the coveted prize.

When it was Cody's turn to challenge Okada the next month, Omega amplified the tension, as *he* teased throwing in the towel for his stablemate. In subsequent episodes of *Being the Elite*, fans were given the indication that neither man trusted the other.

This played out for several months until New Japan's *New Year Dash!! 2018* show. Following a 10-man tag team match, Cody went after opponent Kota Ibushi with a chair after the bell. Unexpectedly, Omega came storming down the aisle, putting an immediate halt to the attack. This satisfied two separate storylines: building heat between Cody and Omega and displaying Kenny's deep affection for his former Golden☆Lover partner, Ibushi, who embraced him after the save.

Later that same month, when Omega lost his IWGP United States Heavyweight Championship to Jay White, Cody, along with Hangman Page, assaulted the blond Canadian. This time, it was Ibushi who rushed the ring to rescue his dear friend.

In an exclusive, *BTE* covered the mayhem that continued backstage after the match.

Everything was now in place for a showdown between Omega and Cody. It was booked as the main event at *Supercard of Honor XII*, Ring of Honor's pay-per-view slated for *WrestleMania 34* weekend, in April 2018. Although the show at New Orleans' Lakefront Arena was a significant drive from WWE's downtown activities and *NXT TakeOver: New Orleans* occurred at the very same time, more than 6,000 fans turned up for the card, shattering a Ring of Honor attendance record.

With nearly a year to prepare for this match, the participants could visualize it practically move for move before the bell rang. The main event went on late, but once Omega and Cody began tangling, the fatigue some fans might have felt earlier was wiped away. The confrontation ended with interference from the Bucks. But whose side were they going to take? They attempted to superkick Cody, but struck Omega instead, leading to a win by the Prince of Pro Wrestling and a number of unanswered plot points.

Primarily, who was the leader of the Bullet Club?

Future AEW star Jungle Boy was already in the business, but the storyline rekindled something in him as a fan. "I'd stopped watching wrestling a long time ago," he remembered. "I fell out of love with the thing I loved the most. And it was Kenny Omega, the Young Bucks and Cody who got me back into it."

By this stage, *Being the Elite* had 205,000 subscribers, some of whom were more taken with the series than they were with the actual confrontations in the ring. "We had a guy in the airport on our way here," Matt told the *Sporting News* in 2018. "And he puts his hand out and said, 'I love your YouTube videos.' He didn't mention anything about pro wrestling."

Outside of WWE, the Bullet Club now had the game's cockiest heel in Cody, who tended to appear in public in finely tailored suits, and most sympathetic babyface in Omega. In Japan, because of Omega's obvious admiration for the culture and dexterity in the native tongue, many Japanese now embraced his claim that he wasn't quite a gaijin. After nearly wresting the IWGP Heavyweight Championship away from Okada on three prior occasions, a sizable portion of the Japanese fan base was rooting for Omega to claim the gold.

He was characteristically adept at hyping the historic rivalry. "I am the gateway drug," he boasted to the New Japan website before an earlier confrontation. "Do you want to take the Okada pill or do you want to see how *far* this rabbit hole goes? Then you'll take the Kenny Omega pill. I'm not trying to be selfish. If I wasn't the best wrestler in the world, I'd say, 'Look, you've got to give it to this guy. He's the leader, and I'll be his warm-up act. That's fine.' But I'm not an idiot. I know the truth.

And the truth is I am the most creative, the best, the man of the hour. Put the belt on me."

As with the Cody match, the Bucks were involved in helping Omega plan his challenge to Okada, scheduled for June 9, 2018, at the *Dominion 6.9* event at Osaka-jō Hall. The duo's friendship with Okada went back to when all three were being mishandled in TNA. Before one particular match, Okada was supposed to bleed, and he expressed his hesitation to the Bucks and Alex Shelley beforehand. Matt and Nick went to TNA management and successfully argued that it really wasn't necessary for their friend to cut himself.

Okada never forgot and was instrumental in arranging for the Bucks to work in New Japan. In the dressing room, he'd pull good-natured pranks on the Bucks, like putting on Matt's gear, and — with his thick Japanese accent — pretending to be a member of the Jackson family.

On the morning of the event, the Bucks met with Omega to discuss the various exchanges that would take place between the ropes. The no-time limit, two-out-of-three fall encounter would combine artful ring psychology with a series of moves that only these two combatants were capable of consistently hitting. In the first fall, Omega seemed to throw everything at his foe, only to be outmaneuvered when Okada dropped down during a sunset flip and scored the pin. The second fall featured one animated near-fall after another until Omega won with his One-Winged Angel.

Both appeared to be exhausted in the third fall. At one point, Okada hit a Rainmaker but seemed too tired to cover his opponent. When Omega tried a One-Winged Angel, he apparently collapsed from the weight. Every gesture and nuance told a story. Among the audience, the suspension of disbelief was universal.

Omega blasted Okada with everything. But Okada wouldn't fold. Omega bounced off the ropes, charged across the ring and smashed his rival with a V-Trigger — a knee to the head. But rather than log the pinfall, Omega seemed to need assurance that the burial was complete, ploddingly rising to his feet to utilize his last reserve of strength and finally secure the IWGP Heavyweight Championship with one more One-Winged Angel.

Dave Meltzer was hardly alone in declaring this the greatest match of all time.

Harold Mejj's international marketing strategy was now firmly in place. In addition to a Canadian IWGP Heavyweight kingpin, another Winnipeg native, Chris Jericho, was the IWGP Intercontinental titlist (he'd later propose a New Japan versus WWE Intercontinental Championship clash, but neither side appeared enthusiastic about making it), while American Juice Robinson was the company's United States champion, and the Bucks held the IWGP Tag Team belts.

Tradition notwithstanding, very few Japanese devotees seemed to be objecting.

24
CHAPTER

When New Japan held its *Wrestle Kingdom 13* pay-per-view in January 2019, approximately 6,000 of the roughly 40,000 spectators had come from other countries. In fact, some of the visitors noted that they were seated in special gaijin sections at the Tokyo Dome. While nowhere near the international level of a major WWE event, it was obvious that the promotion was past the point of being a distinctly Japanese phenomenon.

Yet, the company continued to adhere to certain Japanese customs. Regardless of their national origins, many of New Japan's star performers passed through the promotion's dojos in Japan, as well as Los Angeles, and a facility in Auckland, New Zealand, run by Bad Luck Fale. "Our goal is to bring the wrestler in from the start, and not just teach him the wrestling techniques, but also the Japanese fighting spirit mental part," New Japan president Harold Mejj said.

He mentioned Jay White, who'd become the IWGP Heavyweight champion after Kenny Omega departed the company for AEW. "He's from New Zealand, but he came to our dojo as a young man, where we harnessed his energy. And I think that's something totally unique that fans appreciate."

At the Fale Dojo, the regimen was almost identical to the ones in Japan. Training began as soon as the athletes woke up. Warm-ups included 1,000 squats, 200 push-ups and 200 sit-ups, while sumo, jiu-jitsu, kickboxing and shoot and submission wrestling were among the disciplines taught.

"When we started [the Bullet Club], we weren't just a bunch of gaijin," Fale told the New Japan website. "We were part of all this, and whatever happened, we still had the sense that we were protecting what the company had built. It's tradition. I've seen so many foreign guys come in and show such disrespect to the Japanese guys. They don't understand that this company has stayed alive so long because of that respect. You work together to get things done. We learned that from the Japanese way of doing things."

Despite the rigorous nature of the WWE Performance Center, Mejj claimed that there was one major difference. In New Japan, the competitors still regarded their profession as a sport. "We're not sports-entertainment," he stressed. "This is wrestling."

In addition to winning the 2018 New Japan Cup tournament, British-born Zack Sabre Jr. had been a 2015 PWG Battle of Los Angeles winner, held titles in Revolution Pro Wrestling and Germany's wXw promotion and had gone to the finals of the 2016 WWE Cruiserweight Classic. "Overseas, you still have more focus paid on the entertainment side," he told New Japan's website. "I've always felt most at home when wrestling here."

Even when New Japan staged shows in other countries, an effort was made to recreate the mood of a Japanese arena. "Not only is our style Japanese style," Mejj said, "you'll notice that when we do our ring announcing, we do it in Japanese. We want to give the audience the authentic feel."

New Japan made its first foray, independent of any co-promotion, to the United States in 2017, with two shows at the Long Beach Convention and Entertainment Center in Southern California. Reportedly, the company had planned to do this a year later. But when AJ Styles, Doc

Gallows, Karl Anderson and Shinsuke Nakamura all left for WWE in 2016, New Japan felt compelled to wage war on its rival's turf.

According to New Japan, tickets for the Long Beach cards and meet and greets sold out within two hours. When additional tickets were put on sale, the company said, they were gone in minutes. "I remember that website crashed," Matt Jackson told New Japan's website. "So just saying that people were excited would be an understatement."

With an English-language announce team consisting of WWE Hall of Famer Jim "J.R." Ross and MMA fighter Josh Barnett, and main events that included Kazuchika Okada successfully defending his IWGP Heavyweight crown against Cody on night one, and Kenny Omega becoming New Japan's first United States Heavyweight champion by besting Tomohiro Ishii in the tournament finals on night two, the shows drew fans from 37 states.

Among the audience members was future AEW owner Tony Khan. "He really wasn't kidding when he [said] he was a wrestling fan because [he sent] me a video of him wearing a Bullet Club shirt in the front row," Matt Jackson told CBS' Miami affiliate. "And, actually, I think I went up and I might have 'too sweeted' him or something."

During the Monday Night Wars in 1998, members of the WWF's D-Generation X faction embarrassed WCW by driving in a military jeep to a *Monday Nitro* event and fomenting chaos outside. Nineteen years later, while on a loop through California, Elite members the Young Bucks, Marty Scurll, Adam Page, Cody and his wife, Brandi Rhodes, decided to exhibit the same kind of sedition, piling into a limousine to shoot a segment for *Being the Elite* outside a *Raw* show in the city of Ontario, California. Surrounded by fans, the group marched through the parking lot, just feet from the production trucks, leading admirers in a whooping chant of "Too Sweet."

Although their stay was short, they'd edit the section to make it appear that they'd "invaded" *Raw* and caused mayhem.

Former Ring of Honor wrestler Jimmy Jacobs was a member of WWE's creative team at the time. But when he heard that his old associates were outside, he ran over to them to take a selfie. Apparently, the Bucks warned him that there might be repercussions if he posted the picture on social media. Jacobs is said to have assured them that he had no intention of doing this, then dispatched a photo above the caption, "Pleasant surprise to see old friends in lovely California. #BCInvasion #RAW #youngbucks #bulletclub #villain #hangmanpage #WWE."

A reasonable argument can be made that WWE was left with little choice but to fire him.

"I knew it might make some people upset, but at that point of my life, I didn't care," he told interviewer Chris Van Vliet. "I wasn't trying to not get fired anymore because, for so long, I was there, just not trying to get fired. They did for me what I could have never done for myself. I would have stayed there another 10 years and been miserable and hated life just like most of the other writers there."

In the fallout, WWE sent the Bucks a cease and desist letter for using the "Too Sweet" hand gesture that the company trademarked following the arrivals of Styles, Gallows and Anderson. The Bucks swiftly excised the term from YoungBucksMerch.com and the Pro Wrestling Tees website.

New Japan returned to Long Beach the next year, selling out before one match was announced and coordinating their show with the opening of a new Los Angeles dojo. According to Matt Jackson, the eventual main event — the Young Bucks versus the Golden☆Lovers — could have sold out the Staples Center in downtown Los Angeles.

Although a card at the Cow Palace, in Daly City, outside San Francisco, in the summer of 2018 did not sell out, New Japan still managed to draw 6,000 fans to a building that had seen Pat Patterson, Ray Stevens, Pepper Gomez, Kinji Shibuya, Bobo Brazil, Peter Maivia, Rocky Johnson and Andre the Giant headline.

Since those territory days, the focal point for pro wrestling in northern California had shifted, with *WrestleMania 31* being held in 2015 at the Levi's Stadium in Santa Clara and construction starting on San Francisco's sparkling Chase Center two years later. But in 2018 the storied Cow Palace became relevant again, as a new chapter in history was being created.

25
CHAPTER

In 2016, ITV announced the revival of *World of Sport*, which would kick off with a pilot episode taped in Salford, Greater Manchester, in November, featuring indie stars like Grado, El Ligero and Sha Samuels. The show was slated to air on New Year's Eve and include popular WWE Hall of Fame announcer Jim "J.R." Ross on the microphone. The reverberations would be felt around Europe, particularly in Great Britain, and would epitomize how WWE responded to the expanding indie revolution. Even before ITV's plans were public, WWE declared that it was producing its own British product. The company's first United Kingdom Championship Tournament aired in early 2017 — just after the *World of Sport* relaunch — with a lineup of Pete Dunne, Tyler Bate, T-Bone, Wolfgang, Mark Andrews and Trent Seven among the notable names.

Initially, these wrestlers were told that they weren't being pried away from their indie commitments in the UK. Instead, WWE would pay them a healthy retainer in exchange for, in the event of a scheduling conflict, appearing on the promotion's show. For wrestlers who'd grown up watching Bret Hart, Shawn Michaels, the Undertaker, "Stone Cold"

Steve Austin and The Rock, the notion of regularly performing for WWE was exhilarating.

"The guys who signed told me they were delighted with their contracts," said Brian Elliott, the former editor of *Fighting Spirit* magazine. "It was good money, and this is what they'd worked their whole lives for."

With Triple H heading the effort, the goal was to have WWE's UK product appeal to the traditional British wrestling fan, just as NXT did to the indie follower (at one point, a special match was even presented in rounds). *World of Sport* legend Johnny Saint would be appointed general manager of the brand, eventually called *NXT UK*. The two-night tournament, featuring 16 wrestlers, was broadcast from the Empress Ballroom in Blackpool, in northwest England, a striking facility built in 1896 with a barrel-vaulted ceiling, gold and white patterned panels and 12 glass chandeliers. Traditionally, Blackpool, with its bawdy boardwalk and carny culture, had been a cradle of British pro wrestling.

But the WWE United Kingdom Championship tournament also delivered a nod to the future, with the immensely talented Tyler Bate, then just short of 20 years old, emerging with the title.

To emphasize its commitment to the European market, the company opened up a 17,000-square-foot Performance Center in London in 2019. By this point, there were approximately 30 performers from all over Europe on the NXT UK roster, whose program streamed weekly on the WWE Network.

At the same time, the company began affiliating itself with numerous European indies, as well as purchasing the promotions' libraries to air on the WWE Network.

PROGRESS had been involved with WWE since 2016, when it hosted two qualifying matches for the WWE Cruiserweight Classic. Following his WWE United Kingdom Championship win, Bate continued appearing on PROGRESS cards, along with Pete Dunne, Mark Andrews and Trent Seven.

Ireland's Over The Top (OTT) promotion, founded in 2014, also forged an agreement with WWE. Interestingly, the company was initially formed to create a more adult alternative to what fans were seeing on WWE television. At that point, Irish Whip Wrestling was no longer a commodity, and another Irish company was doing holiday camp cards.

"It was funny because when Fergal Devitt would come back from the New Japan tours, he'd work those shows, just to be with the Irish lads," said Elliott. "You'd hear about him wrestling in some obscure town and you'd say, 'What the hell was Fergal Devitt doing there?'"

OTT's cards initially took place at Dublin's Tivoli Theatre, an old movie house converted into a nightclub. "It was just this cool place with a great atmosphere," Elliott said. "People really felt they were seeing something before everyone else knew about it. I think the speed at which they built their reputation surprised a lot of people. I'm not sure anyone expected these shows to draw 2,000 people. But the local talent was really over."

As with Insane Championship Wrestling (ICW) in Scotland, which also entered into an accord with WWE, the promotion capitalized on local stereotypes. A character called the "Lord of the Manor" Paul Tracey represented the privileged Irish Protestants from times past, while the Lads from the Flats portrayed working class guys raised in public housing. Luther Ward and the Ward Family were depicted as Irish Travellers, an often ostracized itinerant group with its own dialect sometimes referred to as "white gypsies."

Session Moth Martina, who later signed with Ring of Honor, played "a lazy drunk girl with 10 kids who runs riot around her council house [housing project]," Elliott said. According to Irish slang, a "session moth" is a woman who trades sex for alcohol or party drugs. "That's the comedy of it. She'd play it to the hilt. When she went to Japan, she wasn't sure if anyone would understand the gimmick. But they loved her doing drunk comedy. She would trip over her own feet. If she ran the ropes too much, she would tire out. It was pretty unique to the Japanese."

But the WWE link occasionally caused issues for the local promotion. When David Starr — the self-professed "Bernie Sanders of professional wrestling" — wrestled WWE's United Kingdom champion WALTER on an OTT card in 2019, the American grabbed the belt, berated his foe about "selling out" and stomped on it. Although the fans appeared to be entertained, WWE officials apparently were irritated that the title had been so publicly disrespected.

On another indie, a wrestler on the NXT UK brand was placed in an intergender match but was not permitted to direct any aggression at the woman in the opposite corner. To behave otherwise could violate the corporation's ban on depictions of domestic violence.

While fans were happy to see WWE talent turning up on their local promotion's cards, there was concern that the company's demands might start to impact the wrestlers' performances, as well as the camaraderie with longtime devotees. "People were worried that, at some point, things would get yanked away," said former *Fighting Spirit* writer Will Cooling.

In time, WWE distinguished their UK talent by tiers. Tier 1 wrestlers were exclusive to WWE and affiliated promotions like PROGRESS, ICW and OTT, but they could not participate in the other leagues' live-streamed matches. Tier 2 had the luxury of performing on streamed programs. Tier 3 allowed the combatants more leeway, although they could not wrestle on any rival's television show.

Over the past several years, fans had grown accustomed to the concept of their favorite wrestler working with hundreds of potential opponents. The new WWE rules appeared to change the possibilities.

At one point, British-born New Japan regular Will Ospreay expressed his disapproval by sarcastically tweeting, "So who am I allowed to wrestle in the UK now?"

This prompted WWE wrestler Ricochet, a former two-time PWG Battle of Los Angeles winner and one of the most compelling junior heavyweights in New Japan earlier in the decade, to write back that it was time for Ospreay to "join the team."

Ospreay responded to the offer in capital letters: "NEVER!!!"

"Matt Riddle, Chris Hero and Keith Lee were all big draws when they'd come to the UK," said Cooling. "Then they all moved to WWE. So the British companies ended up booking the guys who were left — over and over again. Sometimes, that can make a storyline more interesting. At the same time, you might have some fans who won't go to the shows as much because they'll say, 'I just saw these guys the last time.'"

From the sidelines, many UK followers viewed the shifting landscape with a sense of dread. Some envisioned WWE purchasing one of their favorite promotions simply to shut down the competition.

"The fans were worried because of tighter restrictions over who could work where," said Elliott. "Of course, a fan also wants to see these guys come to their home town, where they can slap their hands and meet them after the show. If you've gotten to know these guys, you begin wondering if the character you're going to see will become some WWE version of them. It's not strange to be sad or mad about that. But you have to look at it from the wrestler's point of view, as well."

During a Fight Club Pro show, Trent Seven, Tyler Bate and Pete Dunne lost a six-man "loser leaves town" match, signifying their departure from the promotion. The problem was that, in addition to being a key component of the NXT UK roster, Seven happened to be one of Fight Club Pro's owners. "For a long time, he was one of the faces of Fight Club Pro," noted Cooling, "and didn't do a lot of days outside it because he wanted his fans to come to his promotion to see him wrestle. But after he went to NXT UK, they had to write him out of Fight Club Pro a lot more."

When WWE affiliated itself with PROGRESS, the group's founders became employees of the international conglomerate. That meant that when WWE needed them, WWE came first, even if it meant being absent from or moving the date of a PROGRESS show. In 2019, Jim Smallman, the comedian who cofounded the promotion, announced that he was leaving PROGRESS to concentrate on his responsibilities with NXT UK.

Even Shaun Ryan, the video artist responsible for some of OTT's most imaginative vignettes, opted to transfer his talents to the NXT UK brand.

Yet, not every issue facing the British wrestling scene in the late 2010s could be blamed on WWE. As the stars of companies like RevPro and PROGRESS were exposed online, there was demand for them to showcase their skills elsewhere, forcing them to cut down their bookings in the UK. "There have been some weeks when I'd wrestle in three countries," Zack Sabre Jr. told New Japan's website. "I have three international flights coming up next week, all within four days."

Given these types of schedules, the argument could be made that, in forming NXT UK, WWE was ensuring that British fans would continue to see their homegrown talent. These included competitors like New Zealand–born and Australia-reared Toni Storm and Kiwi Travis Banks, who were part of the trend of wrestlers from the Oceania region who came to Great Britain at a time when some of the local stars were pursuing work elsewhere.

In 2019, as observers pondered the British wrestling scene's future, Cooling wondered whether it was still possible to create stars who could draw new fans. "And will they turn into fans who were as loyal as the fans from before, fans who go to shows all year long and are willing to travel around the country for professional wrestling?" he questioned.

At the same time, in Germany, wXw COO Tassilo Jung viewed his company's relationship with WWE in positive terms. The affiliation attracted the attention of the German media, which led to more visibility among possible fans. Houses had grown, from between 500 and 700 in Oberhausen to 1,500. "Most of our wrestlers can't live off wXw," he told me as we sat at my friend Handsome Dick Manitoba's punk rock-themed bar in New York, "but the WWE exposure could change that. Guys who've been on nobody's radar are rising to be top talent."

Like the UK during the *World of Sport* era, Germany and Austria had their own wrestling scene in the '70s through the '90s, centered on the Catch Wrestling Association (CWA). As in the UK, the matches were divided into rounds. For much of its existence, the CWA World Heavyweight Championship was the property of promoter Otto Wanz, a stout former boxer and strongman who defended the title in South Africa, as well as AWA cards in the United States. In fact, at one stage in 1982, after cutting a deal with Verne Gagne, Wanz was the AWA World Heavyweight champion for several weeks, exchanging the belt with Nick Bockwinkel.

Yet, despite the fact that he started a wrestling fanzine at 14, Jung knew nothing about this aspect of his national history. "I was a fan of WCW and the WWF," he said. "It took me a couple of years before I even learned who Otto Wanz was."

Westside Xtreme Wrestling was founded in Oberhausen in 2000, debuting with a card in an Essen disco featuring Claudio Castagnoli against his trainer, fellow Swiss wrestler SigMasta Rappo. Jung was the referee. The audience consisted of 17 fans.

"wXw came and went five or six times," Jung said. Owner Pete "Hate" Wiechers "was a tattoo artist and a great guy but didn't know about business. He brought in guys from [the Japanese promotion] NOAH, but spent all the money by the time they got to Germany and couldn't pay his mortgage."

Despite this, the Oberhausen-based promotion developed a small but dedicated fan base. "Everyone wore black and was united by following obscure American indies. ECW was out of business and done as an alternative, but it definitely had an influence. I'd call these people pure indie fans, anti-mainstream to the point that if a TNA wrestler would show up, you'd get a 'Fuck TNA' chant in English."

Among the attendees' favorite promotions was CHIKARA. As a result, Mike Quackenbush was invited to tour Germany, by popular demand.

In 2006, Jung, who'd been working in his father's carpet store, Felix Kohlenberg and Christian Jakobi purchased wXw from Hate. "We had money from whatever jobs we had," Jung said, "and we felt wXw had vocal, loyal fans and a special atmosphere. Even when we'd take a few months off, the same fans always came back. It was about the best thing wrestling fans had in Germany at the time."

The partners set a number of modest goals, among them, staying within their budget and drawing at least 200 spectators to every show. Talent largely came from Germany, Austria, Switzerland and Holland, but Brits such as Doug Williams and Robbie Brookside and Americans Bryan Danielson, AJ Styles and Low Ki also made appearances. When certain Japanese wrestlers were touring Europe, wXw would manage to recruit them onto its shows.

"We were always trying to get to a place where we had 25,000 euros in the budget, so if someone broke his neck or a fan got hurt, we'd have insurance," Jung said. "We were playing a wrestling company, then became one."

Starting in 2006, the company began drawing international attention with its annual 16 Carat Gold single-elimination tournament. Over the years, the winners would include Chris Hero, WALTER, Sami Callihan, El Generico, Tommy End (Aleister Black), Zack Sabre Jr., Ilja Dragunov and Absolute Andy.

Three years after the tournament's formation, wXw did two co-promotions with Japan's Dragon Gate promotion in Oberhausen, as well as Barcelona, Spain.

With its emphasis on death matches, wXw partnered with CZW and Big Japan Wrestling (BJW), putting on shows in the United States and Asia. Big Japan's World Strong Heavyweight Championship would also display the wXw logo. One Philadelphia bloodfest featured a match between wXw death match specialist Thumbtack Jack and American hardcore competitor Drake Younger, as well as a battle for the CZW Ultraviolent Underground Championship.

"Death matches were fun," Jung said, "but this turns away families and turns away venues." In an effort to establish a middle ground, wXw began cleaning up its presentation while creating special death match events. Death match fans would join a mailing list, purchase a ticket, then receive the address of the venue two days before the show. Meanwhile, Jung noticed "more normal people" at the regular wXw shows.

But in 2012, both CZW and Big Japan reported that some of their wrestlers had developed infections during their death match tours. Concerned about the spread of disease, the company phased out death matches. "We lost fans who came for exactly that," Jung conceded, "and we wouldn't get them back." Instead, wXw concentrated on drawing followers of strong style wrestling, forming a brief relationship with New Japan, starting in 2015.

The next year, the company became the first German promotion to have its own streaming network, wXwNOW. "Before, we were a punk rock production," Jung said. "Then we realized that, if we were going to have our own network, wrestlers couldn't come out of a random door. They needed to come out on a big stage with video walls."

By 2018, the company had seven full-time employees and expanded from 20 annual shows to 80. Twice a year, wXw held a four-day festival that incorporated bowling and karaoke events, in which both fans and performers participated.

Despite its WWE ties, some of wXw's appeal involved its specifically German characters. "One running gag in Germany is that everyone named Kevin is a simple-minded idiot," said Jung. The cliché is based on a trend, jokingly called "Kevinism," based on supposedly lower income German parents giving their children exotic or Anglo-sounding names. In response, wXw created an Alpha-Kevin character with a clenched-tooth grin and his own logo.

"Everyone in Germany got it," Jung said. "and he became a huge babyface character."

Likewise, WALTER and Robert Dreissker were dubbed the AUTsiders because of their Austrian nationality. "This was very funny in Germany, but meant nothing anywhere else," Jung said. "Of course, WWE couldn't do this because they weren't thinking only of Germany."

The roots of wXw's connection to WWE can be traced to former Werder Bremen goalkeeper Tim Wiese, who made six appearances for Germany's national team between 2008 and 2012. In 2014, the year he retired from professional soccer, the national hero was a guest time-keeper in Frankfurt for a WWE match pitting Jimmy and Jey Uso against Stardust and Goldust.

Two years later, WWE announced that he'd appear on a show in Munich, teaming with Sheamus and Cesaro in a bout against the Shining Stars and Bo Dallas.

The company asked wXw for help.

"We shipped the ring, the trainer and the [training partners] to Bremen, [Germany], where Tim lived," Jung said. "It was 100 percent kayfabe. But now, we had a relationship with WWE."

The match turned into a showcase for the former goalkeeper. Looking more muscular than he'd been in his soccer days, Wiese shoulder blocked, hip tossed, clotheslined and body slammed the Shining Stars, cousins Primo and Epico Colon, and worked with Cesaro to hit a double suplex on Primo. Then, Wiese won the match for his team by splashing Dallas and tying him up for the pin.

The next day, "everyone in Germany was talking about wrestling," Jung said. "WWE was helping us, and we were smart enough to market from it."

In October 2018, the bond became official. wXw would now enjoy the same kind of association with WWE as PROGRESS, OTT and ICW, and stories about a possible German Performance Center or version of NXT Germany circulated.

When observers warned Jung about the possible hazards, he seemed unfazed. "I don't think WWE wants to hurt us," he answered. "We can use their talent so, day to day, I say they're good for us. I'm not delusional, but right now, it's a wonderful arrangement."

26
CHAPTER

T he night before *WrestleMania 35*, I ran into Robert Odie Brown, an indie referee I'd met a month earlier on the other side of the country. In a tired voice, he told me that he'd just worked his ninth show in four days.

WrestleMania week tends to create schedules like that, and it's a phenomenon WWE never really anticipated. The company obviously set the foundation by making their show a mega-event that attracts fans from all over the world and can sometimes draw an entire city into the festivities. By and large, the indie wrestling revolution did the rest.

During the week of *WrestleMania 35*, at New Jersey's MetLife Stadium, just across the Hudson River from New York City, more than 50 wrestling-related events, staged by groups other than WWE, were held in the metropolitan area. For those who couldn't attend, FITE TV broadcast 35 wrestling shows. Unlike in other sports, the company estimated that 20 percent of these cards were viewed after they'd already taken place — allowing followers to watch events that had occurred simultaneously.

"*WrestleMania* weekend proves that every wrestling fan has different wrestling tastes," said Bertrand Hébert, who, with Pat Laprade, wrote *Mad Dogs, Midgets and Screw Jobs*, the history of Montreal wrestling, along with the biographies of Mad Dog Vachon and Andre the Giant. "They're not loyal to one style. They might be bigger fans of maybe a certain kind of wrestling, but they're open to learning about new things."

Still, it's *WrestleMania* that draws everyone together.

"I've seen fans who got in on the indie revolution, and they'd wear their Bullet Club shirts and replica belts, and chant, 'You deserve it,' and 'You still got it,' and curse out Vince McMahon," said Philadelphia-area fan Paul Carboni. "But the bona fide truth is we all got here by drinking Vince's Kool-Aid and liking it."

According to Jeff Jarrett, the indie revolution never would have existed if it hadn't been for the WWF's Attitude Era: "Between the years 1997 and 1999, you had millions and millions of kids who wanted to be the next 'Stone Cold' Steve Austin or the next Rock. Then, fast forward 15 years, and those kids are in the ring, leading the indie wrestling boom."

And while some indie watchers continue to insist that they'd never support any product tied to the McMahon family, the reality is that professional wrestling is not as tribal as it sometimes seems. "If you watched Ricochet on the indies for 15 years, you had to love it when you first saw him on *Raw*," said Southern California fan Pete Trerice.

Yet, former Ring of Honor owner Cary Silkin theorized that, in 2018, the majority of WWE fans had little awareness of the indies: "If you went to a WWE show in Toronto or Des Moines, and you polled 100 people at random and asked if they had heard of Ring of Honor, maybe 15 to 20 percent would say yes. There are people who only watch *Raw* and *SmackDown*, don't go on the internet to read about wrestling and don't care. If the Young Bucks walked through the audience at a WWE show, how many people would recognize them? I don't know."

FITE TV COO Mike Weber believed that Silkin's approximation was low, theorizing that, at some point, 30 to 40 percent of the WWE audience had watched another promotion.

Either way, the ones who follow different companies tend to be pretty ardent about them.

David Fuller, owner of Iconic Heroes of Wrestling Excellence (IHWE), said that, in 2016, Jim Cornette convinced him to run a show the week that *WrestleMania 32* was held at AT&T Stadium in Arlington, Texas. "We were in Fort Worth, an hour away from everything, on a Thursday night," he recalled. "But we drew 600 fans, including people from England and Ireland and Japan. We had no national television platform. But 50 to 60 percent of the crowd probably came because Jim Cornette talked about us on his podcast. I just sat there, watching his meet and greet line. It was two hours long."

Still, not every group enjoys running *WrestleMania* weekend. When Chicago-area indie AAW staged a show the week of *WrestleMania 34* in New Orleans, the company was disappointed. "It was at 11 in the morning," pointed out promoter and producer Mike Petrovich. "A lot of the fans were at a midnight show the night before. They were drinking all night and exhausted. The guys were working three or four shows a day and didn't act like our show was special. They were just thinking about managing their schedule and getting to the next show."

From a fan perspective, though, no time of year is as exhilarating. During *WrestleMania 35* week, A Matter of Pride, a New York group with a largely LGBTQ roster, drew a vocal and appreciative crowd. An Orange Cassidy–hosted event featured the "freshly squeezed" warrior in all his nonchalant grandeur. Wearing a pair of shades, Cassidy opened the show by picking a random guy at the bar to ring announce. Another match included a prize of a $20 gift card for the Friendly's restaurant chain. Although the ring announcer disclosed that the value was only $16, the eventual winner, Jigsaw, demanded that the ref place the card on his waist like a belt. A showdown between Session Moth Martina and Nate Webb found both "too drunk" to engage in combat. After spitting beer in each other's faces, the pair knocked each other out with a double lariat. Declared the ring announcer, "Everybody wins. Everybody loses."

The rules of a special "dodgeball match" had to be changed after Maxwell Jacob Friedman stole the ball, the announcer told the audience, so the participants had no choice but to wrestle. The crowd greeted the proclamation with a howling chant of "wrestling sucks."

After Teddy Hart came to the ring with his cat, Mr. Velvet, and read a book about furry animals, the fans settled in for the main event:

a Christmas Chaos Deathmatch between Nick Gage and Ultramantis Black. Among the weapons utilized: a Christmas tree covered in barbed wire.

Another happening, this one at the WrestleCon fan convention, was branded Joey Ryan's Penis Party. For the cost of $30, any fan was allowed the luxury of taking a photo with his or her hand on Joey Ryan's dick.

I think it was the Wednesday before *WrestleMania* when Bertrand Hébert told me that he had an extra ticket to EVOLVE.

A little background about myself and Bertrand. We were unwitting competitors at one point. When WWE was looking for a writer to coauthor Pat Patterson's autobiography, Bertrand and I were the final two candidates. He got the gig. I didn't.

Although I like to think I'm pretty good at my racket, after reading Patterson's touching story, *Accepted: How the First Gay Superstar Changed WWE*, it was clear that, in this case, the better man had won.

EVOLVE was started by Gabe Sapolsky in 2010, two years after he left his booking gig at Ring of Honor. Fans who'd been following Sapolsky's career since he'd worked as a Paul Heyman protégé in ECW instantly attached themselves to the league, convinced that his credentials meant that this would be an indie with integrity. For the most part, they were satisfied. Sapolsky forged a relationship with the now-defunct Dragon Gate USA, the American arm of the Japanese promotion by the same name, resulting in a gifted ensemble of Asian talent appearing on the shows. As WWE began scoping out NXT candidates, the promotion turned to Sapolsky in 2015 to scout potential stars.

Like PROGRESS, OTT and ICW, EVOLVE's affiliation with WWE deepened. NXT sent wrestlers to EVOLVE to gain experience working in front of the group's small but passionate crowds. The presence of NXT names helped buttress the gates. In July 2019, when AEW ran its *Fight for the Fallen* pay-per-view, WWE countered by streaming EVOLVE's 10th anniversary show on the WWE Network, sending NXT names like Adam Cole, Matt Riddle and Babatunde, along with Drew Gulak and Akira Tozawa from the company's cruiserweight division, *205 Live*. From EVOLVE's perspective, the event showcased the promotion's regulars, such as Austin Theory and Anthony Henry, and sent the message to indie stars that, when you worked for EVOLVE, both WWE officials and fans would be watching you.

In fact, when Shotzi Blackheart made the decision to go to WWE, NXT general manager William Regal made the contract signing a public event at an EVOLVE show.

For years, Chris Hero had a certain indie cachet for walking away from an NXT deal to return to his roots. But in 2018, he came back and assumed his WWE identity, Kassius Ohno. Late in the year, he was sent to an EVOLVE show in Queens, where, following a victory over Anthony Henry, he sat in a chair, icing his arm, while addressing the crowd from the ring.

"When I went back to NXT, some of my best fans were worried about how I'd be portrayed, if I would be featured, if I could realize my potential," he said. "I want you all to know that WWE and NXT take very good care of me. I feel respected. I feel appreciated. I feel very fortunate to be in the situation that I'm in, where I have a contract. I'm valued and I feel I am changing professional wrestling for the better."

Ohno then switched topics from the humaneness of WWE to the virtues of EVOLVE. With fans cheering for each name, he mentioned Daniel Bryan, Johnny Gargano and Aleister Black. "One thing all those professional wrestlers have in common is, beside from being at the top of their game, they stepped foot in an EVOLVE ring."

The fans began to chant "EVOLVE," over and over.

"And that's exactly where it is, man. It's people evolving. So who's going to step up now? Who does EVOLVE have who's going to step up, be the next Aleister Black, be the next Johnny Gargano, be the next Daniel Bryan, be the next Kassius Ohno? Who's going to do it? Those of you on the independent wrestling scene, I challenge you. Step your goddamn game up."

When Bertrand and I arrived at the Evolve show during *WrestleMania* week, most of the seats were occupied, so we ended up standing near the ring. As Kazusada Higuchi and Curt Stallion exchanged hard chops, I looked at my phone and noticed that it was 12:19 p.m. — leaving me wondering how their chests would feel later in the weekend, after wrestling at the same breakneck pace three or four more times.

The encounter was followed by a video showing Josh Briggs being injured three weeks earlier at La Boom, the Latin nightclub in Queens that was hosting the card, along with tweets wishing him a quick recovery after hip surgery. On crutches, he hopped out to the ring and thanked the crowd for parting to allow EMTs to transport him to an ambulance.

"No matter what I do in my career, no matter what it becomes, nothing will be as special as that moment," he said. "I respect each and every one of you more than you'll ever know."

Given his recent medical challenges, I naively thought that the point of this promo was simply what it seemed to be: an acknowledgment to the fans from a hardworking indie guy who recently suffered a tough break. But before Briggs could leave, EVOLVE Champion Austin Theory, who'd debut on NXT five months later and appear at the following year's WrestleMania, attacked. Then, as Theory mockingly hobbled on his victim's crutches, Briggs rose from his crumpled position on the canvas and surprised Theory with a chokeslam.

One of the most intriguing characters on the card was JD Drake, a crew-cutted, round-bellied brawler who had a surprise match with Angelo Dawkins of NXT's Street Profits and looked like a guy who would have been a solid hand, and maybe even a headliner, in the territory days.

In the main event, Theory defeated a returning Kyle O'Reilly but ended up fighting off Bobby Fish and Roderick Strong, O'Reilly's Undisputed Era faction-mates in NXT. As Theory fled, O'Reilly took the mic and reminisced to the crowd about his time in EVOLVE. Spontaneously, fans broke into an NXT chant. Later, Bertrand and I both agreed that it felt as if a gap was closing — if not between the indies and WWE, than at least between the indies and NXT.

The moment that the show ended, a new crew swept in, changing the banners and other signage, but keeping the ring and everything else intact. While some fans departed for other shows in the New York area, a number lingered to see the wXw card, labeled *Amerika Ist Wunderbar*, that immediately followed the EVOLVE one.

Despite the fact that I wasn't used to watching a live wrestling show that early in the day, I had a pretty good time. Bertrand left, but I spent much of the rest of the afternoon with Israeli wrestler Gery Roif, listening to his assessments of the participants. There were a number of guys I'd already seen on the American indies, including LAX, Darby Allin and David Starr, as well as German talent such as Lucky Kid, Marius Al-Ani and Absolute Andy. In the main event, wXw Unified World Wrestling champion Bobby Gunns beat Japan's Shigehiro Irie, only to be challenged by Joey Janela for a match to take place in Europe.

Given wXw's affiliation with WWE and Janela's then-impending relationship with AEW, I realized that this was a matchup that fans might not be able to see in the near-future.

But it would be six months before AEW's television show debuted, and Janela had a full schedule of indie shows before then, most immediately his two post-midnight Joey Janela *Spring Break* cards slated for Jersey City that weekend. Noted reporter Mike Davis in the *Asbury Park Press*, "If *WrestleMania* is the Super Bowl of professional wrestling, *Spring Break* is the freakshow next door."

The cards were staged by Game Changer Wrestling (GCW), the same people who backed the Orange Cassidy card, and you'll read a lot about them in the next two chapters. Originally, there was supposed to be only one Joey Janela *Spring Break* show, but after it sold out in four minutes, a second night was added.

The climax of the two events was a 60-plus person battle royal dubbed the Greatest Clusterfuck, which continued so late, I wouldn't have been surprised if some fans then directed themselves to the nearby New Jersey Meadowlands to wait for the doors to open for *WrestleMania 35*. Depending on the worldview of the spectator, the Clusterfuck alone might have been worth the flight to Newark Liberty International Airport.

The match started with Necro Butcher — who stapled a dollar onto his own forehead while playing himself in the 2008 movie, *The Wrestler* — coming out of retirement against hardcore icon Nick "Fuckin'" Gage. Within minutes of the next two wrestlers, Marcus Krane and Shlak, entering, there was already a door in the ring. Everything devolved from there — to the enchantment of the crowd. Swoggle, the four-foot-five competitor who, as Hornswoggle, was once portrayed as

Vince McMahon's secret son in a WWE storyline, hit Necro Butcher in the balls with a plastic chicken. Krane attempted to smother Brian Pillman Jr. with a plastic bag. On a stage overlooking the ring, Marko Stunt and Nate Webb performed a song on guitars until MJF rose from the audience, pulled off a mask and attacked them.

Upon entering the contest, Joey Ryan began scouring himself with baby oil. He was joined by SeXXXy Eddy of IWS fame, sporting a towel and rubbing himself down, as well. When proudly effeminate wrestler Effy attempted to join them, he was ordered away by Eddy, who soon had his towel ripped off by Ryan. Eddy was nude now, covering his balls while Effy dropkicked him, ass-first into Ryan's face. Climbing the ropes while still cupping his testicles, Eddy performed a moonsault onto Effy.

Somehow, Swoggle managed to grab Ryan's bionic dick and use the momentum to toss him over the ropes.

Kikutaro, a Japanese wrestler whose mask connoted images of a children's cartoon character rather than a fearsome gladiator, then joined the fray, sticking his fingers in various asses and passing out from the fumes.

The 33rd wrestler to enter the bout was Dustin Thomas, a performer with literally no legs. Nonetheless, he was able to deliver a 619 and swanton bomb to Egotistico Fantastico, then dive outside the ring onto a collection of adversaries.

There were some guest appearances from folks who hadn't been around in a while: the nWo's version of Sting, who last performed as the character in WCW in 1999; Mantuar, a half-man, half-beast persona who mooed at his foes in the WWF in the mid-90s; and 56-year-old Tracy Smothers, who still wore the Confederate flag singlet that made him a babyface in the American South some 30 years earlier.

The match ended indecisively. Led by Session Moth Martina, a group of women stormed the ring, beating up a clown thrown between the ropes, pummeling referees, hitting GCW wrestler Jimmy Lloyd with light tubes and stripping down Joey Janela to his underwear.

It had been a full day of *WrestleMania* weekend events for just about everybody in attendance. But when I caught an Uber with my friend Patrick Jean-Joseph at a gas station down the block, at 3:45 a.m., I was so wired that I could have sat through more.

27
CHAPTER

Of all the promotions I watched while researching this book, I kept circling back to GCW. Just when they did something to shock or amuse me, I'd discover that they were planning another event to surpass the last one. So I'd keep finding excuses to hang out with these guys. I needed another Joey Janela interview. I wanted to ask Shlak something we didn't go over the last time. The company was planning a Japanese tour, and I could help write the program. I was completely marking out for this group, and I wasn't alone.

"One thing we found, because we're heavily a data-driven company, was that some people are fans of very specific types of wrestling," said FITE TV COO Mike Weber, contradicting the observers who claimed that the variety of shows during *WrestleMania* week proved that followers are open to different forms of the mat wars. "GCW fans could care less about Ring of Honor or New Japan or IMPACT. They want Joey Janela or somebody like him, and will only buy that product."

Promoter Brett Lauderdale told me that one of the devices he used to build a loyal base was presenting theme shows, among them *Joey Janela's Spring Break, Joey Janela's Lost in New York, L.A. Confidential* and *Blood*

Sport, a collection of battles in a space without ropes, in which participants could only win via submission or knockout.

GCW grew out of Jersey Championship Wrestling. As the name faded in 2015, Lauderdale and partner Danny Demanto took over. They were fortunate to have Joey Janela as an eager member of the roster. "He'd been around for a few years," Lauderdale said. "All he needed was someone to believe in him and a platform. He needed us and we needed him and *bam*."

A lifetime fan with a decidedly Dirty Jersey taste, Lauderdale was hired as a writer for WWE.com in 2005, shortly after graduating college. But his experience at the company's Stamford, Connecticut, headquarters was not a pleasant one for either party. "I was really young and immature. I thought I knew everything about wrestling. And then, there'd be a dude two seats down from me who didn't care about wrestling, and I'd be like, 'What the fuck is he doing here?' And I'd complain, 'Why does he get to do this? I'm the one who should be doing it.' I'm sure I eventually annoyed enough people where it wasn't worth it to have me around."

Returning to the Garden State, he offered his services to his favorite indie, CZW, writing for its website, cranking out press releases and occasionally refereeing. But for all its allure, a smaller wrestling operation also had flaws, just different ones than WWE. When he had his own promotion, he told himself, things were going to be different.

"You hear so much in wrestling about the unwritten rules. 'You can't do that.' Why not? Who's making these rules? Why do we have to follow them? When you come to one of our shows, the ring and the chairs are set up differently. We don't have guardrails because I want the people to be up on the ring, as close as they can. People say, 'You can't do dives over there because there are people over there.' I say, 'Do the dives. People love it if a dive comes right by their face. And they're going to get out of the way.' There's just a feeling of unpredictability."

Likewise, not many promoters were willing to build a show around Nick Gage, a death match legend in CZW, as well as a convicted bank robber. Shortly after he was paroled in 2015, GCW branded a card the *Nick Gage Invitational*, a death match competition not unlike CZW's annual Tournament of Death. "Nick had been away for four years and three months," Lauderdale said, "and his popularity grew while he was in prison. We were so underground then, nobody knew who we were. But the people who came that day have described it as a life-changing experience."

The event was booked in a parking lot outside an American Legion hall in Warren, New Jersey. Some 450 fans turned up. Nick Gage, on the other hand, did not.

He'd been picked up on a parole violation the day before.

Remarkably, the real-life circumstances gave the event an air of validity. The wrestlers who did show up — Janela, Joe Gacy, Matt Tremont, MASADA, Danny Havoc, and Kyle the Beast (later simply known by the acronym KTB), among others — practically sacrificed their lives to exceed fan expectations. For the next 18 months that Gage was incarcerated, there was a buzz around his name.

The fans knew that when he finally emerged from the big house, he was coming straight to GCW.

Gage was also contemplating his return. "I was getting letters from fans," he remembered. "'Keep your head up.' And it made a difference."

Alone in his cell, he thought about how the death match was often dismissed as a gory gimmick and the things he could do to take it to a new plateau. "It helped me get through my time," he said. "I'd be working out, thinking about what I was coming home to and getting a crew of guys together who could get in the ring and make this work."

He knew that the time spent behind bars would only serve that purpose. "I'm not proud of my past, but everybody knows what I did, so why hide it? It fits my character. When I'm in a death match, the people know I'm legit."

Prior to a death match with Gage in Atlantic City, his opponent, Shlak, a full-time tattoo artist with an inked up face and gap-toothed scowl, was methodically going over supplies with a member of the ring crew: "Two panes of glass, a door, tubes around the perimeter of the ring, barbed wire. Make it real and messy. Remember it's 'Prison Rules.'"

To capitalize on Gage's past issues, GCW had added the stipulation to the contest. And, as Shlak was eager to point out, he was no stranger to the penal system himself. "Young idiot stuff. Assault and drug charges. That's a shoot, and it adds an extra level." In the weeks leading up to the confrontation, he made it a point to pepper jail lingo throughout his promos. "Not everyone got it, but they knew it was real. What you don't understand, you fear."

In anticipation of the brutal encounter, he'd arranged to take the next day off from the tattoo shop. "I'll be in rough shape."

Even referee John Gray was open to the possibility of taking a beating. During a 2016 bout, Gray, who'd driven 16 hours to the Atlantic City show from his home in Alabama, was blasted in the head with a light tube. "I got my stitches, went back out and finished the event."

More frightening than any injury was the concern that an oblivious bureaucracy would do something to diminish everyone's fun. Before one show, Lauderdale was questioned by a health inspector about the light tubes that would be used in the ring. At the next show, he spotted her in the audience, wearing a pair of rubber gloves. "And guess what happened?" he asked. "A light tube broke and glass flew into the crowd. I thought, 'She's definitely shutting us down.' But she kind of shrugged and said, 'Well, these people knew what they were in for.'"

As I continued my conversation with Shlak, I noticed that he was taping a stack of thick magazines to his lower abdomen before slipping on a shirt. "It's body armor," he pointed out. "Nick is going to shank me in the back. Remember, it's a prison match. That's the story we're trying to tell. You can bleed all over the place. You're going to have some blood marks who'll be into it. But it's better to have less blood and tell a better story."

Noted Gage, "In GCW, we have death match guys who can actually work. There's a storytelling to the blood and guts. There are still guys who will go out there and smash each other with weapons. But you need to wrestle, too, and have a reason for everything you're doing."

Outside the dressing room, a fan named Steven Spedden from Salisbury, Maryland, pulled a plastic container of homemade cookies from a bag, handing out the pastries to the ring crew and asking them to bring some backstage to the boys. A CZW fan since 2001 and GCW follower from the beginning, he made it a habit of hauling treats to every show that he attended. He felt particularly motivated, given the degree of punishment that he knew guys like Shlak and Nick Gage would endure that night.

"If you're going to pay the money to see wrestling," he said, "you want some of it to be real. I don't consider myself a blood mark, but you can't deny that the thumbtacks and the barbed wire give it that little bit extra." He paused and smiled. "It's the sugar on the cookie."

During another GCW show in L.A., I saw Shlak and Markus Crane destroy each other in a frenzied death match that, at one point, spilled into the street. Then, while Crane went backstage to pick out the glass from his skin, a bloody, wide-eyed Shlak walked over to the gimmick table, posing for selfies and signing autographs.

Shlak explained to me that his background had been in the punk rock world, specifically "shithole, scum rock." Among his heroes was the late punk rocker GG Allin, who would self-mutilate and defecate onstage, attack spectators and always hold the promise that, one day, he might commit suicide during a live performance.

Instead, he simply died of a heroin overdose.

As a fan of both ECW and CZW, Shlak began "weaving the hard-core stuff into my punk shows. Not shitting all over the place like GG Allin, but I'd cut myself up and use barbed wire baseball bats and things like that."

His band's name: Eat the Turnbuckle.

Ultimately, he began training at CZW. Already accustomed to taking a pounding in his act, he learned that "the bumping hurts more than the cutting. The cutting doesn't prevent you from walking."

With an entrenched group of fans in the Philly punk world, it was easy to draw crowds to his early matches. Because of his antics, he tended to attract a pretty counterculture bunch. But if you were nice to Shlak, regardless of your background or political dogma, he was generally pretty nice to you.

Which led to a very uncomfortable situation.

Before Shlak entered the wrestling business, he was photographed with a group of white supremacists called the Atlantic City Skins, Sieg-Heiling on camera.

As the story blew up on the internet, Shlak responded online, pointing out that, despite all the ink on his body and the numerous bonehead decisions he'd made, never once did he opt to get a White Power tattoo. In fact, he added, when he took the time to think about it, he didn't really like Nazis. "Nor am I a homophobe or racist, and I don't subscribe to any ideology that narrows who I can associate with. All this from a stupid photo I took 15 years ago, mocking a random old guy next to me who looked like Hitler. I take full responsibility and own up to the foolish decision. I used to know some of these guys. That's what the music and tattoo shop scene was like in the area that I grew up in. It was a different time. I am a grown man and will not say sorry for knowing a person. Yet I will apologize to anyone that has been offended by my action. No malice was ever intended, just poor humor."

In total, Shlak told me, he lost two wrestling gigs over the controversy. "But, come on, my girlfriend's Jewish. Every wrestler who's worked with me knows who I am."

And after talking to a number of those wrestlers and watching Shlak interact with hundreds of fans, I reached the conclusion that he was telling the truth. The guy was warped, had developed some unusual interests and very likely had a fetish for the sight of his own blood. But you know what? He wasn't a Nazi.

Nor was he the most twisted guy in GCW. That honor, I'm pretty certain, probably went to Joey Janela.

Janela was never formally trained. But in 2006, when he was 15, he found himself backyard wrestling with an older guy called Dirtbag Dan. Dan was tied to a small-time indie and, soon, Janela was "setting up the ring and chairs and acting like the toughest 15-year-old you've ever seen."

The operation was called National Wrestling Superstars and, even then, Janela considered it "the carniest promotion in Jersey. Anyone who could sell 10 tickets could be on the show. Every show, every week, the heel would get on the mic at intermission and beat up on the local favorite. And then, the big name, who'd just gotten released from WWE, would come out and destroy him."

National Wrestling Superstars special attractions included a teacher's battle royal at a local high school, as well as cop and firefighter battle royals. "The mayor would manage the babyface in the main event, and the heel manager would take a bump for him."

Joey needed to get in on the action. So he told the promoter a lie about training at some school in an unspecified area of Pennsylvania. "I guess I was a professional wrestler. My dreams came true. I learned on the fly."

What he lacked in knowledge, he compensated for in daring, flipping off of the bleachers onto his opponent or delivering a moonsault from the basketball hoop. While delivering pizzas, working for a car service and selling solar panels door to door, he kept showing up at the arena and doing crazy stuff. For a Garfield, New Jersey–based company called Pro Wrestling Syndicate (PWS), he wrestled as Star Man, a video game character in full body suit. In one encounter, he leaped off a 35-foot-high beam onto six competitors. "They caught me, which doesn't always happen."

The altercation went viral.

A month later, he purchased a ticket and wore his Star Man gimmick to *Monday Night Raw*. When a couple of fans recognized him and began chanting his name, he played to the crowd and was escorted out of the building.

"I had a really bad attitude," he said. "At the time, I was like 20 years old. I thought I was a bigger name than I was. I paid no attention to etiquette. A lot of times, I was one of the few wrestlers who could say he got beaten up before he even left the dressing room."

Eventually, the association with PWS fell apart. "I couldn't use the Star Man gimmick because they put someone else in the costume. I kind of wanted to be myself anyway. Joey Janela."

Looking for a change of scenery, he began driving to the Carolinas and working for free. "I was building my work ethic and keeping my mouth shut and, after a while, some of the veterans began looking out for me."

On weeknights, back in Jersey, he trained at CZW's facility, run by Drew Gulak. With a new perspective, Janela managed to ingratiate himself with the future WWE Cruiserweight champion and get bookings on the CZW cards. "I already had fans, so when I got out there, there were people in the crowd who liked me. I was one of the few guys in CZW not getting heckled out of the building."

Lio Rush was also a recent arrival to CZW, and, in 2015, he and Janela began to talk shit about each other on Twitter, triggering a long feud that the Bad Boy compared to the rivalry between RVD and Jerry Lynn in ECW. The culmination was a ladder match in which Janela hung on a beam 25 feet in the air, then elbow dropped Rush across two ladders. "Lio and I had complete control over our whole deal. He was just phenomenal. We were doing crazy shit, and our matches were being live streamed."

Like most indie fans from south Jersey, Janela was enamored with CZW founder John Zandig, who was not beyond bringing a weed wacker to a death match and once raised a little heat by getting hung from meat hooks. Zandig had retired in 2009, citing a combination of injuries and financial stress, and sold his share of the promotion to DJ Hyde. But he came back the next year — "Just when I thought I was out, they pull me back in." — retiring again in 2012.

In early 2016, Janela was taunting Zandig online, hoping he could provoke him into another return. In February, Lauderdale visited Zandig at home, and the pair came up with the idea for a GCW event labeled *Zandig's Tournament of Survival*. One match would take place in a "log cabin" made of light tubes. Another would involve panes of glass and a bed of nails, and another clash encouraged fan participation: the wrestlers agreed to use whatever weapons the spectators brought to the arena.

Despite all the projected blood spilling, though, it was universally agreed that nothing would be as sick as the Janela-Zandig match.

Up until this point, Janela had never incorporated barbed wire or glass into his confrontations. But he was fixated with a spot that Zandig had once executed with "Sick" Nick Mondo off a roof through a collection of perilous debris. As soon as Janela arrived at Game Changer World, GCW's home arena in Howell, New Jersey, Zandig led him outside the building to a pickup truck. As a full-time construction foreman, Zandig had built an elaborate menagerie of wood panels, barbed wire, light tubes and glass in the truck's bed. Peering upwards, Zandig explained how they were going to tumble off the roof — a much higher roof than Mondo had gone off, Janela noted — but the suspension in the truck would break their fall.

"I was scared," Janela said, "but I wasn't going to back out."

The bout itself was a typical enough death match brawl, until the crowd spilled into the parking lot, while Zandig and Janela fought their way up to the roof. On the ground, the weapons in the back of the truck were set on fire. Around that time, both men realized that the truck was parked a little too close to the building. So, as Zandig lifted Janela, the veteran decided to jump into the bed, feet-first, guiding his opponent to the proper spot.

"He was standing on the gutter, right at the edge of the roof, and it almost collapsed," Janela said. "Then we were going through the air."

Janela closed his eyes. The two hit their mark, crashing through a piece of plywood, but the stunt was anything but safe. "Zandig broke his back in three places and now walks with a cane," Janela said. "He was saying, 'My back is broken. My back is broken.' But I thought he was exaggerating. I looked at my thumb and it was half-way sliced off. I cut it on the barbed wire and nearly lost it because all the tendons and ligaments were severed.

"But we'd done the planned ending of the match. And, miraculously, we both walked away."

In the parking lot, attendants cut barbed wire out of Janela's long hair. Then, back in the dressing room, EMTs stitched and taped him. "I looked over at Zandig and said, 'That was crazy.' We hung out together for about two hours, had a few beers, watched the other matches and went to the hospital."

Footage of the altercation ended up on ESPN. While fans went wild on the internet, wrestling purists were aghast. People like Joey Janela, they exclaimed, had no place in an industry that had been graced by the likes of Karl Gotch, Danny Hodge and Lou Thesz. Conveniently, none of the critics seemed to remember the original Sheik stabbing opponents with a pencil, Abdullah the Butcher carving people with a fork and the barbed wire cage bomb death match between Atsushi Onita and Hayabusa.

The reality is that, in the course of nearly killing himself, Janela broke through to a place in the business where he might not have ever gotten to had he heeded the cautious admonitions of others.

"Them going off the roof of that building was probably irresponsible on everybody's part," Lauderdale said. "At the same time, nobody was forced. It was their idea. They wanted to do it. And I trusted in those two that no fans would get hurt, nobody was going to die. Roll the dice. What do you have to lose?"

28
CHAPTER

I n December 2016, GCW staged a Christmas-themed card entitled *Deck the Halls with Ultraviolence*. In the main event, KTB successfully defended his GCW World Championship against Matt Tremont. "It was not a memorable event in terms of a draw," remembered Brett Lauderdale. "But we made a real profit. It was our 'get over the hump' show."

Two months later, Tremont captured the title in a match highlighted by the two tumbling through a hole in the ring. It was an angle fans had seen before, but as Lauderdale watched the audience go nuts, he had a revelation. Why shouldn't GCW get in on the action during *WrestleMania* week? The next day, he and his associates began planning a card in Orlando in the days leading up to *WrestleMania 33*.

"Most Mania week shows are planned 10 months in advance," he explained. "These days, I find myself looking for inside tips on where *WrestleMania* is going to be a year and a half from now, so I can book a building before anyone else can get to it." Nonetheless, the first *Joey Janela's Spring Break* came together in seven weeks.

"It was such a reach for us. The company was just in its infant stages. So how could we do a show during *WrestleMania* week, and think that anybody was going to care? We needed a hook. And that hook was Joey Janela."

Despite his rising star status on the indies, Janela was dismissed as too unknown or small-time to carry an important event on his back. Displaying his old arrogance, Janela peppered Lauderdale with ideas that he knew few other promoters were willing to try — both for his own match and the others on the card.

"There were a lot of veterans out there who a lot of people thought nobody cared about," Lauderdale said. "Marty Jannetty had been wasting away on the indies for years. But people were still into him. He just hadn't been presented in a way that was interesting. We matched him up with Joey."

In one vignette leading up to the show, Janela was shown having a dream about Jannetty. "Not the guy who'd been running around on the New Jersey indies," Lauderdale pointed out, "but the star who'd teamed with Shawn Michaels in the WWF in the '80s. It went up on YouTube. It went up on Facebook, and it spread."

Dan "The Beast" Severn was a former NWA World Heavyweight champion and UFC Hall of Famer, but, like Jannetty, he'd been on the indies a long time. GCW announced that, at *Spring Break,* he'd be battling Matt Riddle, a UFC fighter from 2008 to 2014, who'd appeared on Spike TV's *The Ultimate Fighter 7* and racked up a four-fight UFC win streak before testing positive for marijuana.

"Now it wasn't just a match with Dan Severn, indie guy," Lauderdale said. "It was a match between two serious MMA fighters. You have to look at opportunities that other people don't. 'Nobody cares about Dan Severn. Nobody cares about Marty Jannetty.' Yes, they do, if you *make* them care."

Ray Lloyd had had a WCW run as Glacier, a character based on *Sub-Zero* in *Mortal Kombat* two decades earlier. Although he later worked backstage for TNA and made some CHIKARA appearances, no one had seen him in the ring for about 10 years.

Lauderdale booked him in the Clusterfuck battle royal. The crowd was so rapturous that Glacier's indie prospects were suddenly revitalized. Ring of Honor used him in a similar capacity that summer.

Prior to the event, Lauderdale had downplayed the prospects of turning a profit. If he only sold 200 tickets, GCW would take a $2,000 loss, he estimated, but would hopefully walk away with some added attention. "If we sold 300 tickets, I figured we might break even. If we sold more, that would be awesome. There ended up being 750 people there."

The Severn-Riddle match felt like a shoot. There were single leg takedowns, a side takeover, a knee bar and a dragon sleeper among other MMA moves. But in the end, Severn passed the torch, succumbing to his opponent's rear chinlock variation, the Bromission, while both competitors were on the mat. In spectators' eyes, Riddle assumed the role that Severn had once played, an authentic hooker who could humiliate anybody, regardless of sports background, in an actual fight.

The Joey Janela–Marty Jannetty clash had an entirely different energy. The pair brawled through the crowd until Janela superkicked the referee, bringing out a brigade of officials who tried to restore order. At one stage, iconic CHIKARA ref Bryce Remsburg, who was doing commentary, stood up like he was going to enter the ring. Instead, the legendary Earl Hebner, of NWA and WWE fame, raced to the squared circle, as the building combusted.

Hebner took control, shoving Janela down. But when Janela shoved him back, yet *another* arbiter turned up. It was Virgil, the former valet of "Million Dollar Man" Ted DiBiase, apparently attempting to extend his time in the wrestling business as a referee. For years, Virgil had set up shop at flea markets, autograph shows, even the Coney Island boardwalk in Brooklyn, hoping to sell his eight-by-tens. There was even a website, "Lonely Virgil," showing the grappler sitting alone at a table, pining for attention. Now, he finally had it. The arena exploded, with the audience chanting his name.

Similarly, Jannetty popped the crowd by doing his old move, the Rocker Dropper, to Janela on a chair. It was a nostalgic moment, but it didn't make sense for Janela to do the job. Ultimately, the Bad Boy won the contest with a superkick.

Afterwards, Jannetty seemed to contemplate hitting Joey with a chair, then decided against it. Both combatants got on the microphone and put each other, as well as GCW, over. At this stage, though, the fans didn't need to be told that they were watching a very cool promotion.

For the rest of the weekend, those who hadn't attended the card were badgered by those who were there, as they gloated about witnessing the hottest thing to happen in wrestling that week, if not in years.

When Nick Gage was finally released from prison in 2017, GCW knew exactly how to exploit the development. At the company's second *Tournament of Survival*, fans were stunned by Gage's surprise appearance. Sending everyone home happy, Gage defeated GCW World champion Matt Tremont in the final to claim the strap.

But now, the company had to keep pushing limits to maintain its credibility, forcing Lauderdale to constantly come up with different sources of wonder. As followers were still tingling from Gage's title win, the promoter managed to convince the man Lauderdale considered the world's best death match wrestler, Masashi Takeda, to appear on a GCW show.

That summer, the company worked with Mexico's Desastre Total Ultraviolento (DTU) — Total Ultraviolent Disaster — league, selling out the famed Arena Aficion in Pachuca de Soto, the capital of Hidalgo state.

In Milwaukee, GCW structured a card around Danny Havoc, a veteran of CZW, CHIKARA and others who'd been known for combining his technical knowledge with hardcore. "Danny was a Midwestern farm boy who'd done backyard wrestling in his family's barn," Lauderdale said. "He was retiring and this was his final hurrah in this part of the country. We were in uncharted territory, and we packed the building."

Elsewhere, Gage entered into a series of riotous matches with Teddy Hart. "When we first met Teddy, he was living in Florida and was the guy working at the strip club who made sure the strippers got to their cars," Lauderdale said. "People told me, 'Teddy Hart's done,' but I'd heard that before about other people and didn't believe it. I mean, what was the worst thing that could happen?"

When Hart arrived at GCW, he didn't even have his ring gear. He swapped out his sweat pants for some trunks, then borrowed elbow pads and ring boots. "From the very first match," Lauderdale said, "he delivered."

Since GCW's start, wrestlers had bounced back and forth between the promotion and CZW. The arrangement made sense, given that both groups were located in New Jersey, put out a similar product and often shared fans. Plus, an argument could be made that much of what Lauderdale knew about professional wrestling came from his time working at CZW. But, according to the promoter, CZW had issued an edict barring its talent from wrestling in GCW. Although the rule was frequently ignored, he maintained, CZW found other ways to hurt its Garden State adversary, including contacting immigration officials and reminding them to check the documents of GCW performers from outside the country.

"There was a lot of bad blood," Lauderdale said. "So Giancarlo Dittamo, who was a producer for both promotions, pitched a CZW versus GCW feud."

Dittamo's idea involved a GCW invasion at CZW's *Cage of Death 19* card in December 2017. "I'd always had a line of communication with [CZW owner] DJ Hyde," Lauderdale maintained. "Even if it was me sending him a text saying, 'You're an idiot.'"

But a day before the show, Lauderdale said that he was uncertain about whether the angle would take place. That night, he saw Hyde at another event and asked if they were going to be working together. Lauderdale said that Hyde laughed, replied "no" and walked away.

As a result, Lauderdale claimed that he stayed away from the Rastelli Complex in Sewell, New Jersey, while *Cage of Death 19* was taking place. The show had already started when Dittamo texted.

"Let's do this," he allegedly wrote.

Nick Gage and Lauderdale drove to Sewell and waited in the parking lot until Dittamo sent another message: "Now."

Running into the arena, Gage and Lauderdale hopped the guardrail, throwing fans fliers for GCW's show the next week, and slipped into the cage where a number of performers were situated. As Lauderdale handed *them* fliers, more wrestlers entered the ring. The interloping promoter expected to be knocked out. But there was too much focus on Gage, who grabbed the microphone, and informed the audience, "This is a straight fuckin' shoot."

Matt Tremont and Gage exchanged shoves — a perfectly logical interaction, since they were fighting each other at the upcoming GCW event — while Joey Janela raised his arms in despair and placed his hands on his head. Security rushed Lauderdale out of the ring. Gage hung out for a while, lifting the fabric of his GCW shirt and flaunting it to the crowd. Leaving the cage, he offered to fight anybody in the dressing room. Then he coolly climbed back over the guardrail.

The crowd patted him on the back and serenaded him with chants of "Nick Fuckin' Gage."

By the time police showed up, Gage and Lauderdale were gone.

"I was waiting for DJ to call me and say, 'What do we do now?'" Lauderdale said. "But he never called — to his detriment. The whole thing added to our outlaw image. It was the biggest shot in the arm we could have gotten, and it wasn't even our show."

As GCW was planning its second *Spring Break* event, scheduled for the week of *WrestleMania 34* in New Orleans in 2018, Joey Janela was on a card in Indiana, sharing a dressing room with Pierre Carl Ouellet, who'd been Pierre of the Quebecers and pirate Jean-Pierre LaFitte in the WWF. But Ouellet was a very different performer than he'd been in the past. Although approximately 50 years old, he now billed himself as PCO. He was jacked and intense, executing stunning aerial moves between the ropes.

Janela contacted Lauderdale. "PCO killed it. Let's put him on *Spring Break*."

PCO made the 2,600-mile drive from his home in Montreal. It would be well worth it. When *Joey Janela's Spring Break 2* ended, fans were raving about PCO the way they had Matt Riddle and Marty Jannetty the year before. The eccentric French Canadian was a cult hero, and the performance would lead to not only a contract with Ring of Honor but a stretch as the company's champion.

This was a starkly different performer from the guy who, as a member of the Quebecers, had done a Canadian Mountie gimmick alongside Jacques Rougeau. It was a disappointing time. Both Quebecers were accustomed to wrestling a hard, or "stiff," style, and expected to have physical matches. Instead, they were depicted as cartoonish. Even their WWF Tag Team Championship win over the tough Steiner Brothers bordered on the ridiculous. As a special stipulation, the match took place under "Quebec Province Rules," allowing the titles to switch via disqualification. That was achieved when Jacques tricked Scott Steiner into swinging a hockey stick at him. "Our run with the belts could've meant a lot more if we were booked a little stronger," PCO told the *Sporting News.*

Ouellet left the industry in 2011, feeling largely unsatisfied.

"I never retired," he told me. "I took a sabbatical. I wanted to touch the people in a way that reminded them of a good memory, a bad memory, a movie memory, a horror memory. I was thinking, 'Let life throw me something.' Call it fate or whatever you want to call it."

At a certain point, he ran into an old-school strongman known as Mike "The Destroyer" Roy. In his prime, Roy was a professional arm wrestler who'd also perform stunts like bending nails and bars and tearing decks of cards. Although he'd been about 300 pounds, he changed his diet and exercise regimen to drop to 130. "I thought he was incredible and asked him to be my trainer," PCO said.

One night, as the coach watched PCO do abdominal exercises with his arms in straps, Roy noted that his charge reminded him of Frankenstein. And so a gimmick was born. A series of vignettes were created based on the trainer, now a shadowy figure called D. Destro, discovering the aging wrestler's carcass in a cemetery. Spewing black gunk from his mouth, Destro, described by PCO as his "special entity," shocked the former Quebecer to life with a car battery.

"When fans are in trouble, when their car breaks down, they know they have the jumper cables," PCO explained. "They relate to the electricity that comes out of it because of the revival, the boost, the energy."

In another video, Destro funneled blood into PCO after driving a nail through his nose.

"It's what I was looking for all my life," PCO said. "I really *did* come to life. It was a very real story."

Enrolling in gymnastics courses, PCO returned to the indies with a new routine, doing backflips and moonsaults more fluidly than before.

"There's a lot of pain I can endure," he told *Newsweek.* "I have a body that even my doctor can't explain. I'll have severe cuts or get concussed or whatever, and I'll be fine. It's just weird and the doctor says I'm not normal."

Determined to live his gimmick, he felt gratified when his young daughter remarked that her friends asked if her family lived in a castle.

Once again melding yesterdays and tomorrow, GCW matched up PCO with future WWE United Kingdom champion WALTER at *Joey Janela's Spring Break 2*. Utilizing every lesson he'd acquired from his coach, PCO embedded himself into the crowd's memory. At one point, he executed a moonsault that missed WALTER and took out the referee. Taking advantage of the circumstances, WALTER power-bombed PCO through a table. After another arbiter rushed to the ring, WALTER attempted to tie up PCO for a pin, but, incredibly, PCO kicked out.

Regenerated, PCO punished WALTER with a somersault senton outside the ring, then a top rope hurricanrana. WALTER replied with an overhead suplex. But because PCO was the man who couldn't die, his in-ring resurrection was completely believable.

After blasting his adversary with a rolling senton, PCO hit a springboard moonsault and ended the match with a senton bomb.

The fans were rhapsodic. As they left the arena, Lauderdale stood by the door, shaking hands and asking what they liked best about the show, making mental notes on the type of program they wanted to see next.

"All that stuff adds up," he said. "When I look at talent, I'm not just looking for guys who are popular. I'm looking for guys who are hungry and guys who have that same mindset when it comes to fans. I don't want guys who are calling fans 'marks.' That fan interaction is very important to me.

"I remember in, like 1996, I ordered something from ECW and they screwed it up. I had to keep dialing the phone number. But once I got a hold of them, they sent me two shirts and a tape to make up for it. I never forgot that."

L.A. Confidential was presented at the Hi Hat nightclub in Los Angeles two nights before WWE hosted the *2018 Survivor Series* at the Staples Center. Joey Ryan had been scheduled to wrestle Nick Gage but tore a pec less than a week earlier. Around the same time, Joey Janela received a text from actor David Arquette.

"You have anything?"

Noted Janela, "He almost booked his own death."

In 2000, David Arquette starred in the WCW movie, *Ready to Rumble*, and, as the company was struggling to remain relevant, was awarded the WCW World Heavyweight Championship. The move was largely condemned, but Arquette continued to find his way back to wrestling. When he heard about the vacancy on the GCW card, he volunteered to have a death match with Gage.

Just two weeks earlier, Arquette had had a conversation with ECW's "Innovator of Violence," Tommy Dreamer, and began thinking about a hardcore collision.

The day before *L.A. Confidential*, Arquette and Gage met at a restaurant. "He wanted to do balls to the wall," Gage said. "I let him know this wasn't a joke to me. This is what I do. I told him, 'I'm going to go hard on you, and you're going to get hurt. You're going to get cut.'"

The *Scream* star did not seem intimidated, and Gage was happy to give his opponent plenty of offense. At one point during the *L.A. Confidential* clash, Arquette delivered a diamond cutter to Gage on the broken glass. "The match was going great," Janela remembered. "The fans couldn't believe David Arquette was doing something like this."

Gage rubbed glass into Arquette's forehead. Then a sharp piece cut an artery on Arquette's neck and he started bleeding.

The actor briefly left the ring, but he quickly reentered and lunged at his foe. "He bugged out." Gage recounted. "He tried to turn it into a shoot. I looked at the cut and saw it wasn't squirting, so I just gave him a judo throw and pinned him. I could tell he was done."

To Janela, Gage was being charitable. "Nick Gage, a convicted felon who robbed banks without even covering his face, has literally died in a death match." He was referring to a 2010 encounter in which a blood-saturated Gage's heart briefly stopped while he was being air-lifted to a nearby hospital. "He could have really hurt David. But he didn't want to."

When the action ended, Arquette's friend, the late actor Luke Perry, whose son, Jungle Boy, was also on the show, rushed Arquette to the emergency room.

The next night, Arquette was seen at the *NXT TakeOver* card that preceded the *Survivor Series*, having a great time and sporting a Ric Flair t-shirt. But then, an infection developed, necessitating another visit to the hospital. "After a few days, he watched the match and realized he was at fault," Janela said. "He called Nick on the phone, and everything was okay."

The confrontation received international coverage, pleasing everyone involved. "It's cool," Gage said. "David's a good guy, and it gave us a little light. Some people don't like that stuff, but a lot of people love it. And now, more people knew about it, and were running to us."

Observed Janela, "A bad buzz or a good buzz is just buzz."

On social media, Arquette's sister, actress Patricia Arquette, begged her brother to refrain from any further death matches. He responded by explaining his motivations to fans: "Last week I was injured in a wrestling death match. I wanted to make sure to address the photos and videos that have surfaced from the event, as this is not the type of wrestling you watch on TV. I knew it was violent and potentially bloody, but I truly did not know the extent of what I was participating in. However, I take responsibility for putting myself in that situation. I also want to apologize to the professional wrestling world for any negative attention this might have brought forth. I am looking forward to getting back into the ring under much different circumstances."

Before I end this chapter, I want to mention one other event unique to GCW: Jimmy Lloyd's birthday party. In 2018, Lloyd, a former child actor who blew off commercials and made-for-TV movies for death matches, turned 20. To commemorate this landmark, 150 GCW fans gathered at a New Jersey warehouse, starting at 10 p.m. After a local stripper gave Jimmy, who billed himself as "A Different Boy," a public lap dance, the spectators were treated to a lucha match, pitting Ciclope versus Miedo Extremo; a classic three-way involving Teddy Hart, Jack Evans and Jody Fleisch; and a death match featuring Dan O'Hare and Shlak against Jeff Cannonball and Matt Tremont.

As the participants brawled at ringside, a fan held up a cell phone camera and asked a bloody Tremont if he had any birthday wishes for Lloyd.

"Fuck you, Jimmy!" Tremont yelled.

In Lloyd's match, a gory victory over Kit Osborne, fans substituted the usual "*This is awesome*" chant with "*Hap-py Birth-day.*"

This was followed by an appearance by ECW legend, the Sandman. Swigging beer, he paraded to the squared circle, with the crowd singing his theme song, "Enter Sandman," a capella, with one audience member on cowbell.

Playing heel, GCW co-owner Danny Demanto entered the ring and began taunting Jimmy Lloyd. "I got you the Sandman to show up to your shitty birthday party," Demanto sneered, before Sandman bashed him with a Singapore cane — the way the special attraction had battered Tommy Dreamer in ECW's glory days — and offered Lloyd a beer.

There was also a musical performance, a rap song written for Lloyd that included these lines:

> *Climb the ladder*
> *Do the drop*
> *Do the muthafuckin' drop*
> *Pin him for the win*
> *And then, we're going to the sandwich shop*

"It got rave reviews all over the internet," Lauderdale recalled. "People bought DVDs and watched MP4s of it. This kid's birthday, it was so crazy, people wanted us to grow it into an annual event."

Thus far, that's exactly what GCW has done. I know because I was one of the guests the next year in Atlantic City when Jimmy turned 21.

After defeating Eric Ryan and Markus Crane in a three-way death match, Lloyd continued the merriment by slamming and smashing Ryan in the barroom next door. As fans cheered, cuts opened on both of the combatant's heads. Since there was no official ring, and people were running to wherever the brawl happened to spill, I found myself at one stage alongside Teddy Hart, who was holding his cat, Mr. Velvet, upside down and petting his stomach, while Tony Deppen, Orange Cassidy and Jungle Boy lounged nearby.

When I turned around, I noticed referee Ryan Torok, still in his striped shirt, sprawled out on the floor. But before I could inquire about the situation, there was Joey Janela, beaming in street clothes and glasses, stepping through a huddle of spectators to throw a series of worked punches at Lloyd.

Standing there, I contemplated the fact that this kind of scene never lasts forever. By the end of the year, Janela, Jungle Boy and Cassidy would be signed by AEW. There would still be time for fun. But I wasn't sure if these off-the-clock altercations would spring up so extemporaneously.

Still, I was experiencing an indie wrestling moment that would linger in the minds of everyone there. Just as others reminisce about the time Vince McMahon took the Road Warriors' Doomsday Device on a dance floor or when Brock Lesnar practically slammed Mr. Perfect through the emergency door on a flight back from England, this would be a time that Jimmy Lloyd and Eric Ryan and Joey Janela would revisit in the distant future — a time when their bodies could still withstand a post-match pounding, and professional wrestling was less about the money and all about the love.

29
CHAPTER

espite all this excitement, other indies continued to exist in isolation. Whether or not an indie boom had ever occurred, these organizations would still be there, simply because some promoter in a remote corner of the world felt possessed to share his or her love of the sport of kings with the neighbors.

"It's tough to promote wrestling here," noted Brian Wescott, the timekeeper and historian for the Idaho Wrestle Club. "If we're lucky, maybe we get a WWE show once a year. We're not really close to anywhere. It's hard to get here. But when it comes to unemployment, we're number seven in the nation. And wrestling is the purging of the emotions, a catharsis. What we're doing is a public service."

According to Wescott, an Idaho scene sprung up in 2015 after California transplant Anthony Garibai, aka The Lost Soul, decided to purchase a ring and train the talent he needed to start his federation. When the annual Harvest Festival was held in Middleton, the Idaho Wrestle Club had a total of three wrestlers. If everyone doubled up on their tasks, it was enough to stage an event.

Over time, the roster expanded to 32 performers and acquired a television slot, enabling potential fans to familiarize themselves with names like The Sun God Tanatiuh, Adriel Noctis, Kiki "The Gem" Starling, Theodoric Lionheart and "Puppetmaster" Brad Zane. Almost all of the wrestlers were Idaho natives, although Wescott knew of at least one wrestler who drove in from Oregon. A typical show stretched about 90 minutes and consisted of four to seven matches.

Garibai's Lost Soul character was inspired by a time in his life when he was homeless. "I did feel lost," he told the *Idaho Press-Tribune*. "I was obviously in a dark place. But even though I was in a dark place, I still had faith. The Lost Soul is a connection to everybody because everybody has been lost once in their lives, and needed to find themselves."

His early years in pro wrestling were spent working for some 20 small promotions in bars, malls and parking lots, never earning more than $50 a shot. It cost him $4,000 to buy Wrestle Club's ring, but it took him about a year before he was able to find a venue, organize the talent and host a show.

Most of the group's cards were fundraisers, pulling in about 40 fans. A New Year's Day show in front of the Idaho State Capitol Building in 2017 drew 100. When one of the wrestlers suffered heat stroke during a 2018 match at the Comic Con in Boise, he was quickly tended to by the ring announcer, a certified nursing assistant, and one of the heels who happened to be an EMT.

"The Idaho wrestling community is very close," said Wescott. "If you go to a baby shower, a wedding, a birthday party, the same people will be there. We're almost like a family. Our wrestlers might be a long way from WWE, but we all share something we couldn't if it wasn't for wrestling."

Away from the center of the indie universe, carny elements sometimes have a disproportionate influence over certain promotions. "Indie wrestling is still populated with promoters who think that $20 and a hot dog is enough for you," said Tom Green, who previously helped promote Indiana groups like Fight Sports Midwest and School of Roc. "These wrestlers are conditioned to believe that you should walk barefoot for 10 miles up a hill made of glass for the honor of stepping into a wrestling ring. And then, they'd be told that pro wrestling etiquette dictates that you don't talk about this stuff."

Other promoters have the best objectives but are doomed to fail, simply because they don't understand how easy it is to lose money in wrestling, Green continued. "There's a term I heard: 'tax-return wrestling.' These guys just got some money back from the IRS, and they're going to burn it all opening a wrestling promotion."

Marko Stunt was born in 1996 in the middle of the Monday Night Wars. In the years that followed, the only pro wrestling he was exposed to was the indies, and with that, the questionable business practices and attitudes that come from existing on the fringes.

At five-foot-two and 144 pounds, Stunt and his younger brother, Logan, were frequently mistaken for children even after both had become professional wrestlers. When I asked if they had some type of genetic condition, the man sometimes called "Mr. Fun Size" answered, "No, but my mom is also tiny, just four-foot-ten. I've been graced. That's the way I look at it. I'm unique in professional wrestling. You don't see people like me very often."

The son of a Baptist missionary from Olive Branch, Mississippi, Stunt was never an active WWE fan. After attending a number of indie shows, he began training in his teens. Despite the sometimes risqué content on the local indie cards, his father approved of Stunt's goals. "He grew up watching Memphis Wrestling — Jerry 'The King' Lawler, Bill Dundee — and would drive me to shows."

There was little about Stunt's coaching, in rural Mississippi, that resembled a WWE Performance Center or New Japan dojo. Indeed, once he'd appeared in AEW and had interactions with professionals in the business, Stunt was uncertain if the wrestling people he initially met were incompetent or brutal. "In one of my first matches, my partner told me, 'Stand up. I'm going to superkick you.' I said, 'Why?' and he busted me in the jaw. I don't think he broke it, though. I could still talk."

Logan Stunt's experience was equally as unsettling. "I was training for less than a week when they threw me in a ladder match. I wasn't ready to wrestle, and they said, 'You're going to wrestle.'"

He avoided injury when he was eliminated from the contest before he had a chance to mount the metal stairwell.

Meanwhile, Marko said that he developed a platonic friendship with his coach's girlfriend, sparking resentment from the older man. Before a six-man tag match, the trainer was scheduled to be in the opposite corner and asked one of Stunt's partners, Motley Cruz, for a favor. "Tag out to Marko," the coach apparently requested. "I want to get in the ring with him."

According to Stunt, Cruz didn't wish to see his friend get beaten up and refused.

Although he avoided a thrashing, Stunt also found himself marginalized by the local promotion. "That kind of killed it for me," Marko said. "I didn't get called again for five or six months."

Finally, a promoter in Tennessee, who'd seen Stunt work in Mississippi, had a spot on one of his shows and wanted the youngster to fill it. But Stunt was cautious. "After being away for so long, I was thinking, 'This might not work for me.' But just being in another promotion with a different group of wrestlers changed everything. The more I wrestled, the more I became a fan."

He never realized how far he'd go in such a short period. By the time he was 21 years old, he'd gained international attention, after appearing on the biggest indie card in North America since the demise of WCW.

All In signaled a new age in professional wrestling. And Marko Stunt was there from the very start.

30
CHAPTER

It was the Ring of Honor show that was held over *WrestleMania 33* weekend in 2017 that inspired the bet that led to the *All In* pay-per-view.

The Lakeland, Florida, card was loaded. Marty Scurll retained his Ring of Honor Television Championship over Adam Cole. Jay Lethal defeated Cody in the Rhodes family specialty, a Texas bullrope match. And, the day before they made a surprise return to WWE, Matt and Jeff Hardy dropped the Ring of Honor World Tag Team straps to the Young Bucks.

After drawing more than 3,500 fans, Cody was confident when Dave Meltzer opined that no North American company besides WWE could garner a house of 10,000 or more. Cody maintained that he needed three months of promotion to accomplish the feat. Ultimately, it took 15 months to organize *All In*.

"Hangman" Adam Page credited *Being the Elite* with pulling the crowd into the Sears Centre Arena. "It all sprouted from a YouTube series that these guys made on their cell phones every week," he said. "It wasn't something they were paid to do. It wasn't something they *had* to do. No one told them what they could or couldn't do. And if someone did, they had the power to ignore it. Wrestling outside the machine, we answered to the fans and not to anyone else. And that's a luxury we were afforded."

It was Tommy Dreamer who — embodying the link between the ECW era and the indie revolution — texted the NWA World Heavyweight champion at the time, Nick Aldis, and delivered the news that Cody was interested in challenging him for the title at *All In*. The two agreed to do a number of social media angles in which Aldis appeared to be disinterested. Then, at a Ring of Honor show in London, the pair faced off, setting the conditions for the match. "That was when I knew we were going to do something big," Aldis told the *Inside the Ropes* podcast, "because the reaction was so strong, like not only in the building, but online. Even though [fans] know I'm from England, they know I don't live there. So they thought to themselves, 'This guy flew all the way over to England just to walk out in a suit and confront him and accept the match.' That's the thing. It's the commitment. It's the effort. We went, 'Wow. We're a part of something.'"

Few expected tickets to sell out so quickly. "It was a perfect storm," said former Ring of Honor owner Cary Silkin. "The people were with them. I'm pretty close with the Bucks, and if they'd sold half the tickets the first day, then slowly sold more, they would have been happy."

Likewise, Marko Stunt had no expectations about appearing on the high-profile show. Stunt had only gained a national forum recently, during *SummerSlam* weekend in 2018, when Kyle the Beast, or KTB, had issued an open challenge during *Joey Janela's Lost in New York*. In the crowd, Stunt raised his hand. Seemingly incredulous, KTB dared the young man to step into the ring.

Recalled Janela, "Everyone thought Marko was a child."

"How old are you anyway?" KTB dared.

"You want to know how old I am? Old enough to fuck your mom."

KTB charged, but Stunt ducked out of the way several times. Then he hopped onto the turnbuckles and delivered a flying head scissors. When KTB tried to slam his agitator, Stunt flipped around in mid-air and hit a code breaker.

Although Stunt was eventually squashed, a new indie star was born.

And because of live streaming, the whole world knew about it. "The show hadn't ended when someone told me, 'Hey, man, Cody Rhodes is looking for your number,'" Stunt said. "I woke up the next day and looked at his text. He said, 'Send me your match graphics. I'm going to put it on my Instagram.' I reread it a couple of times. *Cody Rhodes is texting me?*

"What was even weirder was when I got to *All In*, Cody, the Bucks, Kenny Omega and Marty Scurll all knew who I was."

Excalibur's announcing experience had largely been confined to his home promotion, PWG. Then, Matt Jackson messaged him and asked if he was interested in calling *All In* with Don Callis and Ring of Honor's Ian Riccaboni. Excalibur readily agreed, even though he admitted to being somewhat in awe of Riccaboni.

"For as young as he was, he had more experience working big shows than I do. When I'm announcing for PWG, I'm producing myself. I don't have to worry about anyone in my ear or in the truck or relays or anything like that. It's just me talking into a microphone for three hours, whereas he's dealing with notes and a highlight video coming up in 15 seconds. And he's amazing at that."

Although the Bucks were enthusiastic about having Excalibur at the announcer's table, Cody appeared uncertain. "He's very traditional," Excalibur said, "didn't like the mask. We talked about a dress code. He always wears a suit, and I never wore a suit. I like wearing a t-shirt. So I asked, 'Do I have to wear a suit?' And he said, 'I prefer that you wear a suit, but you need to do you.' That's when I realized he'd probably listened to my work and was starting to come around."

Ultimately, Excalibur opted to wear the outfit he generally used when he announced at PWG: a t-shirt, jeans and a pair of Vans with a blazer.

Adding to the uniqueness of the event, podcaster Conrad Thompson organized Starcast, where fans could meet wrestlers — both *All In* participants, as well as old-timers — purchase merchandise, participate in Q&As and watch live podcasts. The convention, stretching from the Thursday preceding *All In* to Sunday, sold 11,000 tickets.

Since the show was taking place near Chicago, Pro Wrestling Tees turned a section of its warehouse into a showroom. By the time the weekend ended, 2,500 fans had visited. Owner Ryan Barkan would also participate in *Zero Hour*, the pre-show leading up to *All In*, firing merchandise at fans from a t-shirt cannon.

Ring of Honor provided the ring crew and production expertise, ensuring that the pay-per-view's satellite transmission went smoothly. "All the credit goes to the Young Bucks and Cody," Ring of Honor COO Joe Koff said. "We were the infrastructure for the show, but it was still *their* show." Between the card and broadcasts of Starcast events, FITE TV grossed more than a million dollars in internet pay-per-view sales.

Yet, the card was nearly thrown into disarray when Cody had an altercation with a stranger the night before.

He was walking his dog, Pharaoh, near the hotel when a person he never met went chest to chest with him and demanded that he put the Siberian Husky on a leash. Cody's first instinct was to fire off a punch. But he quickly realized that his reaction could put the show in jeopardy.

"I just shoved him as hard as I've ever shoved anyone in my life," he told interviewer Kenny McIntosh during an *Inside the Ropes* Q&A in Dublin. "And he went flying into the bush. And the guy runs into the lobby. I was in the lobby signing [autographs] for the fans while doing an interview with the police officer."

Although the "Prince of Pro Wrestling" was fined $50 for taking Pharaoh off his leash, Cody's antagonist decided not to press charges, saving the star a trip to the police station. "I still would have made it [to the show]," Cody said. "But it would have been a very different *All In*."

On September 1, 2018, in the opening match of *All In*, Frankie Kazarian and Scorpio Sky defeated Ring of Honor World Tag Team champions Mark and Jay Briscoe in an exciting non-title clash. To the wrestlers gathered around the television monitors backstage, the bout set the tone for the rest of the show. "There was a bit of nerves because it's a big production," Joey Ryan said on 'Stone Cold' Steve Austin's podcast. "There are guys working who have WWE experience, so they kind of know how to build a show, how to present a show, but you're worried about feeds, you're worried about times. So I think we were all really nervous when Frankie Kazarian and Scorpio Sky and the Briscoes went out because it was like, 'Okay, is this where it falls apart? Are they going to be blowing spots?' Because, obviously, WWE shows — there are go-throughs, there are people to help you with your match, so everything is polished before it goes out onstage.

"I think them hitting a homerun to lead it off just for morale and the spirit of the locker room was the key to it being a successful show."

Despite the novelty of this type of event, there was the underlying message that *All In* was tied to wrestling history. As Tessa Blanchard left the dressing room before defeating Dr. Britt Baker, Chelsea Green and Madison Rayne in a four-way match, her father, WWE Hall of Famer Tully Blanchard, and step-father, Terry "Magnum TA" Allen — in a wheelchair because of injuries sustained in the 1986 car accident that ended his in-ring career — both hugged her. Later, during Jay Lethal's successful Ring of Honor title defense against Flip Gordon, the champion attempted to channel the late Randy "Macho Man" Savage, twirling his finger and twitching the way the WWE great did. Adding to the richness was the presence of the Macho Man's brother, "The Genius" Lanny Poffo, in Lethal's corner. At one point, when Lethal was struggling, Poffo tapped him three times on the shoulder, transforming him into an avatar of the Macho Man. With the crowd cheering for Lethal as if he actually were Randy Savage, the titlist delivered his idol's signature elbow drop from the ropes three times.

Joey Janela knew the Bucks from their mutual appearances in PWG. When the Bad Boy first heard about *All In*, he playfully texted Matt Jackson, asking, "Where can I send my VHS tape and eight-by-ten picture?"

Jackson replied by telling Janela that the Bucks wanted him on the show.

Janela was matched up against "Hangman" Adam Page, who'd been depicted on *Being the Elite* beating Joey Ryan to death with a telephone. Since then, Page had apparently been racked by guilt, with his boots coming to life and taunting him about the murder on the webcast.

"Somehow, the *BTE* editing team were able to capture the visual images of actual nightmares I was having," Page joked to me.

Page and Janela had become friendly in the Carolinas, where the Hangman started wrestling as a teenager. Page was also familiar with his opponent's valet — and on-again, off-again girlfriend — Penelope

Ford and agreed to have her interfere in the match, executing gymnastic backflips, as well as a plancha off the top rope onto the floor. "Penelope and I had been doing spots like this all over the northeast," Janela said. "But for people who'd never seen it, they hadn't experienced a valet doing moves like this since Lita," who delivered flying moves on behalf of Esse Rios in the WWF in 2000.

Since Cracker Barrel was an *All In* sponsor, the combatants made sure to insert a giant barrel with the restaurant chain's logo into the hardcore encounter. That was before Ford handed Page a black trash bag containing the talking boots that had been harassing him on *BTE*. Although seemingly rattled, Page managed to dispatch Ford with a superkick, beat Janela with the phone that purportedly killed Ryan and win the match after climbing a ladder and executing a Rite of Passage — a belly-to-back piledriver.

What followed was the most unusual portion of the show, involving a routine that some hated but everybody talked about.

On a big screen, fans saw a seemingly dead Joey Ryan. Suddenly, beneath his trunks, his dick appeared to get hard. Ryan's eyes opened, as announcer Don Callis noted that the hunky performer had been resurrected. Marching to the ring, Ryan was met by a column of walking penises, a parody of the Undertaker's druids in WWE. Inside the squared circle, he meted out revenge on Page, grabbing Hangman's hand and bringing it to the throbbing pelvic area. As much of the crowd howled, a frightened Page was then dick flipped to the mat.

"When you put a card together for a whole show, [former WCW president] Eric Bischoff told me right before *All In*, 'Make it a buffet,'" Cody said to *Inside the Ropes*. "'Hey, here's the serious thing. Here's the emotional thing. Hey, here are some penis druids.' Make them laugh."

Although some claimed that the angle cheapened the event, Ryan countered that the fans were thoroughly entertained, particularly because the *BTE* storyline had been stretched over months. "I go to leave, and the crowd starts chanting, 'Rest in penis,'" he told Steve Austin's podcast. "It starts slow. 'Rest in penis.' By 30 seconds later, 10,000 people are chanting 'Rest in penis,' and I just stop in the ring and I just have goosebumps. And I'm like teary-eyed. Oh my god. Like, this stupid shtick that I'm doing — it was like the most surreal moment that I've had in my career."

By contrast, the most realistic portion of *All In* occurred when Cody challenged Nick Aldis for the NWA World Heavyweight Championship. "It related to Cody going after the belt that Dusty wore," said David Marquez, owner of NWA-affiliated Championship Wrestling from Hollywood and an announcer on *NWA Power*. "Everyone, deep down inside, loves that belt."

Now, the participants hoped to restore the title's former glory.

Following a 2012 lawsuit, Houston-based attorney and promoter R. Bruce Tharpe reached a settlement for ownership of the NWA name and trademarks, sometimes appearing as a heel manager on shows. By and large, the championship was defended out of the public eye, with Tim Storm winning the belt from Jax Dane in 2016 at a small event in Sherman, Texas, that wasn't even live-streamed.

The next year, Smashing Pumpkins lead singer Billy Corgan, who'd briefly served as TNA's president, bought the NWA, vowing to restore it to its former glory.

Shortly after leaving TNA, Corgan, along with Dave Lagana, a writer, producer and director who'd worked at TNA and WWE, had visited Marquez at a Championship Wrestling from Hollywood show. "We were all sitting in a conference room, and Billy was talking about starting a new company," said Marquez, whose grandparents operated an Olympic Auditorium concession stand where attendees could purchase lettuce, tomatoes and cabbage to throw at the heels. "I said, 'Don't start a new acronym. There's already an NWA.'"

Corgan argued that the NWA no longer seemed to have value. "I don't want to say that he had an ECW mentality, that Shane Douglas killed it by throwing down the belt, but it felt like that," Marquez said. "Lagana was the one saying, 'Why don't we do this?'"

"Billy has a really good sense of nostalgia. So I told him, 'The NWA World Heavyweight Championship is like Donald Trump. To his supporters, he can never do wrong.' I've traveled around the world with the NWA. People flock to it."

Marquez credited Lagana with advocating for Nick Aldis to win the Ten Pounds of Gold. The hulking Brit had the rugged look, star quality, a background as a TNA titlist and followers in the UK, North America and Japan. Once he won the gold on CZW's *Cage of Death* show in

December 2017, the organization began booking Aldis on indie cards that were already drawing attention.

"The Aldis Crusade" was a series of international title defenses held over the course of 60 days. "What's more retro cool than the traveling champion routine?" Aldis told *Inside the Ropes*. "It totally works with all these great independents."

Recounted Marquez, "Lagana calls me one day. He asks, 'What do you think of Cody Rhodes becoming World champion?' This was three months before *All In*. Nick was into it. He knew he was going to be winning the belt back at the NWA 70th anniversary show in Nashville. And Cody was into it because the NWA was so special to him. We all understood the lineage."

As an extra touch, it was decided that Bill Apter, the writer and photographer who'd covered some of the greatest matches of every major NWA kingpin since Dory Funk Jr., should be at ringside with his camera. "He was the conduit to wrestling for millions of us," Marquez pointed out.

To enhance the big fight feel, each wrestler had a number of notables in his corner. Jeff Jarrett, Shawn Daivari and Tim Storm were among those seconding Aldis, while Cody's cortege included his wife, Brandi, Tommy Dreamer and Diamond Dallas Page. "Cody and I would have a lot of these moments where we were always on the same page," Aldis told *Inside the Ropes*. "Leading up to it, we would text each other with certain ideas. Cody was the one who texted me about entourages because I had thought about it, and then just didn't give it any more thought. And I was like, 'I'm glad you said that.'"

As he would in AEW, Cody also included Earl Hebner, who refereed many of Dusty's matches, as the third man in the ring. "He had to do pre-match instructions," Cody told Kenny McIntosh in Dublin. "He came into the locker room and told me what he was going to say. He was very proud. And I said, 'Perfect. You know what you're doing. You're the most senior referee in the industry. Say whatever. You're the boss.' It seemed like it was all good."

But when Hebner was standing between the two headliners, his nerves appeared to overtake him. As he opened his mouth to deliver instructions, he paused. "It is only a millisecond," Cody said, "but you can see the look on my face of, 'I put this show together. It's about to fuckin' go downhill right here.'"

The match was generally well-paced, conjuring up memories of the classic NWA title clashes from the 1970s and '80s. Then, as now, there were moments when outside forces appeared to shift the tide. At one point, Daivari attempted to interfere for Aldis, only to be victimized by Diamond Dallas Page's Diamond Cutter. When Brandi tried to use her body to shield her husband, she was hit with Aldis' elbow drop.

Eventually, Cody was busted open, the blood soaking his blond hair the way it did Dusty's and Ric Flair's back in the day. Noted Jeff Jarrett, "The purpose of blood has always been, by design, to add drama and emotion to a wrestling match. And done correctly, done at the right time, it always does."

In the end, Cody won the Ten Pounds of Gold after Aldis tried a sunset flip and the challenger blocked it and held on for the three-count. Fans leaped from their seats, shouting, some teary-eyed, all realizing that Cody and Dusty were the only father and son tandem to ever hold the NWA World Heavyweight Championship.

Even those who'd criticized The American Dream for selfish and repetitive booking decisions during the Jim Crockett Jr. era were filled with a sense of longing for the late Son of a Plumber.

As Excalibur called the action, he tried to separate the emotion inside the Sears Centre Arena from the reality of pro wrestling in 2018. "Not to disparage the title, but in a world where WWE was the be-all and end-all, how could a title that's defended on indie shows be seen as an important title? But they brought it back. They gave it meaning. Nick Aldis was already bringing prestige to the title by defending it all over the world. Then, by having it in a prominent place at *All In* and us treating it as an important institution, it added to it."

Since the championship match was positioned in the middle of the card, there was still a great deal of anticipation for the other confrontations. But because the performers were taking their time to deliver their best stuff, there was concern that the final contest — the Young Bucks and Kota Ibushi against Rey Mysterio, Rey Fenix and Bandido — would seem rushed. In fact, Nick and Mike Jackson did cut a number of their flashy moves. But that was so Bandido, the least-known participant in the bout, could shine.

Shortly after Kenny Omega pinned Pentagon Jr., the lights went out. When they switched back on, a man in a Pentagon Jr. suit delivered two codebreakers to The Cleaner.

It was Chris Jericho — whose presence in the building had been hidden from most of the other talent — making his first non-WWE appearance in the United States in close to 20 years.

"I guess Chris Jericho is kind of that wrestling outlaw," Cody told ESPN. "I think he's capable of making magic, and I think he wanted to make it with us."

As fans lingered in the parking lot and the wrestlers and announce team boarded a bus back to their hotel, Excalibur was unaware of the event's impact until he opened Twitter on his phone. "That was when I understood what we'd done," he said. "I remembered thanking Cody and the Bucks after the show, and they said, 'Oh, yeah. There's going to be another one. There has to be.' I didn't know about AEW at the time. But I realized this wasn't going to be a one-off."

31
CHAPTER

Something had changed in professional wrestling and, on a nearly daily basis, there were hints that a major announcement was on the horizon. In the cases of Finn Balor, AJ Styles and Adam Cole, WWE had pursued the biggest names on the indies and brought them into the machine. Would Kenny Omega, the Young Bucks and Cody follow the same path? "Contract season's here, right?" Matt Jackson told Fightful.com. "I think it's been 20 years since there've been wrestlers who have the leverage that we currently have. We know the position that we have. Next year will be the year that we get paid, no matter where we're wrestling."

Hoping to broaden their possibilities, the Young Bucks tried to procure ownership of the Bullet Club name from New Japan but were unsuccessful. There was also disenchantment over the fact that all new Bullet Club members, including those who joined the faction via Ring of Honor, had to be approved by New Japan. "New Japan never saw the value in Matt and I," Nick Jackson complained to Kenny Herzog in a *Bleacher Report* article. "They never paid us good. We would have had to work with New Japan for another two decades to even get close to retiring, and the style they demand is back-breaking."

At an October event at Ryōgoku Kokugikan (Sumo Hall) in Tokyo, "Switchblade" Jay White, Gedo and Jado aligned themselves with the Bullet Club. "We hadn't even been talked to," Cody told *Inside the Ropes* during a Dublin Q&A. "And, you know, you don't owe us that, but the part of wrestling that is real, especially in New Japan, is the factions. I was as excited to be in the Bullet Club as I could possibly be, and I was incredibly lucky to attach myself to the hottest thing in wrestling. However, I wasn't going to just let it be, 'Hey, I'm the Bullet Club guy now.' There can't be 80 people in it. It's got to be something different."

There had been pro wrestling–themed cruises before, but, because of its timing, Chris Jericho's Rock 'N' Wrestling Rager at Sea, scheduled for October 27 through Halloween 2018, was receiving a disproportionate amount of attention. FITE TV would be broadcasting not only the matches, but also related podcasts and other events. As Cody and the Bucks commiserated about their situation, they vowed to do something on the Norwegian Jade cruise ship that would alter the direction of the indie wrestling revolution.

In 2015, Jericho and his band, Fozzy, had been invited to play a KISS-themed cruise from Miami to Jamaica. "It was such a great experience, as a professional, as a fan, as a performer, all across the board," he told *Sportskeeda*. "I was just really impressed with how much fun it was. You get up in the morning, you hang for a bit, you do your gig, you go back to your cabin, take a shower, then you've got the rest of the night to do whatever you want to do. I said, 'Dude, I want to do this.'"

Chris Jericho's Rock 'N' Wrestling Rager at Sea would feature wrestling, along with concerts, comedy, paranormal acts, podcasts, autograph signings, trivia contests and Diamond Dallas Page conducting his DDP Yoga classes at poolside. Jericho officiated a wedding, and WWE Hall of Famer Pat Patterson, who attended with his coauthor, Bertrand Hébert, hosted a number of karaoke sessions. "It was all done without WWE or any major television promotion," Hébert said. "And it sold out. I was walking around, thinking, 'It's a whole new world and an open market.'"

As fans from such locations as the United Kingdom, France, Hong Kong, Australia and New Zealand journeyed from Miami to Nassau, Bahamas, and back, they had the opportunity to see IMPACT World champion Johnny Impact, Ring of Honor titlist Jay Lethal and IWGP Heavyweight kingpin Kenny Omega all defend their titles. As with *All In*, the wrestling logistics were largely coordinated by Ring of Honor.

Among the biggest challenges was having a team of engineers secure a ring on deck, and prevent, in Jericho's words, the squared circle from slipping into the ocean.

"It was like *All In* in a couple of ways," said Hébert. "You felt like you were part of something, part of the gang. The fans and wrestlers were together all the time. The place where I saw the least amount of talent was the 'Talent Only' area. When I went to the buffet the first day, there was Cody and the Young Bucks, with their families, having lunch with Kenny Omega. Of course, fans asked for autographs, but they understood that there was a difference between the character and the regular person whose privacy had to be respected. It was a big change from the days when fans didn't know those boundaries."

Ryan Barkan of Pro Wrestling Tees truly felt like he was living "in a whole 'nother world. Here I was in the middle of the ocean and, everywhere I went, I was surrounded by 2,000 of my customers."

The wrestling itself was spread out over several days and received well by the passengers. Former Ring of Honor champ Dalton Castle appeared as his old CHIKARA character, "Smooth Sailing" Ashley Remington. Scorpio Sky, known to get on the mic and rile up the spectators by bashing their hometown, turned his ire on the Atlantic Ocean, declaring, "This is the worst body of water I've ever been on." Sami Callihan beat Marty Scurll in an "Anything Goes Anywhere on the Ship" clash. Mark and Jay Briscoe engaged in a brother versus brother conflict, battering each other with chairs. Flip Gordon won the "Sea of Honor" tournament.

The main event, Cody, Scurll and Omega over Jericho and the Bucks, was thrown into uncertainty when the Ayatollah of Rock 'n' Rolla left his wrestling gear behind in Florida. His trunks and boots were swiftly flown to Nassau and rushed to the dock so the man who orchestrated the cruise could compete.

But that wasn't what fans remembered. Following a victory over Delirious, Cody delivered an insight into the future by declaring that, although he'd savored the prospect of making a surprise appearance at the 2019 *Royal Rumble*, it wasn't going to happen. Furthermore, he emphasized, he had no intention of re-signing with WWE.

And during Chris Jericho's podcast, Cody and the Bucks announced that they were leaving the Bullet Club, along with Omega, "Hangman" Adam Page and Marty Scurll, to form a new faction simply called The Elite.

"Once again," observed Hébert, "these guys pulled off a major angle, and they didn't need TV to do it."

As the year wound to a close, the intrigue built over where the various Elite members, as well as their backstage allies, would end up. Rules were being flouted and indie promotions, both large and small, seemed to reap the benefits. In November 2018, IWGP Heavyweight champion Kenny Omega squared off against Fenix, champion of Mexico's AAA promotion. This unique clash took place not in Tokyo or Mexico City, but Poughkeepsie, New York, a small, former manufacturing city about 90 miles north of New York City. The match, presented by the Northeast Wrestling group, drew about 2,700 fans to the Mid-Hudson Civic Center, where the WWF had taped a weekly television show prior to the *Monday Night Raw* days. Many attendees left the building saying that the non-title bout, which Omega won with the One-Winged Angel, was the greatest match they'd ever witnessed.

Meanwhile, Cody seemed to be mocking WWE from afar. After a particularly lackluster *Raw* that month, he tweeted, "Y'all being negative. Is it really that bad?"

BTE became another forum to poke fun at WWE. On the web series, Cody appeared to be intrigued by another WWE run, only to be dissuaded by Christopher Daniels, who'd intone, "The power of Crockett compels you," a warning to remember Dusty's battles with Vince McMahon while booking for Jim Crockett Jr.

During a November episode, Daniels and SoCal Uncensored partner Frankie Kazarian had received gifts of whistles, apparently from Triple

H. This was a parody of WWE's recent habit of assigning indie veterans to coaching positions in NXT. Mixed in with the gag was the clear message that Daniels and Kazarian had bigger things to do.

The scene was not based purely on fiction. Reportedly, WWE had been making lucrative offers to a number of *BTE* regulars. Hangman Page was supposedly offered main-roster money to wrestle for NXT, while the Bucks were promised the same type of salary as top star AJ Styles. To further entice the Jacksons, WWE was said to have pledged to allow them out of their contracts in six months if they weren't happy and to air *Being the Elite* on the WWE Network.

"For a moment, I thought that we would probably be going to WWE," Matt Jackson told CBS' Miami affiliate. "That was the closest that it's ever come to us going there, for sure. And they were great. They were respectful, and they told us what our value was. It was hard to turn down because it would have been life-changing. I can't stress enough how friendly and how great they were to us."

Although the performers never discussed the details of these discussions on *Being the Elite,* fans had a fairly good sense of what was transpiring. During a December episode, Kazarian dressed as Triple H to make an offer to the Young Bucks, only to be dispatched with a double superkick. On the same show, Page found a note that the Jacksons had left to someone named "H."

"Although this is a difficult decision, we watched an episode of *Raw* and saw what you guys did to the tag team division. I know in this business the saying goes, 'Never say never,' but for now, we wish you the best in your future endeavors."

Once again, the Elite was mocking the time-honored patterns of the wrestling business. Previously, when WWE released a talent, a corporate statement would wish the person well in his or her "future endeavors." Now, the Bucks were using the same language to reject a highly profitable contract from the biggest company in the industry.

With the internet humming with suppositions about the next step for the various headliners, *BTE* introduced a storyline in which Scurll was inviting friends to a party on January 1, but virtually no one would commit. This fueled rumors that Scurll was going to remain under contract, at least in the short-term, to Ring of Honor, while his companions' deals would change as soon as 2019 began.

"We definitely made aggressive attempts" to re-sign top Ring of Honor talent, the company's general manager Greg Gilleland told Baltimore's CBS affiliate. "More aggressive than we've had with anybody in the past. Sometimes people have a dream, and you can't negotiate against dreams."

When *Final Battle*, Ring of Honor's last pay-per-view of 2018, occurred at New York's Hammerstein Ballroom on December 14, I wandered the backstage area, watching the Elite and SoCal Uncensored chatting and laughing with other Ring of Honor talent, as well as executives. On the surface, everyone appeared to be on the same team. When I mentioned to Cody that I was writing a book on the indie wrestling revolution, though, he laughed and said, "Keep an eye on what happens tonight."

In his challenge to re-capture the Ring of Honor World Championship from Jay Lethal, Cody was turned away, while Frankie Kazarian and Scorpio Sky dropped the Ring of Honor World Tag Team straps to Mark and Jay Briscoe during a three-way ladder match that also included the Bucks. And Adam Page fell short in his effort to win the Ring of Honor World Television Championship from Jeff Cobb. The conclusion, for those who'd been following behind-the-scenes developments, was that Cody, the Bucks, Page and SoCal Uncensored were all departing.

This was reinforced as soon as the show ended and all of the above-listed wrestlers came down the entrance ramp, shaking hands and saying goodbye to audience members.

On *BTE*, Cody, the Bucks and Page were shown leaving the Hammerstein Ballroom as the crew cleaned up the building and dismantled the ring. The episode ended with Matt Jackson declaring, "Let's go change the world."

The next month, at *Wrestle Kingdom 13*, there were more clues about which wrestlers were parting ways with New Japan: Kenny Omega dropped the IWGP Heavyweight Championship to Hiroshi Tanahashi, Chris Jericho lost the IWGP Intercontinental belt to Tetsuya Naito, and Juice Robinson took the IWGP United State Heavyweight title from Cody.

"Is New Japan okay?" the company's president, Harold Mejj asked on the company's website. "Yes it is. Is this the beginning of the end? Twitter's getting ahead of itself. Talent will come and go. That's life. What counts is that, while here, people produce the best product possible for us."

Having recognized the pattern of departures ahead of time, New Japan was prepared for 2019. Bullet Club members included Bad Luck Fale, Tama Tonga, Tanga Loa, Chase Owens, Taiji Ishimori and Yujiro Takahashi. The Bullet Club's leader, New Zealander "Switchblade" Jay White, would become the IWGP World Heavyweight champion in February.

"We always rebound bigger and badder than before," Tonga told *Sports Illustrated*. "Jay White is our new guy, and we have now entered a new era, the 'Cut Throat Era.'"

For a period, Australian Robbie Eagles was also in the faction, selling the most Bullet Club t-shirts in Japan since the Young Bucks' departure.

But what about the Bucks? Since October, rumors had been circulating about a new league attempting to recruit discontented wrestlers from New Japan and WWE, as well as superstars from the smaller indies. This would not be a knockoff of WWE, but a unique promotion with a wrestler-centric sensibility. WWE Hall of Fame announcer Jim "J.R." Ross was said to be involved, along with wrestling super-agent Barry Bloom. And, unlike the money mark–driven promotions of the past, this effort would be funded by a family of billionaires, with the ability, if they so chose, to outspend Vincent Kennedy McMahon.

32
CHAPTER

Shahid "Shad" Khan was born in Lahore, Pakistan, and moved to the United States in 1967 to study industrial engineering at the University of Illinois at Urbana-Champaign. While in college, he worked at Flex-N-Gate, a manufacturer and supplier of stamped metal and welded components, assemblies and plastic parts for the automotive industry, and was hired as engineering director as soon as he graduated. In 1980, he purchased the company and combined it with a separate business that he had founded, Bumper Works, which manufactured bumpers and fenders. As he acquired more companies, Khan's clients grew to include Ford, Toyota, Suzuki and Volkswagen. His corporation eventually operated plants internationally, in more than 50 locations.

In 2012, Khan became the first ethnic minority to purchase an NFL team when his ownership of the Jacksonville Jaguars became official. The next year, he added the Premier League team, Fulham FC to his portfolio, buying it from Mohamed Al Fayed, whose son, Dodi, had been fleeing the paparazzi with Princess Diana when they died in a Paris car crash in 1997.

According to *Forbes*, which had once labeled him the "Face of the American Dream," Khan was worth an estimated $7.9 billion.

His son, Tony, born in 1982, had been a wrestling fan his entire life. Among the promotions he followed were Mid-South, Continental, Memphis and Smoky Mountain Wrestling, along with New Japan and All Japan Pro Wrestling. He'd later compare the battle between the Young Bucks and Lucha Brothers at AEW's *Double or Nothing* pay-per-view to the memorable clash that pit Octagon and El Hijo del Santo against the "Terror Team" of Art Barr and Eddie Guerrero at AAA's *When Worlds Collide* in Los Angeles in 1994.

Despite his demanding schedule, Shahid Khan supported his son's obsession, accompanying the boy to a 1996 ECW card that included one of Chris Jericho's final appearances for the company, as well as a Paul Heyman Q&A.

Twenty-three years later, when Tony, who regularly filed match results and feedback to Dave Meltzer's *Wrestling Observer* newsletter, was a guest on *Talk Is Jericho*, he conceded that he wanted to own a wrestling company his entire life.

His goal was to start a promotion that could reel in lapsed wrestling fans, as well as appeal to young people who never started watching at all. And with so many greats on the indies, he told his father, the roster possibilities were unbounded. "There's a huge amount of talent that's on the street," Shahid Khan noted at Yahoo Finance's All Markets Summits in 2019, "whereas in the NFL, the top talent is already there."

The senior Khan was persuaded to bankroll the effort. But when the Bucks finally met Tony Khan, they took a cynical approach. "It was all hypotheticals," Matt Jackson told the CBS affiliate in Miami. "'What if we did this, and what if we did that?' At first, it was almost like I was rolling my eyes a little bit, like, 'Oh, we've heard this a million times from people wanting to get into the wrestling business.' We're the biggest doubters and skeptics in the world because everything changes on a weekly basis in wrestling. One day, you're promised you're going to be the champion, and then you show up that day and they're like, 'Oh, we changed it.' Or your match gets cut from a pay-per-view."

Ultimately, the brothers discovered that, as a lifelong student of the business, Khan's wrestling philosophy was similar to theirs. "Tony came to us at the right time, and he made the right offer," Matt Jackson told reporter Chris Van Vliet. "I'm not talking financially. I'm talking, 'Hey, you guys can run this thing, and I want you guys to hire your people.' It's like someone saying, "I want you to make a movie and you can hire all the cameramen — all your friends can be with you.' He gave us the keys to this thing. You can't say no to this."

In a statement coordinated with the launch of All Elite Wrestling, Khan elaborated, "A new family has formed, bonded by love and respect for wrestling, but armed with a vision and resources that have never before been available to the wrestling community."

While Khan would be listed as AEW's president, the Bucks, Cody and Kenny Omega were given executive vice president titles. The company's chief brand officer was Brandi Rhodes. After building the Bucks' brand online, Matt Jackson's wife, Dana Massie, was placed in charge of AEW's merchandising.

"AEW is run by wrestlers," signee Jungle Boy pointed out. "I'm not asking a guy in a suit what I can do. I'm asking the Young Bucks."

As for the non-wrestling employees, Cody pledged to favor applicants whose product knowledge extended past the Attitude Era. "If you don't know who Lou Thesz is," he told *Bleacher Report*, "you can get out. It's that simple."

Khan promised to utilize the same type of analytics employed by the Jacksonville Jaguars and Fulham FC, tracking the wrestlers' wins and losses and breaking down the various maneuvers executed between the ropes.

And while promoters of the past could be arbitrary in how they treated injured talent, AEW intended to take the financial burden off the combatants. At a press event, Cody told the media that the promotion's goal was "to care for wrestlers like the television industry takes care of its actors on set."

In other ways, though, AEW would be markedly different from the entertainment industry. In particular, Cody vowed to keep the dressing room free from the influence of the script writers blamed for inauthentic promos in WWE. "We certainly don't need to script a great deal of the product we're planning," he told journalist Steve Gerweck. "There won't be a writer hired for All Elite Wrestling any time soon. Because wrestlers are the writers."

The proclamation would satisfy future AEW talent, among them, Jon Moxley, who characterized the introduction of script writers as one of the wrestling industry's most regrettable decisions. "Their job shouldn't exist," he told the *Wade Keller Pro Wrestling Podcast*. "If you need a writer to write a promo for you, you fuckin' suck at your job. The best writers in WWE, writer guys I like who aren't idiots, cannot write a promo for me because they're not me."

The official launch of AEW occurred precisely at midnight, pacific time, on New Year's Day 2019. On a special edition of *BTE*, Cody, the Bucks and Adam Page were shown at the Tokyo Dome, watching their cell phones tick down, until the AEW logo appeared. On Page's phone was the message: "All In 2 Double or Nothing."

When *Wrestle Kingdom 13* ended, the Elite boarded an aircraft and made the 7,100-mile journey to Jacksonville, Florida, for the rally kicking off AEW. It occurred in the center of the Khans' empire, just outside TIAA Bank Field, home of the NFL's Jaguars. With fans crowding the parking lot, Scorpio Sky, Frankie Kazarian and Christopher Daniels did their SoCal Uncensored shtick onstage, before Cody and the Young Bucks came out to resounding cheers. Although the promotion had yet to secure its own television outlet, the group declared that its premier pay-per-view, *Double or Nothing*, would debut on May 25, 2019, at the MGM Grand Garden Arena in Las Vegas.

"Matt and I didn't even want to announce the start of the company until closer to May," Nick Jackson would tell *Bleacher Report*. "We even thought of the idea of announcing the company at *Double or Nothing*, and Tony was completely against it. He wanted to announce it as soon as possible. As soon as we announced it in January, we were like, 'We've got to start working and start getting shows ready, got to find buildings, build a ring. Right away, we felt the pressure of getting everything going.'"

As the festivities continued in Jacksonville, Brandi Rhodes spoke about AEW's women's division and introduced one of her first signees,

Dr. Britt Baker, who'd been working the indies for three and a half years while earning her degree from the University of Pittsburgh School of Dental Medicine. She was the type of modern-day performer that AEW hoped would distinguish it from its rivals; if Baker could manage to become a seasoned wrestler and dentist at the same time, she'd later joke, she could overcome any obstacle inside the ring.

As podcaster Conrad Thompson relayed AEW's goals to both the live audience and the 499,000 fans streaming the event on YouTube, he was interrupted by Maxwell Jacob Friedman, or MJF, arguably the most mesmerizing young heel on the indies. "Now, I'm not going to lie to you people," he acknowledged. "When I got the phone call that I was going to be here on such a historic evening, for the first-ever All Elite Wrestling Press Conference, I was really excited. Trust me, I was. But that excitement quickly turned into a great deal of depression when I realized it was going to be held in the dumpster fire of America known as Jacksonville, Florida."

It was cheap heat, but it worked. As fans booed and MJF turned his rage toward the Jacksonville Jaguars mascot, Joey Janela, accompanied by valet Penelope Ford, appeared and laid out the villain. Then other signees showed up, including PAC — the former "Neville" in WWE — and Hangman Page, and the show appeared to be over.

It wasn't. As the pyro began to go off, Chris Jericho took the stage to a roaring reaction, raising his arms and cupping his hand to his ear like the Hulkster, while, somewhere in the crowd, a fan waved a flag emblazoned with the word "ELITE."

"It really does feel like the culmination of our entire career," Matt Jackson told CBS in Miami. "Like everything we've done for 15 years has gotten us to this point. I think everything we've learned along the way, all of our failures, all of our successes, it certainly feels like this is what we were destined to do."

Cody told ESPN that it was important for AEW to supplement the established names with dynamic young talent. There was also an understanding that certain wrestlers were going to maintain their relationships with the promotions that initially took a chance on them. While Janela would be obliged to appear on AEW's television broadcasts and major events, for instance, he would still return to GCW for *Joey Janela's Spring Break* and other important cards.

"I always wanted to make it in WWE," he told me, "wrestle at *WrestleMania*. But now, I know I can make it elsewhere."

With AEW's pyro lighting up the skies, the reverberations could literally be felt at the Jacksonville Veterans Memorial Arena, where WWE was preparing for a live broadcast of *SmackDown*. In fact, some fans went directly from the AEW rally to the *SmackDown* show. While AEW contended that the two companies just happened to be in the same city that day, Jericho, who'd maintained communication with Vince McMahon while negotiating a three-year contract with the upstart company, didn't believe it.

"I was laughing because that fireworks display at the end of [the rally] was at the top of the Jacksonville Stadium, so it was like the end of a *WrestleMania*," Jericho told *Busted Open Radio*. "I just know that inside that Jacksonville Arena somewhere, the old man was in there going, 'Will you shut that pyro off? Goddamn it. I'm trying to do a meeting here, trying to run a show.' It was very strange; obviously no coincidence that it was done the same day."

Publicly, the Bucks argued that they'd never fathomed going to war with WWE. To do so, they elaborated, would "be irresponsible of us." But Jericho knew McMahon well enough to understand that he viewed the situation differently. "This is a war," Jericho told Scott Fishman at *TV Insider*. "Even if you don't want it to be, it just is. There hasn't been any competition for WWE on a national basis [for years]. I think this is something they didn't really want. But it's great for the fans and great for the guys. I think in the long run, it's going to make a difference because it gives people a choice, and it's always good to have a choice."

33
CHAPTER

I n the buildup to *Double or Nothing*, the AEW signees helped garner interest with surprise appearances at various small promotions.

Although AEW's indie status would later be questioned, at this point, the newcomer was unashamedly associating itself with the mom and pop leagues that had produced most of its talent.

During a January 2019 event for Bar Wrestling — a group founded by Joey Ryan that staged wildly entertaining cards in bars (at one show, Ryan and multiple WWE women's champion Bayley engaged in a Falls Count Anywhere thumb wrestling match) — Frankie Kazarian, Christopher Daniels and Scorpio Sky were facing Yuma, Watts and Kevin Martenson at the Bootleg Theater in Los Angeles. As officials began to lose control of the action, Ryan ran out to help SoCal Uncensored, followed by "Hangman" Adam Page. Despite their adversarial history on *Being the Elite* and *All In*, the two declared a public truce.

Still, Yuma, Watts and Martenson appeared dedicated to harming their opponents, prompting more run-ins — from Cody and Brandi Rhodes, then the Young Bucks. Following a flurry of superkicks delivered by the Jackson brothers, SoCal Uncensored scored the victory. Then

Cody took the microphone and declared that everyone in the crowd was now an AEW employee.

Brandi immediately fired the new hires.

A few days later, Matt Jackson posted a cryptic tweet of a scene from the *Hunchback of Notre Dame*, in which the character Frollo asks, "How dare you defy me?" That night, at a DEFY Wrestling show in Seattle, the message suddenly made sense. In the middle of a 10-team tournament, the Bucks' music hit, prompting Matt and Nick to storm the ring and superkick everyone.

On Super Bowl weekend, the brothers turned up in Norcross, Georgia, at a show called *Come Hell or High Water,* interrupting the Lucha Brothers — Pentagon Jr. and Fenix — as they battled SoCal Uncensored to ask the Mexican athletes, "Why don't you come wrestle for AEW?"

In the Chicago area, Mike Petrovich and Danny Daniels from AAW noted that the Lucha Brothers would be working for them about three weeks later and decided to get involved. "I texted the Bucks and told them, 'Pentagon and Fenix will be here. Why don't you come to the show?'" said Daniels. "They texted back, 'We were thinking of doing that exact same thing.'"

Observed Petrovich, "It helped everybody. The Bucks got to promote AEW, and the fans said, 'If this is where the Young Bucks want to be, it's where we want to be too.'"

In the changing indie landscape, AAW occupied a unique position. "We're too big to be a small indie, but too small for someone to invest millions of dollars in us," said Petrovich. "At the same time, we don't have contracts with any larger promotion, so we've been able to use wrestlers from AEW, EVOLVE, MLW and IMPACT all on the same show."

Prior to the Lucha Brothers, AAW's biggest draws had included Tyler Black in his pre–Seth Rollins days. "Tyler Black from Davenport, Iowa," said Daniels. "He was 18, very hungry, very opinionated. He'd travel anywhere, do ring crew. He asked a lot of questions. Sometimes, we butted heads. He wanted to do cool moves, and I wanted everything in the match to make sense. But he learned on the job and formed his own style."

Despite their exposure on *Lucha Underground,* it was in AAW that Pentagon Jr. and Fenix became real indie idols, attracting followers who'd previously been indifferent to lucha. At the company's *The Art of War* show in late February 2019, the Lucha Brothers were defending their AAW Tag Team Championship in a triple threat match with LAX and Myron Reed and AR Fox when the arena went dark. The fans screamed, anticipating what would occur next. When the lights came back on, the Young Bucks were in the ring, attacking Pentagon Jr. and Fenix, and enabling LAX to capture the belts.

After the match ended, the Jackson siblings issued a challenge. If the Lucha Brothers didn't like what just transpired, the Bucks said, they could get their revenge against the Jacksons at *Double or Nothing* in May.

But the four would tangle the next month at the Acropolis in Puebla, Mexico, after the Lucha Brothers defeated Los Mercenarios — Rey Escorpion and El Texano Jr. — for the AAA World Tag Team Championship. As in Chicago, the lights went out and, when they went up, the Bucks were there. On this occasion, they engaged their rivals in a quick, impromptu match, snaring the gold with a Meltzer Driver.

Each of these incidents received copious amounts of social media coverage, building momentum for the pay-per-view. In addition to *Being the Elite*, the Bucks and their friends now put up a second web series, *The Road to Double or Nothing*.

A month after the rally that officially launched the promotion, AEW had held another high-profile event, a *Double or Nothing* ticket-selling party, poolside at the MGM Grand in Las Vegas. Nyla Rose, a tough, transgender wrestler known as the "Native Beast" because of her Oneida heritage, was welcomed to the roster, along with Sonny Kiss, a flamboyantly gay performer who proudly described himself as "gender-neutral." Given the highly polarized political environment in the United States, some accused AEW of trying to force a certain agenda on the wrestling public. But Kiss told *Wrestling Inc.*'s podcast, "People think that they are just hiring people due to their sexuality, and that's not what they are doing. They are hiring authentic people, transgender and homosexuals, such as myself. They are hiring people like that to give representation to really good wrestlers." Although there had been gay caricatures in wrestling since the advent of television, he continued, the way that these particular performers were being depicted was new and, arguably, more consistent with the roles LGBTQ people were playing in society.

Nyla Rose later told me that she had no interest in being portrayed as a babyface simply because she was trans. After all, a wrestler who slammed smaller opponents through tables was supposed to get booed. "The vast majority of fans get it," she said in an article I wrote for *The Daily Beast*. "They hate me because they're supposed to hate me. Or they like me."

Her trainer, James Zaveski, or "Sweet Jimmy Z," a full-time assistant principal at a Morgantown, West Virginia, middle school, explained that, even when Rose was jeered, her position in AEW benefitted a lot of lives. "We've got kids in my school who are identifying as non-binary. And that's here in West Virginia. And seeing Nyla on TV week after week just normalizes it for them."

Emphasizing the company's international reach, the speakers at AEW's ticket-selling party hyped their relationship with Oriental Wrestling Entertainment (OWE) — then located in China — and AAA, as well as efforts to recruit Japanese female talent. It was all positive stuff, but the fans needed that one special moment to excite them. They received it as the event was winding down and Kenny Omega suddenly appeared, proclaiming himself a full-time member of the AEW roster. This brought out a cocky Chris Jericho to humble his fellow Winnipegian. But when the two finished brawling, it was Omega who was standing at the podium, wearing Jericho's hat.

While all this was transpiring, WWE eyed its new competitor warily; at the same time, AEW attempted to exploit the dissatisfaction of both WWE fans and wrestlers.

In June 2019, Kenta Kobayashi, aka KENTA, returned to New Japan after six years in WWE, becoming a member of the Bullet Club a month later. He'd joined the largest wrestling organization in the world with high expectations, he told Japan's *Weekly Fight Magazine*. But as Hideo Itami in NXT and WWE's cruiserweight division, *205 Live*, he felt micromanaged and "defanged."

In March, WWE *Raw* Tag Team champions Scott Dawson and Dash Wilder had been walking back to the dressing room in Elmira, New York, and seemed to go out of their way to take a photo with a fan wearing an AEW t-shirt. It was unusual behavior, and such that might have gotten the tag team fired in a period when wrestlers had fewer options. During a short conversation about their career prospects, the spectator said, "I'll see you in May," a reference to *Double or Nothing*, and reminded them, "Money isn't everything."

Reportedly, either Dawson or Wilder replied, "Ain't that the truth."

When another fan tweeted a photo of his three-year-old nephews sporting replica *Raw* Tag Team belts, and the caption, "Look out, Dash Wilder and Scott Dawson," Wilder responded, "Don't wish being *Raw* Tag Team champs on them. For their sake."

Although AEW was one of the few major indie groups not to stage an event during *WrestleMania 35* weekend, the group's presence was felt everywhere. During the WWE Hall of Fame ceremony, Triple H, Shawn Michaels, the late Joanie "Chyna" Laurer, X-Pac, "Road Dogg" Jessie James and Billy Gunn were being honored for their roles in the promotion's D-Generation X faction during the "Attitude Era." In the course of bantering onstage, Gunn, who'd had several tenures with WWE and recently was hired as an AEW producer, joked that Vince McMahon could no longer fire him. The remark triggered an AEW "chant" from some of those in attendance at Brooklyn's Barclays Center.

Replied Triple H, "Billy, let's be honest. He would buy that pissant company just to fire you again."

On *The Road to Double or Nothing*, Cody delivered his rebuttal, focusing specifically on Vince McMahon and his booking methods. "You mean to tell me some pissant bodybuilder making every match a DQ, meandering around the crowd, throwing the jib cam at his opponent compares with a Kenny-Okada match?"

Despite these jibes, WWE profits continued to increase, the result of television rights fees, advertising and sponsorship revenue, changes in American tax law and lucrative shows presented the year before in Australia and Saudi Arabia. With so much in its coffers, the company could dissuade talent from working for other leagues. In the months after AEW's founding, NXT contracts for newcomers were extended to five years from the standard three-year deals, and established performers were offered raises.

"Everyone in WWE owes Chris Jericho a thank you because the moment I signed with AEW everyone started getting these huge raises to not go," the Ayatollah of Rock 'n' Rolla boasted to Scott Fishman at *TV Insider*. "It was very similar to what happened to [hockey great] Bobby Hull in the early 1970s when he signed with the WHA [World Hockey Association, a National Hockey League rival from 1972 to 1979] for a million dollars. Every other player got a huge raise to not jump with him. My dad [Ted Irvine] went from $35,000 to $100,000 a year because they didn't want him going to the WHA. It's the same thing that Vince is doing with WWE. Vince doesn't want anyone coming to AEW, doesn't want there to be a mass exodus, whether you are an opening match jobber or a main-event Roman Reigns."

Yet, sometimes, people left anyway. Shortly after *WrestleMania 35*, Dustin "Goldust" Runnels announced that he was parting ways with WWE. Even at 50 years old, he was convinced that he still had great matches yet to perform. "It's frustrating when you have so much to give and you're getting older," he told Kenny McIntosh at an *Inside the Ropes* Q&A in Las Vegas, claiming, like Cody, that his creative suggestions were often ignored in WWE. "It's like a prison where they're taking care of you, but . . . it's prison."

On *The Road to Double or Nothing*, fans learned that Dustin would be wrestling his half-brother Cody at the pay-per-view. It was a match both had previously wanted to perform at *WrestleMania*, playing off their differences in upbringing and competition for their father's approval. "We're telling a story that has not been told," Dustin said. "You get one of these matches once or twice in a decade."

Cody was in full promo mode when he described the upcoming clash as a fight between wrestling philosophies. "This match is generation versus generation," he said on *The Road to Double or Nothing*. "I am not here to kill Dustin Rhodes. I am here to kill the Attitude Era. My entire lot, my whole class of peers have been compared to these late '90s to early 2000s [wrestlers] for over a decade, and it's an utter sham. Sure, you paved the roads for us but, gosh, you set the speed markers at 35 because you are terrified of any of us putting our fuckin' foot down on the pedal."

34 CHAPTER

I f I was going to write a book about one ambiguous wrestling personality, it would be Jack Pfefer, who, in 1933, following a falling out with some business partners, exposed the industry's "fakery" to the *New York Daily Mirror*. A Lithuanian-born Jew with a thick Yiddish accent and, according to what the Fabulous Moolah once told me, an aversion to personal hygiene, Pfefer was both an innovator and a con man. In a U.S. Justice Department report, Fort Worth promoter R.G. McElyea described Pfefer as "one of the loudest, vulgarest . . . and most objectionable" humans he had ever encountered. Yet, Pfefer ingratiated himself so deeply to renowned shooter Stu Hart, who didn't have a lot of tolerance for those who disrespected the business, that the Calgary promoter asked the apostate to be godfather to the 10th Hart child, Ross.

I'm not sure if it was courage or a complete lack of shame, but even after revealing wrestling's most sacred secret, Pfefer kept showing his face, forming allegiances and making enemies by, among other things, arranging for former circus strongman Dick Shikat to shoot on Danno

O'Mahony, who held a version of the world championship in 1935. As a result, O'Mahony was only able to retain his title "via disqualification."

Later, the wily Pfefer became known for promoting an ensemble of oddities, like the Elephant Boy and the Swedish Angel, whose acromegaly — a growth condition that also affected Andre the Giant — resulted in an unusually large and misshapen head. For a while, Pfefer booked shows featuring unknowns with names similar to top stars, including Bummy Rogers, Bruno Sanmartino, Hobo Brazil and Lou Kez. If you read the autobiography I coauthored with "Classy" Freddie Blassie, you already know the story I'm going to tell next. But it's a good one, and I don't mind repeating it.

When the actual Lou Thesz demanded that Pfefer stop promoting an imitation version of him, the promoter offered the gifted grappler the same fee as the imposter.

"How much is that?" Thesz asked.

"Fifteen bucks."

How a man of Pfefer's bearing and character was able to briefly step into a slot previously occupied by a dignified impresario like the late Vincent James McMahon, aka "Vince Sr.," is a question that should be pondered by scholars. But in 1959, it happened.

McMahon and partner Toots Mondt had been doing well at Madison Square Garden, then the premier arena in the United States, structuring their shows around popular Antonino Rocca. But Pfefer had somehow managed to charm Rocca's real-life manager, Kola Kwariani, a native of the former Soviet Republic of Georgia and onetime Greco Roman champion in Europe, and sow dissension from there. Suddenly, McMahon and Mondt were out, and Kwariani was the booker and matchmaker at Madison Square Garden, working alongside Buffalo promoter Pedro Martinez and Pfefer, who supplied the talent.

On January 2, 1960, this new alliance was responsible for a record 21,950 house at the fabled arena, headlined by a card featuring Rocca against the Great Zuma. Prior to the coalition with Kwariani, Pfefer had fashioned Zuma as a Rocca knockoff, instructing the wrestler to work barefoot and execute acrobatic maneuvers, while emphasizing his Argentinian nationality. From my research, I've determined that Pfefer had a hankering for the name "Zuma." Previously, the promoter had billed another athlete as "Zuma, the Man from Mars."

But the Rocca-Zuma clash was as good as it got for Pfefer and his cronies. When a main event featuring the tandem of Rocca and Bruno Sammartino failed to sell out the Garden, Pfefer and friends had the two wrestle each other at the fabled coliseum on November 15, 1960. The card, which included a competitor named Haystacks Muldoon — some Pfefer amalgamation of 601-pound Haystacks Calhoun and 1880s champion William Muldoon, I'm guessing — only drew 12,815.

Pfefer had another show scheduled for the following month, but it was cancelled, and Vincent James McMahon reclaimed the promotional rights. For the next 58 years, no one outside the McMahon family would promote wrestling in Madison Square Garden again, until the combined Ring of Honor and New Japan *G1 Supercard* that occurred on April 6, 2019, the night before *WrestleMania 35*.

WWE had not run a pay-per-view in the building since 2011, when The Rock returned from a hiatus to team with John Cena at the *Survivor Series*. While *WrestleMania 35* was being staged at MetLife Stadium in New Jersey, supplementary events — *NXT TakeOver,* the WWE Hall of Fame, *Monday Night Raw* and *SmackDown* — were all being held at the Barclays Center in Brooklyn. "Look, they were being shunned by WWE," Ring of Honor COO Joe Koff said of the Garden. "WWE chose to partner with Barclays, and we asked Madison Square Garden to partner with us and New Japan. And it took a little bit of convincing."

Reportedly, WWE had pressured the Garden not to host the *G1 Supercard*, but Ring of Honor's parent company, the Sinclair Broadcast Group, threatened a lawsuit. "We finally got to the point of contract and, out of courtesy, Madison Square Garden called WWE to let them know we were doing the show," Koff said. "From what I understand, that upset the people at WWE, to the point that Madison Square Garden said, 'Maybe we shouldn't do this.' And I said, 'Maybe we should.' It got a little bit contentious."

Koff did not specify what the various parties said to each other. But the Friday after the announcement, a WWE spokesperson told the media, "Madison Square Garden is, of course, free to work with Ring of Honor however they want."

Some 60 percent of the tickets were sold through Ring of Honor's subscription service, Honor Club. The next day, when Madison Square Garden offered tickets to its mailing list members, between 10 and 12 percent of the remaining ducats were sold. When tickets were finally made available to the general public, everything else disappeared in 16 minutes.

"It was a perfect storm brewing," said Koff. "We'd just come out of *All In* in September. We had the relationship with New Japan, which added some cachet. And there were all those wrestling fans coming into the city that weekend."

The day before the show, Ring of Honor and New Japan presented their own version of WWE's fan gala, Axxess, with a "Festival of Honor" at Madison Square Garden's Hulu Theater, a smaller hall adjacent to the main arena. In addition to the promotions presenting the *G1 Supercard*, fans were able to meet wrestlers from two allied companies, Mexico's CMLL and the UK's Revolution Pro Wrestling.

"It's pretty surreal, man," Jay Briscoe, who wrestled on Ring of Honor's debut show in 2002, told me while taking a break from an autograph signing. "If you said to me that first day that we'd be selling out Madison Square Garden, I'd say you were crazy and didn't understand reality."

Surveying the scene, Bandido took a breath before revealing in Spanish, "This is very emotional. I started wrestling at small arenas in Mexico and now, I'm in Madison Square Garden."

Sixteen years earlier, Jeff Cobb had competed in the Garden as an amateur athlete, but never as a pro wrestler. "In a year's time, I've wrestled in Korakuen Hall, the Tokyo Dome, the ECW Arena and the Cow Palace — and, now, the granddaddy of them all. This is magical, man."

On Eighth Avenue, across from Madison Square Garden, a group of New Japan wrestlers posed for a swarm of Japanese photographers on the wide steps below the Corinthian columns of the James A. Farley Building, the former General Post Office, named for the nation's 53rd postmaster general. It was raining lightly as I edged into the scrum, spotting Tetsuya Naito, Kazuchika Okada, Evil, Sanada, Bushi and Shingo Takagi. But even though I'd been born in the Bronx and enjoy the birthright to walk anywhere I want in New York City, the Nipponese media contingent turned protective and territorial, demanding to see my credentials and physically blocking my view of the visiting stars. Since I was only there as a voyeur anyway, I walked back to the Hulu Theater, where I killed some time chatting with Bully Ray, Bill Apter and Cary Silkin.

Someone must have told the Japanese press corps why I was there because, a little while later, a couple of the people I'd seen earlier found me and led me to a room where New Japan president Harold Mejj appeared to be waiting.

The *G1 Supercard*, he said, was "a culmination of 47 years of history. Wrestling transcends borders. We bring a different kind of wrestling and wanted to showcase what we were made of. And the best place to showcase that was Madison Square Garden."

I admired the way he was putting the Garden over; as a fan, no one loved the arena more than I did. But his goals obviously reached beyond New York. Before the year ended, New Japan would journey to Melbourne and Sydney and hold its largest card ever in England, immediately selling close to 6,000 seats, despite the fact that the company didn't even have a television platform in the country.

The Garden show was yet another way to grab new followers. Besides being broadcast on pay-per-view, it was streamed via Honor Club, FITE TV and New Japan Pro-Wrestling World. Although I'm fairly certain that a sizeable portion of fans at the Garden had purchased their tickets when Kenny Omega, the Young Bucks and Cody were all working for New Japan and Ring of Honor, as I walked around the building, nobody seemed disappointed. In fact, with the lineup of talent, particularly from New Japan, fans were buzzing with anticipation. Everywhere I went, I saw people I knew. At one point, I found myself in one of the bars at the Garden, watching the television screens as the Guerrillas of Destiny (Tama Tonga and Tanga Loa) took both the IWGP Tag Team and Ring of Honor World Tag Team Championships in a four-way with Jay and Mark Briscoe, *Los Ingobernables de Japon* (Evil and Sanada) and PCO and Brody King. To my left was Walt Schwenk, who co-hosted the *Awesome Truth: A Wrestling Book Club* podcast with Steve Cimino. To my right was Pat Laprade, the Quebecois author, historian and broadcaster. Among the others in our conversation was Jaymie Hutchinson, my favorite wrestling fan from Australia and a regular at the various shows during *WrestleMania* week.

All of us had already received the news that across the East River in Brooklyn, some nut had tried to jump Bret "The Hit Man" Hart while he was inducting his late brother-in-law and tag team partner Jim "The Anvil" Neidhart into the WWE Hall of Fame. As we animatedly dissected the circumstances, Enzo Amore and Big Cass — who'd recently been released from WWE — hopped the barricade on the television screens. Now, we had something else to talk about. Was it a work or was it a shoot? As it turned out, it was a work. But I later heard that not all the talent had been informed and, for whatever reason, the angle went nowhere.

Either way, there was much about the card that fans would find hard to forget.

In the match preceding the pay-per-view, the crowd popped when the legendary Great Muta, then 56 years old, was the last entrant in the Honor Rumble battle royal, battling with another Japanese icon, 54-year-old Jushin "Thunder" Liger in the final moments before Kenny King, who'd been loitering outside the ring, returned to the squared circle and eliminated them both.

With Revolution Pro Wrestling founder Andy Quildan holding the belt at ringside, technical master Zack Sabre Jr. retained his British Heavyweight Championship by forcing eight-time IWGP Heavyweight champion Hiroshi Tanahashi to submit.

Matt Tavern dethroned Jay Lethal for the Ring of Honor World Championship in a frenzied ladder match also involving "The Villain" Marty Scurll.

In a match so frenetic, I could barely keep track, Kota Ibushi beat Tetsuya Naito for the IWGP Intercontinental title, seemingly bursting into tears as he was handed the belt.

And in the main event, Kazuchika Okada used a rainmaker followed by a spinning tombstone piledriver to vanquish "Switchblade" Jay White and begin a fifth reign as IWGP Heavyweight champion. For the first time ever, New Japan's primary title had changed hands outside Japan.

Before I left the building, I spotted an exuberant Cary Silkin at the English-language announcers table, embracing Ian Riccaboni, Colt Cabana and Kevin Kelly. When Cary called me two days later to ask about my thoughts, I told him that the final moments of the *G1 Supercard* reminded me of another experience. It had also occurred in Madison Square Garden, been coated with a historical sheen, and, when the show ended, I left the "world's most famous arena" with the feeling that I had witnessed the beginning of something.

That first event, held on March 31, 1985, had been *WrestleMania I.*

35
CHAPTER

s *Double or Nothing* drew closer, AEW again used the indies to
build intrigue for the show. On May 3, 2019, approximately three
weeks before the card, Cody attended a Southern Honor Wrestling
(SHW) event in Canton, Georgia, and announced that local wrestler
Sunny Daze would appear on the pay-per-view. Suddenly, Chris Jericho's
music hit. As the building rocked with excitement, Jericho began bashing Daze with chair shots, until another surprise guest, Kenny Omega,
stormed the ring to brawl with his *Double or Nothing* foe.

Once again, the AEW founding members had created a fervor without television. But on May 15, 2019, the company announced AEW
would soon receive an added advantage. Starting in the fall, AEW was
going to have its own two-hour weekly program on TNT, the same network that previously aired WCW in the United States. The deal with
TNT's parent company, WarnerMedia, had been put together by Tony
Khan and Bernie Cahill, one of the organizers of Dead & Co., a touring
group that included several former Grateful Dead members. It seemed
to be an ideal matchup. Like indie wrestling fans, "Deadheads" viewed
their passion with a religiosity that transcended entertainment.

As with *All In*, AEW wanted a celestial announce team for *Double or Nothing*. Jim Ross, WWE's former senior vice president of talent relations, was now an AEW guy, hired as a commentator as well as a senior advisor. And Excalibur was invited back. "The Bucks said my style of calling matches was so complementary of their style of wrestling, they couldn't imagine *Double or Nothing* without me," he recounted. "It was a big compliment, and I took it pretty seriously. And they also said, 'You're not penciled in. You're penned in.'"

Knowing that I needed to experience *Double or Nothing* to do this story justice, I penned myself in for the May 23, 2019 event in Las Vegas, as well.

On the flight out, I scanned the other passengers, trying to gauge if AEW and *Double or Nothing* meant anything to people outside my orbit. Other than a guy in a PWG shirt who was trying to catch some sleep a few rows back, I couldn't tell if the rest the passengers were flying west for a bachelorette party, Cirque du Soleil, gambling or Nevada's legal brothels.

But as I was checking into my hotel, I spotted two guys in the lobby, one in a Bullet Club shirt, the other wearing a slogan promoting the NWA. At Battista's Hole in the Wall, a restaurant started by an Italian immigrant who ventured out to Vegas to become a singer and instead purchased a dive behind the Flamingo in 1970, I sat down with Kenny McIntosh and Sandra Ruth Wesseldyke Reinstein from *Inside the Ropes*, only to look over at the next table to see a vendor I'd met at a GCW show in L.A. the month before. The next morning in the gym, I found Haku on an exercise bike, smiling, reminiscing and talking about the new opportunities the boys had today. Outside, Shane Douglas and Madusa stood separately by the palm tree–shrouded pool, Bill Apter did his Bruno Sammartino imitation — if you ever meet him in person, I guarantee he'll do it for you too — and I heard another guest tell his friend about a breakfast hosted by Jimmy "The Mouth of the South" Hart.

Now, *this* was more like it, I thought. A wrestling weekend.

The indie scene had "transformed into a sub-genre of people," noted John Thorne, owner of Cleveland's Absolute Intense Wrestling (AIW).

"There are people who only know each other from coming to these events. This is who they are. This is what they do. This is where they feel comfortable."

In the past, he maintained, indie promoters had been reliant on DVD sales. "Now, it's gone back to the live experience. People want to see these wrestlers and these matches live. It's something they can't miss."

As AEW would grow, so would the number of indie shows presented around the company's pay-per-views. "I want them to succeed," MLW cofounder and CEO Court Bauer told *Bleacher Report*, "because it's proof of concept — to networks, licensing companies, international touring companies, advertisers and everyone — that non-WWE leagues are viable."

But longtime indie performers already knew that.

In March 2019, after filing a lawsuit claiming that his *Lucha Underground* deal restricted his opportunities, Joey Ryan and a number of other wrestlers were released from their contracts. Because of his indie history and participation in *All In*, there was speculation that he was headed to AEW. Reportedly, WWE was also interested in Ryan, as a coach and NXT performer. But in late May, at a Bar Wrestling event, Ryan informed the fans that he was going to navigate a different path.

"When my *Lucha Underground* contract ended," he announced, "and I started getting so many offers . . . it felt great to be the hottest free agent in wrestling. When I was negotiating these offers, I came to the realization that if I go exclusive, this incarnation of Joey Ryan goes away forever. So for better or for worse, I choose you, independent wrestling."

As fans pounded the ring apron and chanted Ryan's name, he elaborated on his decision: "With independent wrestling, I might be a big fish in a small pond. But it's my fuckin' pond."

In the weeks leading up to the match against his brother at *Double or Nothing*, Dustin Runnels trained and dieted. In his mind, he'd later say, the collision "couldn't get here quick enough."

At a weigh-in before the bout, Dustin astonished the crowd by invoking his real-life friction with Cody, displaying a t-shirt declaring, "Dusty's Favorite." The moment was covered extensively on social media.

The night before the card, Dustin walked through the MGM Grand Garden Arena, taking in the atmosphere. "I am looking at the railings, the entrances and the big mat there that says, 'AEW,'" Dustin told *Talk Is Jericho*. "I am looking at it and thinking, 'Holy shit.' Here I am. It is a different backyard, a different ballpark and it feels good.'"

The regressive attitudes of the past were fading. AEW was taking wrestling somewhere it had needed to go for a long time, its supporters argued. In an acknowledgment that some of the *Double or Nothing* attendees would be on the autism spectrum, the arena staff had been trained on how to assist people with sensory disorders. In addition, spectators and their families could arrange for noise-cancelling earmuffs and fidget toys, among other items, or watch the show in a quieter room with lower lighting and bean bag chairs.

Over the course of the weekend, Cody emphasized that "diversity will be a way of life" in AEW, as opposed to "a publicity stunt." When questioned about his interracial marriage, he told a story about explaining to his wife, Brandi, that when he looked at other human beings, he didn't "see color."

According to Cody, Brandi replied, "Well, then you don't see my experience."

The anecdote was posted on social media by, among others, Rep. Alexandria Ocasio-Cortez, the widely known Democratic-socialist congresswoman from New York City. "This exchange is a promising peek into what growth looks like in our national discourse on race," she wrote. "Thanks for sharing your experience in this powerful moment, @CodyRhodes."

Backstage before the show, Joey Janela changed into his wrestling gear, feeling a sense of wonderment about preparing for a pay-per-view in Las Vegas. "I just thought, 'This is weird,'" he said. "It feels like yesterday that I was being kicked out of dressing rooms."

The bout preceding the main portion of *Double or Nothing* was billed as a "Casino Royale," a battle royal in which the wrestlers entered in groups of five, each named after card suits. Every three minutes, another set of grapplers came in until the final competitor, listed as "Lucky Number 21," emerged.

Dustin "No Legs" Thomas, from GCW's Greatest Clusterfuck, was among the first collection of wrestlers. The second included Shawn Spears, who, earlier in the year, had requested a release from WWE after performing there as the "Perfect 10" Tye Dillinger.

He was greeted with outstretched fingers and shouts of "10, 10," his gimmick in WWE. But by the time he appeared on his second AEW card, Tye Dillinger seemed to no longer exist.

Marko Stunt was part of the last unit to enter the ring. "I was more nervous than I'd ever been in my life," he said. "I heard the crowd, the cheering, the countdown." But before he left the backstage area, there was some type of music miscue. "Somebody messed up, and people were screaming, 'Let's go. Let's go.' There's always going to be some problem, so I just went with it. Then I got out, and it was like being on any indie show."

Accompanying Stunt down the aisle was six-foot-five-inch Luchasaurus — known as Austin Matelson without the dinosaur mask — who was fond of mentioning that, although he had a masters degree in European history, specifically English history and literature, he'd yet to wrestle in the UK. "I've know him since I was 10 years old," pointed out Jungle Boy, who was also in the match. "I always wanted to be a wrestler, and my parents let me train at Ric Drasin's wrestling school [in Sherman Oaks, California]. Luchasaurus was there, and so was Rusev from WWE."

In AEW, Jungle Boy, Luchasaurus and Stunt — the most comedic member — formed a popular team. "Riding the shoulders of a dinosaur to the ring might seem preposterous," Jungle Boy said. "But it's fun. And that's what wrestling's supposed to be."

The match included at least one nod to the history of renegade promotions. When Tommy Dreamer tossed a garbage can into the ring, fans responded with an "ECW" chant.

Other exchanges could have taken place on any quirky indie. Yet, they also seemed to work in front of the large audience. After Janela sat on the mat, puffing on a cigarette, Jimmy Havoc stapled the item to the Bad Boy's forehead. Later, No Legs pulled himself up to the top rope and zapped Janela with a 450 splash. At one stage, Orange Cassidy showed up, seemingly uninvited, and executed several slow motion moves on his rivals until Dreamer chucked him over the top rope.

Adam Page eventually appeared to secure the triumph by eliminating Luchasaurus. But Page was then jumped by MJF — who'd been making himself inconspicuous outside the ring — forcing the Hangman to spin around and fire back, purging the ring of his irritant.

Regardless, MJF's actions, along with his smug facial expressions, sent the message that he had the potential to become a heel along the lines of the late Roddy Piper.

Just before the official pay-per-view portion of *Double or Nothing* began, the Bucks, Cody and Brandi Rhodes and Kenny Omega greeted the crowd, as the *Being the Elite* theme played behind them. In a parody of WWE's alleged habit of inflating figures, Matt Jackson boasted that there were 20,000 fans in the 12,000 capacity building, with Cody describing the number as an all-time record.

Throughout the night, AEW seemed dedicated to impressing on its first-time viewers that the promotion told stories a little differently than what fans had been accustomed to seeing. A concerted effort was made to avoid ref bumps, and every single match ended with a clean finish. At the same time, the company worked hard to incorporate the element of surprise into this critical show.

Before a Triple Threat match pitting Nyla Rose against Kylie Ray and Dr. Britt Baker, Brandi Rhodes proceeded to the ring, apparently ready to wrestle. But instead of locking up herself, she took the microphone and introduced the newest member of the AEW roster, 272-pound Awesome Kong.

"She got this insane, loud pop," remembered Janela. "And I was just standing there, one of the fans, watching."

Kong had wrestled in WWE as Kharma and been a TNA Knockouts champion. In 2012, she shocked fans by appearing as a surprise entrant in the men's *Royal Rumble* but had not been a high-profile professional wrestler since her last run with TNA in 2016. "I was afraid they weren't going to remember me," she admitted. "When I heard that pop, I knew they did."

Although Baker eventually won the match, Kong had been its star. "I thought about every discouraging thing anyone ever told me," she said. "And I felt validated."

Like at *All In*, Cody wanted Earl Hebner to referee his match. Hebner had known both Cody and Dustin since they were children. "In fact, their dad was the one who gave me this job," he said on Bill Apter's YouTube show, *1WrestlingVideo*. "When I've got two great kids — well, men now — who I've loved all my life [in the ring] . . . it was a lot of stress on me."

As Cody was making his way to the ring, he passed a throne, not unlike the ones Triple H had used for his *WrestleMania* entrances. Cody first waved dismissively at the object and continued to ringside. But when he got there, Brandi handed him another Triple H device, a sledgehammer, prompting Cody to march back to the ceremonial chair and smash it to pieces. He'd later say that the purpose of this bit of performance art was grandly obliterating his connection to WWE.

"Plain and simple, I was a huge fan of Triple H," he told Chad Dukes on *106.7 The Fan* in Washington, DC. "I learned a great deal from Triple H. But when push came to shove, I thought I was better than 99 percent of the people he was putting ahead of me. He didn't see that. So I knew I was walking out to a sold-out crowd, wrestling in a match that people, at one point, deemed unworthy, and the place was literally shaking. This was the perfect time to do it, to fire my own shot."

This was the match that both brothers had wanted The American Dream to see. When the crowd began chanting "Dusty" at the beginning of the bout, Cody and Dustin wiped their eyes, visibly moved. "I was in a different place," Dustin would tell Kenny McIntosh during an *Inside the Ropes* Q&A the next day. "I could have missed a couple of spots and it wouldn't have mattered. I could do no wrong. Cody could do no wrong."

In the crowd, a fan shouted, "McMahon should have done this match!" All around him, observers responded with "AEW" chants. "I hate to say it because it's AEW," Dustin recalled, "but this was a *WrestleMania* moment for me. And fuck you for not letting us do it in your company."

Given the predilections of the Runnels clan, spectators expected to see blood in the bout and received an abundance of it: after Cody undid the turnbuckle, Dustin hurled himself at his opponent and hit the exposed metal instead. And like his father on many occasions, Dustin might have sliced himself too deeply. "Let's face it, I lost almost a fuckin' pint of blood," he said. "Cody was looking at me, legitimately terrified, saying, 'Maybe we should go [finish the match].' And I said, 'No, this is our moment.'"

As the battle spilled to ringside, Brandi — who walked a fine line, as AEW's chief brand officer and a heel in her husband's corner — went airborne and speared her brother-in-law. Playing the law and order role, Hebner demanded that she go back to the dressing room. When she demurred, Diamond Dallas Page materialized, lifting her up and hauling her to the back.

In a now familiar homage to his father's clashes with Ric Flair, Cody clamped on a figure-four leglock and Dustin reversed it, forcing Cody to roll to the bottom rope and desperately grab onto the strand. Seemingly frustrated, Cody removed his weightlifting belt — adorned with the words, "Attitude Killer" — and slapped his brother with it. Dustin wrested it away and used it to beat his younger sibling's bare ass.

By now, Cody was bleeding, too, with red streaks permeating his platinum blond locks. At times, it looked like his older brother would actually beat him down and pull out a win. But shortly after Cody sustained a turnover suplex, "The Prince of Pro Wrestling" rebounded with a Gori Especial backbreaker, followed by his signature crossroads — a neckbreaker variation delivered from behind — to end the brawl.

Given Dustin's age, and the satisfaction he undoubtedly felt about putting on the high quality match with Cody, some fans expected the elder Runnels brother to announce his retirement at this point. With tears mixing with his blood, he lifted the Attitude Killer belt and pondered it, apparently wondering if, as Cody forecasted, the Attitude Era really was officially dead. As he began symbolically removing his boots, he was serenaded with chants of "Thank you, Dustin." But Cody stopped him from proceeding further.

"You don't get to retire here," Cody proclaimed. "You don't get that because I have to ask you a favor." He needed Dustin, he continued, in a tag team match against the Young Bucks, scheduled to headline *Fight for the Fallen*, an AEW event that summer in Jacksonville, Florida, that would raise money for victims of gun violence.

"I don't need a partner," Cody said, his voice cracking. "I don't need a friend. I need a brother."

With the fans cheering, the crying combatants hugged, their blood co-mingling.

When the match ended, and the crimson-smeared canvas was covered, there was a solemn moment in which the AEW World Championship belt was revealed — by Bret "The Hit Man" Hart, five-time WWF World Heavyweight champion and two-time WCW World Heavyweight titlist. His unexpected appearance stunned and then enraptured fans, who interrupted the "Excellence of Execution" with repeated chants of "Holy shit," viewing his presence as an all-star endorsement of the new league.

Once again, AEW attempted to mix the nostalgic with the new by having MJF march to ringside and cut a promo on Hart, who broke character and laughed when the intruder mentioned the fan who snuck up on the legend at the WWE Hall of Fame ceremony.

The pace was picking up now. Following a blizzard of flashy moves, the Young Bucks retained their AAA World Tag Team Championship over the Lucha Brothers after Matt Jackson hit Fenix with a Meltzer Driver. For the next three weeks, the Californians retained possession of the Mexican title before dropping it back to Pentagon Jr. and Fenix south of the border in the Yacatan capital of Merida at AAA's *Verano de Escandalo* show.

In the main event, Jericho and Omega faced off once again, this time in an AEW ring. "A lot of people are asking, 'Why don't you wait for that [matchup] and build toward it?'" Jericho explained to *TV Insider*. "There is no waiting. There is no assumption there is going to be a second show. We have to come out of the gate with the best show possible."

Jericho played with the crowd before he left the dressing room. A spandex-clad man with long blond hair appeared at the head of an entrance tunnel, his back turned to the audience as the Lionheart logo from early in Jericho's career flashed on the big screen. Then the arena suddenly went dark. When the lights returned, another figure occupied the stage, his face obscured by the "List of Jericho," a silver clipboard that the star had used during a WWE run that started in 2016. After darkness descended again, another character was seen, this one sporting a black leather jacket illuminated with flashing lights — the same gimmick Jericho wore while he was feuding with CM Punk in 2013.

Finally, The Painmaker — Jericho's modern persona — came out, dressed in a fedora, scarf and studded leather jacket.

The brutality started quickly. Some seven minutes into the match, Omega broke his nose. But he was used to working through pain, and the encounter continued at a manic pace. Following a One-Winged Angel from Omega, Jericho appeared to take on a superhuman quality that enabled him to, out of nowhere, execute a codebreaker followed by his latest finisher, a spinning elbow called the Judas Effect, for the victory.

That's when the night truly took off in another direction. Jericho was cutting a promo, boasting about the attributes he brought to AEW, when Dean Ambrose, who'd recently requested his release from WWE, surged through the crowd. Interestingly, the fans were so dedicated to the indies that when they shouted his name, they didn't use his WWE handle but instead the moniker he'd used when he was warring with B-Boy and Nick Gage in CZW in 2010.

"It's Moxley!" they screamed. "It's Moxley!"

The spectators weren't the only ones kayfabed. Marko Stunt had been hanging out in the crowd, listening to Jericho's promo, when a security guard asked him to step back. "I looked over and I saw this guy walk by all covered up, and I was like, 'Who's that?'" Stunt said. "And then I started thinking, 'It's Jon Moxley. It's got to be Jon Moxley.' I wanted to mark out — I was shaking inside — but I managed to keep my mouth shut."

Inside the ring, Moxley hit both Jericho and referee Paul Turner with his WWE finisher, Dirty Deeds, now called the Paradigm Shift. Then, the battered Omega tackled him through the ropes. The pair fought through the crowd and onto a platform where some oversized poker chips had been positioned. As they battled onto the props, Moxley delivered another Paradigm Shift, propelling The Cleaner toward the floor.

Penelope Ford had been watching the main event, but she stopped after Jericho was declared the victor and went back to the changing area. "I was packing up, and then I heard this noise," she said. "And I was thinking, 'Why's everybody going crazy?' I ran out and looked at the screen and said, 'Holy shit.'"

Less than two weeks later, Moxley stormed into New Japan, capturing the IWGP United States Heavyweight Championship from Juice Robinson at Ryōgoku Kokugikan (Sumo Hall).

His scheduled clash with Omega for *All Out* — AEW's pay-per-view commemorating the first anniversary of *All In* — sold out in 15 minutes. Although an injury prevented Moxley from appearing, his replacement, PAC, stunned the crowd with an upset victory that, for the time being at least, reinforced the idea that nothing in AEW was predictable.

Since *Double or Nothing* occurred on a Saturday night, the Starcast festival continued on Sunday for fans not yet ready to leave Vegas. As the day wore down, though, and vendors started to pack up, I noticed Awesome Kong at one of the autograph tables, still trying to make sense of what had transpired at the MGM Grand Garden Arena.

"We know the game is changing," she mulled. "The question is how?"

Excalibur compared the idealism that helped create AEW to the philosophy behind Pro Wrestling Guerrilla. "Except they just happen to have one of the richest families in the world backing them." As with PWG, he noted, the promotion was largely controlled by wrestlers, each with a different definition of the industry. "Just judging by what happened with us, people's roles will change. Not all the partners will end up doing what they set out to do. They'll say, 'Oh, there's a gap here,' and someone will step in to fill that gap, and it will just become part of their job. Maybe, for example, Kenny Omega will be the one worried more about business development. This is all new and it's a real corporation, so you have to bring in people from the outside to worry about payroll, logistics, travel, fulfillments — all these things you never think of. I mean, as far as I know, there aren't any wrestling accountants."

With months to meditate over their looming clash with WWE the company's brain trust was already in too deep to call off a plan that likely frightened all of them. But, to a person, each was aware of his or her influence on what the wrestling business would be in the future.

"I'd like everybody to get out of this saying that we gave them a chance," Tony Khan told *Talk Is Jericho*. "I'd like everybody to say that when we got into this, it was a pivotal moment that changed things for the better for everybody who loves wrestling."

Dustin had spent the night bleeding on the pillows in his hotel room. "I cried this morning," the bruised athlete revealed during his *Inside the Ropes* Q&A. "I cried last night."

He was sad for opportunities missed and grateful to still be able to use his body to tell his family saga the way his father taught him, between the 'buckles with blood and perspiration in his eyes. It was an opportunity that almost eluded him; an opportunity he would have missed had his younger half-brother not decided to take a risk and burn a bridge. Even here, with an intimate group of admirers laughing at his cracks and applauding his observations, the emotions swelled again as Dustin mused about the craft he'd learned to love by sitting at ringside in Greensboro and Augusta and Tallahassee.

"I want substance," Dustin said, no longer speaking for himself. "I want storylines. I want *wrestling*."

36
CHAPTER

On the night of his last local show before he started full-time with AEW, Joey Janela planned to sleep in his own bed. There would be two overnight guests in the house, Marko Stunt and Jungle Boy. In the morning, the pair would slide into Janela's car and drive with him from south Jersey to Washington, DC, for the premier broadcast of *AEW Dynamite*.

"My mom's going to think you're eight years old," the Bad Boy teased Stunt.

"Oh good," Marko replied, his bushy hair flaying out from below an extra-large baseball cap. "Maybe she'll give me some Mountain Dew."

But that would be after a GCW card dubbed *Curtain Call*, a tribute to Janela, Stunt, Jungle Boy and Orange Cassidy before they went on the road with AEW.

In the dressing room, the four interacted with the indie guys who were staying put, the air heavy with anticipation and uncertainty. Would the decision to go to AEW pay off? Once they got there, who would flourish and who'd be left behind? "I'm unsure," Janela conceded. "No one knows what's going on. There's no pecking order in AEW. No one knows their position. I'm top of the food chain here. But over there . . ." He shrugged.

Quite appropriately, *Curtain Call* was being held in an Asbury Park, New Jersey, building labeled the House of Independents. Other events hosted at the facility included a Billy Joel tribute, an ABBA dance party and church services. A section of the downstairs area had been cleared of chairs, so most of the 300 or so attendees could stand during the matches. Since there was no elevator or loading dock, the crew had to carry the ring down the stairs in pieces.

GCW co-owner Brett Lauderdale tried to view the future optimistically. "We're in the same position we've always been in," he said. "Despite our success, we still are the underdog. They say Joey will come back for the *Spring Break* shows, and he'll probably be around for other things, too. But anybody can leave at any time. So it's up to us to keep reinventing. We all know Joey Janela. Who's the next one?"

Outside, GCW commentator Kevin Gill watched the ring crew unload equipment from a truck parked across the street at the Asbury Ale House, comparing the night's event to the World Wrestling Federation "Curtain Call" in 1996, when champion Shawn Michaels defeated Diesel at Madison Square Garden, then began hugging and kissing his real-life friend Kevin Nash in the middle of the ring. They were joined by Hunter Hearst Helmsley and Razor Ramon — Triple H and Scott Hall — who'd wrestled each other earlier in the card. Faces and heels were all blending together, laughing and embracing. But the dramatic display of affection had nothing to do with storyline. Rather, the four close friends were defying management by showing their love for each other before Hall and Nash departed the WWF for WCW.

It was a flagrant violation of kayfabe, and Triple H paid the highest price, having his scheduled win at the *King of the Ring* tournament scratched in favor of 'Stone Cold' Steve Austin. But the act of rebelliousness also motivated the company to shake things up and helped usher in the Attitude Era.

"I was there in Madison Square Garden," Gill said, "sitting in the crowd, and didn't know what the fuck was going on. I don't think anyone understood what that 'Curtain Call' would lead to. It's a little bit different today. Over here, we know we're on the burning edge of history."

As fans began dribbling into the building, Janela stood by the merch table, repositioning his t-shirts to ensure that they were properly displayed. Orange Cassidy placed himself near the door, clad in shades, hands in pockets, responding to fan questions with a slight nod. For much of the past year, I'd been chasing him around the United States, asking for an interview virtually every time we met. But in an era when fans think they know everything about professional wrestling, Orange Cassidy was one of the few performers old school enough to never break character, at least on the record.

Teddy Hart arrived, followed by his small entourage that included a guy in a fur coat holding the eccentric athlete's Persian cat, Mr. Velvet. While many of those in the building were speculating about AEW, Hart's mind appeared to be on the company that initially signed him at 18. "I can't go back in time and wonder what happened in WWE," he said. "I hope there's an opportunity when some of the guys in power decide that maybe Teddy Hart deserves another chance. In my forties, I'm in better shape than a lot a lot of guys in their twenties. I like to do way cooler shit than most of the wrestlers on the planet ever did."

All he needed was to get back in, he insisted. Once you put him in the ring, the rest would take care of itself. "I can earn it. If they give you enough rope, you can either hang yourself or turn it into some kind of magic whip."

Nick Gage contented himself with running the GCW locker room, speaking as a voice of authority and mediating misunderstandings. "My actions back up my words," he said, "and the boys know it." Although it was natural to imagine getting signed by one of the larger companies, he didn't anticipate receiving an offer in the near future. "It's not the main objective." he maintained. "The main objective is going out there and making sure the people enjoy everything they see."

As for Shlak, he tried being realistic about his marketability. "I see that Jungle Boy's going to AEW, and good on Jungle Boy. I could have played jazz music, but I played death metal. Sometimes, it's better to be infamous than famous."

But other indie journeymen wondered where their lives would have gone had they come up in the business at the right time. Even at close to 46 years old, Dan Maff was one of the most believable badasses I'd seen on the northeastern circuit. "If you ask all the top dogs, they know who I am," he told me a few months earlier at an Impact Championship Wrestling (ICW) show in Queens, New York. "A lot of people would look at me like my train has passed. I've had a long career on the independents. Unfortunately, I never left. I've always been here. I just never got my chance. That can happen to anybody.

"I'm an older, seasoned vet. I've seen everything. I've been everywhere. I've wrestled everyone. Some of the kids always tell me, 'Maff, you have all the answers.' And I tell them, 'Yeah, I have all the answers because I made all the mistakes.' I've always worked from the bottom up. I've earned everything I've ever gotten. And, now, I try to pass on as much knowledge as I can. I have a lot to give."

Shortly after I finished the first draft of this book, Maff squared off with PCO in Ring of Honor. He did so well that the company hired him.

It was the first wrestling contract he'd ever signed.

By contrast, at 22 years old, Jungle Boy happened to become an adult at the precise moment that pro wrestling needed someone like him. "I'm in the exact place I need to be," he said in the House of Independents dressing room. "Wrestling had a drought, then the indies became hotter than ever. Then, AEW came out of the blue. I'm fortunate to be around right now."

Nonetheless, he felt some disquiet about making the transition from small buildings to large arenas. "It's kind of weird," he remarked. "I'm at the end of one journey and at the start of another one."

In the not so distant past, Marko Stunt had expected to spend his entire career wrestling in front of audiences of a few hundred fans at best, primarily in the deep south. "Then, I went on the road," he said, "and met a few people. But I still think I don't belong. I know who I was before. I mean, in the ring, you know, I'm confident. But I'm still nervous."

On the AEW pay-per-views after *Double or Nothing*, Janela enticed viewers with the unruliness he'd once displayed during his crazed encounters with John Zandig and Lio Rush. At *Fyter Fest* in June 2019, he delivered a hurricanrana to Jon Moxley into a barbed wire–draped chair, then belted him with the weapon. After Moxley delivered a release suplex to Janela onto an assortment of thumbtacks, the Bad Boy begged for more — and was hit with a Paradigm Shift onto the sharp objects. During a Triple Threat with Jimmy Havoc and Darby Allin at *All Out* in September, Janela was punished with a staple gun while seated on a chair. Havoc followed up by monkey flipping a seated Janela, who landed upright on the chair and smiled at the crowd.

It was a routine he'd done before but never in front of such a large audience. Still, he was concerned about how people would perceive him.

"AEW has put me in these hardcore matches, and I'm more than just a hardcore guy," Janela said. "Now, I have to prove to all these new fans who don't know me that there's a lot of other things I can do."

He was also making lifestyle adjustments he'd never considered in the past. "I'm dieting and getting in shape," he admitted. "A lot of people on the internet who didn't know me said I didn't look like a wrestler, and I kind of had to agree with them. There's a lot of pressure now."

Just two nights before AEW's first show on TNT, Jungle Boy received a rapturous cheer from the GCW crowd at Asbury Park as he entered the ring and fist-bumped spectators, ready to lock up with his close friend, Jake Atlas, who'd soon sign a contract with WWE.

The fans also loudly applauded the referee, Bryce Remsburg, whom they'd watched in CZW and CHIKARA and now, would be departing for AEW, as well. Despite GCW's reputation for hardcore, the combatants had a fast-moving, largely technical match before Jungle Boy went over. As spectators stamped their feet and shouted his name, Jungle Boy blew kisses, held his palms in front of him in gratitude and embraced Atlas, who left the ring to let his rival enjoy the moment.

Marko Stunt had only been associated with GCW for about a year, but his man-boy gimmick was over strong. Now that he was on his way out, the company opted to reboot the bout that initially endeared him to its audience.

He came down the aisle as fans hurled streamers and pounded the ring to his theme music, Pat Benatar's "We Belong." Swathed in an orange streamer, Stunt spun around and around, then made the crowd laugh by taking the microphone and grunting, "I'm blown up."

Instead of being the kid out of the audience, he was now the focal point of the encounter with his original GCW foe, Kyle the Beast, aka KTB. Amid competing chants of "Marko, Marko, Marko" and "Beast, Beast, Beast," Stunt delivered all his shtick: a flying head scissors, dropkick, dive through the ropes, moonsault. After kicking out of a KTB powerbomb and piledriver, he put away his much larger adversary with a somersault from the top rope. Once again, both rivals shook hands and embraced, with KTB raising Stunt's arm and wishing him luck.

The Orange Cassidy collision with Ethan Page contained the comedy elements that helped the "Freshly Squeezed" grappler tie up his AEW deal. Without removing his hands from his pockets, Cassidy ran the ropes, ducked under punches and clotheslines, nipped up, hit a dropkick and splashed his foe from the ropes. At one point, Page became frustrated with the officiating and shoved Remsburg, who brought the house down by countering with a flying head scissors. Seemingly infuriated, Page kicked Remsburg in the balls, bringing out Super Humman — a YouTube character known for hurling himself onto barbed wire and other uncomfortable objects — who hit the heel with a Stone Cold Stunner, setting him up for another splash from Cassidy, followed by a pinfall.

With so many GCW events named after him, Janela's match was the most touching of the night. Fans had watched the Bad Boy risk his body and use both physical comedy and sarcasm to entertain them, and there was an acknowledgment that, without him, GCW might not keep the spot it had in their hearts. In addition to chairs, doors and the usual hardcore elements of his bout with Jimmy Lloyd, there were headlocks and leg scissors and other aspects of technical wrestling. Following an exchange of superkicks and neckbreakers, Janela did what was best for GCW, setting himself up for a dominator into a piledriver variation and doing a clean job for his younger opponent.

It only made the fans love him more. As Brett Lauderdale handed Janela a bottle of champagne, the GCW icon stood alongside Stunt, Jungle Boy and Teddy Hart. "Even though I look the way I do," the Bad Boy told the audience, "with my little, chubby, jelly belly, I come in here and I prove I'm the best wrestler in the fuckin' world."

Still, he continued, it would be the GCW regulars like Jimmy Lloyd, Tony Deppen and KTB who'd write the next chapter.

"Dude, we really did change the game," he crowed. "We changed the business." And, he added, he'd rather "go back to delivering pizzas" than compromise his passion.

"I love professional wrestling and I fuckin' love you guys," he said, showing the same emotion that Dustin and Cody had exhibited in Las Vegas. "I love you guys so much."

Everyone vowed to come back soon. But now, Janela, Jungle Boy and Stunt needed to concentrate on arriving at the Capital One Arena in DC for the AEW broadcast, without committing some scandal that would end their run prematurely.

It had been just over a year since Joey Janela had stood outside the Sears Centre Arena in suburban Chicago, smoking a cigarette and looking at the crowd walking into the building for *All In*. Back then, he thought about Kenny Omega and Cody and the Young Bucks and what it would take to get to their place in the wrestling hierarchy. And now, as he passed through the doors of the House of Independents on the way to the next phase, some other worker was staring at the Bad Boy and contemplating the same thing.

"Don't worry about the money," he stated, playing the role of indie wrestling sage. "Go out. Take bookings. Don't stick to a formula. Be different."

It would be the only way that the indie wrestling revolution was going to continue.

Goodbye! Goodnight! Bang!

EPILOGUE

The debut of *AEW Dynamite* on TNT, on October 2, 2019, heralded a new chapter in the indie wrestling revolution. Despite the fact that the story wasn't over, I knew that my publisher wanted to get this book out. The premiere was as good a cut-off point as any.

The next few months were electrifying. In anointing Chris Jericho as the organization's first champion, AEW capitalized on a recognizable name who both dazzled the public and elevated the people around him. Learning from the mistakes of WCW and TNA, Jericho opted not to surround himself with fellow old-timers whose best years had been in WWE but instead a posse of supremely talented younger people.

Santana and Ortiz of LAX were rebranded Proud-N-Powerful and roared into AEW the month before at *All Out*, the pay-per-view that marked the one-year anniversary of *All In*, executing a sneak attack on the Young Bucks. On *Dynamite*, Jericho inducted the pair into his faction, the Inner Circle, along with "The Spanish God" Sammy Guevara, whose matinee idol looks and charisma leaped through the screen.

Rounding out the group was Jake Hager, the former Jack Swagger in WWE, whose recent MMA career added legitimacy to his enforcer gimmick.

Like the Four Horsemen, the Inner Circle behaved like a street gang. In a January 2020 mob assault, they jabbed a spike into the eye of Jon Moxley — similar to what the Road Warriors did to The American Dream in a 1988 angle — who seemed impervious to punishment and thrived when the numbers were stacked against him.

But at the very same time on the USA Network, NXT was putting on programming of equal intensity. At one stage, the Undisputed Era possessed every men's title of the brand, with Adam Cole holding the NXT Championship, Roderick Strong the North American crown and Bobby Fish and Kyle O'Reilly the tag team gold. Among the others commanding attention on WWE's Wednesday night program was the unique tandem of the Broserweights — former WWE United Kingdom champion Pete Dunne and Matt Riddle — who won the 2020 Dusty Rhodes Tag Team Classic (although Cody said that he owned the trademark, he allowed his former employer to continue to honor his father by using the name) on an edition of *NXT* on USA.

Like AEW, NXT maintained a general indie vibe to its presentation. But the influence on WWE's main roster was considerable. During the 2020 women's *Royal Rumble*, for instance, the NXT stars commanded a lopsided amount of fascination, with former titlist Shayna Baszler and Bianca Belair each dispatching a record eight competitors.

In what felt like a shoot, CM Punk — who'd left WWE under acrimonious circumstances in 2014 — had appeared on FS1's *WWE Backstage* program a few days earlier, advocating for Keith Lee to win the men's Rumble. "He is a big fish in a little pond right now, not to say that NXT is little by any means," said Punk, who insisted that his new role as commentator was due to an arrangement he'd made with Fox and not WWE. "We've got to get going with Keith Lee here. I think he needs to chuck Brock [Lesnar] over the top rope, and he needs to win that whole thing."

Ultimately, former NXT champion Drew McIntyre won the Rumble and a title shot against Lesnar at *WrestleMania 36*.

With so much focus on the Wednesday night wars, there were bound to be casualties. In the period after the *G1 Supercard* in Madison Square Garden, fans appeared to be turning away from Ring of Honor. Cody, the Young Bucks, Kenny Omega and "Hangman" Adam Page had migrated to AEW, and New Japan was staging its own shows, without the organization's help.

But in early 2020, there were some positive signs. Rather than joining the other members of the Elite in AEW, Marty Scurll decided to stay with Ring of Honor. It was said that The Villain would receive "WWE main-roster money" in exchange for far fewer dates, share booking duties with Delirious and work as a liaison to other promotions. In addition to Bandido also renewing his contract, the company fortified its association with the NWA, meaning that Nick Aldis could defend the Ten Pounds of Gold on Ring of Honor shows. And the *Supercard of Honor*, slated for the night before *WrestleMania 36*, would feature a number of New Japan regulars, with KENTA, Jeff Cobb, Dragon Lee, El Phantasmo, Jay White, Will Ospreay and Slex among the promised attractions.

Although the relationship between New Japan and AEW was apparently strained, both Moxley and Jericho appeared at New Japan's *Wrestle Kingdom 14*, which expanded to two nights in early January 2020. On night one, Moxley became a two-time IWGP United States champion following a crazy brawl with Lance Archer. And on night two, Jericho wore his belt to the ring for a clash with Hiroshi Tanahashi.

Despite Jericho's triumph, New Japan allowed its announcers to hype the possibility that if Tanahashi won, he'd travel to the U.S. and challenge for the AEW World Championship.

In terms of ratings, AEW was performing well enough that, four months after the launch of *Dynamite*, TNT agreed to extend the company's deal through 2023 and add another night of programming. Out of every wrestling promotion on U.S. television, AEW had the youngest viewers and the ones most likely to watch via DVR. While always competitive, NXT had only beaten its rival once in the Wednesday night wars — on an evening when even wrestling fans were distracted by hearings related to President Donald Trump's impeachment.

Although every major wrestling company pointedly avoided mentioning the polarizing WWE Hall of Famer, Trump's essence was always there, filling viewers' minds with bluster before they sat down in front of the television. Just as MJF ranted about Cody's "cat piss stained blond hair and beaver teeth," the commander-in-chief was responsible for such online missives as, "Shifty Adam Schiff is a CORRUPT POLITICIAN, and probably a very sick man."

On a single day in December 2019, the president fired off 123 tweets.

Wrestling was supposed to be escapism. But it was hard to view the sport of kings without acknowledging that the news of the day impacted both the fans and the performers. Just hours before Braun Strowman unseated Shinsuke Nakamura for the Intercontinental title and the Usos and Roman Reigns chained King Corbin to the ring post and covered him in dog food on *SmackDown*, the Republican-led U.S. Senate voted to block witnesses from testifying at the president's impeachment trial, assuring that Trump would be acquitted of abuse of power and obstruction of Congress charges.

In the same 24-hour period, Great Britain officially left the European Union after a period of more than 40 years.

Sheffield's former Lord Mayor Magid Magid was one of the 70-plus British members of the European Parliament contemplating post-Brexit job prospects. "Many people don't know, but I used to do MMA," he told ITV. "I had the nickname 'Magic Magid the Submission Machine.' So I'm basically thinking about a career in professional wrestling."

Once again, everything came back to wrestling.

From the moment that I started researching *Too Sweet: Inside the Indie Wrestling Revolution*, I knew how well it was going to be received. In a business that's supposed to be a work, the sentiments expressed by virtually every person I met were genuine. As Brandi Rhodes told me at one point, "What's real speaks for itself." But when I completed this epilogue, in January 2020, I realized that there had to be a sequel, chronicling occurrences that had yet to transpire, against a backdrop of significant world events.

At the time, I assumed that the American presidential election and Brexit were going to loom as the more prominent ones. In the meantime, the first year of the third decade of the 21st century promised to be the best ever to be a wrestling fan. But that was before an international pandemic resulted in empty arena matches, hundreds of cancellations and an abnormal version of *WrestleMania* that forced WWE to do some of its most creative work ever.

KEITH ELLIOT GREENBERG

APRIL 14, 2020

ACKNOWLEDGMENTS

n addition to the multitudes mentioned in this book, the author wishes to thank a number of people who assisted in the process. Before moving to AEW, Rafael Morffi and Shawn "Bird" Carr were with MLW and Ring of Honor, respectively, and went out of their way to make me comfortable backstage. Oly Ossatian of *Inside the Ropes* helped me navigate the company's growing archive. Mark Gilson provided perceptions into the New York indie scene, particularly the subtleties of the various promotions in Queens. Terrence Breen, a regular companion from the Brooklyn Pub, offered suggestions and background information about groups and personalities in the south Jersey/Philadelphia area. At ECW Press, I was not only aided by executive editor Michael Holmes, who played a role in coming up with the book's concept, but copublishers David Caron and Jack David, copy editor Laura Pastore, editorial coordinator Shannon Parr, digital and art director Jessica Albert, marketing and publicity director Susannah Ames, and sales and rights director Emily Ferko. While my parents Abe and Norma aged and struggled with various health challenges, they respected my time when I'd camp out in their home to work on this project. As in the past, Dylan, Summer and Jennifer were supporters, as well as family. And then, there's Dr. Elicia Rosen-Fox, who not only adjusted a few vertebrae following an accident that could have delayed the writing process, but worked hard to understand and enjoy the subject matter. She also posed a question I guess anyone would ask if he or she had never attended a death match before: "Why's there a door in there?"